THE 100 MOST INFLUENTIAL WOMEN OF ALL TIME
OF ALL TIME

THE BRITANNICA GUIDE TO THE WORLD'S MOST INFLUENTIAL PEOPLE

THE 100 MOST INFLUENTIAL WOMEN OF ALL TIME

EDITED BY KATHLEEN KUIPER, MANAGER, ARTS AND CULTURE

Britannica®
Educational Publishing
IN ASSOCIATION WITH
ROSEN
EDUCATIONAL SERVICES

Published in 2010 by Britannica Educational Publishing
(a trademark of Encyclopædia Britannica, Inc.)
in association with Rosen Educational Services, LLC
29 East 21st Street, New York, NY 10010.

Distributed exclusively by Rosen Educational Services.
For a listing of additional Britannica Educational Publishing titles, call toll free (800) 237-9932.

First Edition

Britannica Educational Publishing
Michael I. Levy: Executive Editor
Marilyn L. Barton: Senior Coordinator, Production Control
Steven Bosco: Director, Editorial Technologies
Lisa S. Braucher: Senior Producer and Data Editor
Yvette Charboneau: Senior Copy Editor
Kathy Nakamura: Manager, Media Acquisition
Kathleen Kuiper: Manager, Arts and Culture

Rosen Educational Services
Jeanne Nagle: Senior Editor
Nelson Sá: Art Director
Nicole Russo: Designer
Introduction by Kristi Lew

Library of Congress Cataloging-in-Publication Data

The 100 most influential women of all time / edited by Kathleen Kuiper. — 1st ed.
    p. cm. — (The Britannica guide to the world's most influential people)
"In association with Britannica Educational Publishing, Rosen Educational Services."
Includes index.
ISBN 978-1-61530-010-5 (library binding)
1. Women—Biography. 2. Women—History. I. Kuiper, Kathleen. II. Title: One hundred
most influential women of all time.
HQ1121.A14 2010
920.72—dc22

                                                                        2009029761

Manufactured in the United States of America

Cover photo: Jodie Coston/Photodisc/Getty Images; p. 16 © www.istockphoto.com/Diane Diederich.

CONTENTS

Introduction	8
Hatshepsut	17
Nefertiti	19
Sappho	23
Cleopatra	25
Mary	31
Hypatia	34
Theodora	36
Wuhou	38
Irene	41
Murasaki Shikibu	43
Hildegard	45
Eleanor of Aquitaine	47
Margaret I	51
Christine de Pisan	54
Joan of Arc	55
Mira Bai	70
Isabella I	71
Teresa of Ávila	78
Mary I	80
Catherine de Médicis	83
Elizabeth I	89
Artemisia Gentileschi	103
Okuni	105
Christina	107
Maria Theresa	110
Catherine II	115
Elisabeth Vigée-Lebrun	125
Marie-Antoinette	126
Mary Wollstonecraft	128
Germaine de Staël	131
Jane Austen	136
Sacagawea	144
Sojourner Truth	147
Dorothea Dix	149
Charlotte and Emily Brontë	151

20

32

153

Victoria 159
Susan B. Anthony and
    Elizabeth Cady Stanton 170
Florence Nightingale 177
Harriet Tubman 182
Elizabeth Blackwell 184
Mary Baker Eddy 186
Cixi 192
Mary Cassatt 195
Sarah Bernhardt 197
Sarah Winnemucca 201
Emmeline and
    Christabel Pankhurst 203
Jane Addams 206
Annie Jump Cannon 208
Marie Curie 209
Gertrude Bell 213
Maria Montessori 215
Rosa Luxemburg 217
Colette 220
Gertrude Stein 223
Isadora Duncan 225
Margaret Sanger 229
Helen Keller 230
Marie Stopes 233
Anna Pavlova 235
Virginia Woolf 237
Coco Chanel 253
Eleanor Roosevelt 255
Karen Horney 260
Martha Graham 262
Soong Mei-ling 267
Amelia Earhart 270
Irène Joliot-Curie 271
Golda Meir 274
Marlene Dietrich 276
Simone Weil 279

Katherine Dunham   281
Dorothy Crowfoot Hodgkin   282
Mother Teresa   286
Lucille Ball   288
Rosa Parks   291
Jiang Qing   292
Elizabeth Stern   295
Sirimavo R. D. Bandaranaike   296
Indira Gandhi   299
Eva Perón   301
Rosalind Franklin   303
Rosalyn S. Yalow   304
Nadine Gordimer   306
Elizabeth II   307
Anne Frank   310
Violeta Barrios de Chamorro   312
Sandra Day O'Connor   313
Ellen Johnson-Sirleaf   316
Gro Harlem Brundtland   318
Wangari Maathai   319
Martha Stewart   320
Christiane Nüsslein-Volhard   323
Billie Jean King   324
Mary Robinson   327
Aung San Suu Kyi   329
Shirin Ebadi   330
Hillary Rodham Clinton   332
Oprah Winfrey   338
Rigoberta Menchú   340
Diana, Princess of Wales   342
Glossary   345
For Further Reading   348
Index   350

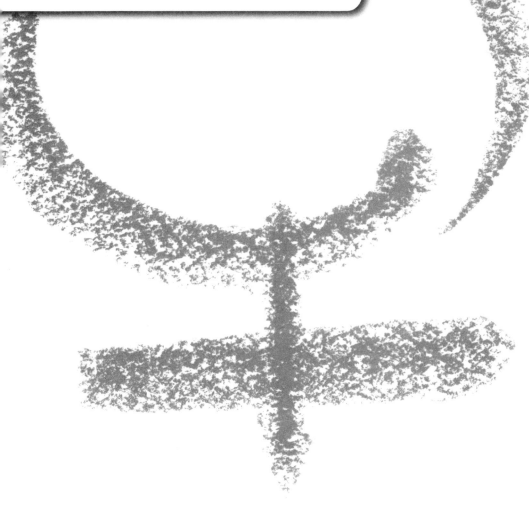

The world is filled with fascinating women, each with her own compelling story. Clearly, no single tome can hold all the intricate details of their collective lives. But this book, filled with profiles of striking individuals who serve as outstanding representatives of their gender, covers many of the most outstanding, influential women from around the globe. Coverage runs the gamut from queens to commoners, with a tip of the hat to those who have made their mark in the arts and sciences, in their country's political arena, and on the world stage.

Most of these women managed to flourish in the face of adversity. Some withstood opposition from outside sources, while family intrigue was a malevolent force in the lives of others. For centuries, merely being a woman was an obstacle these individuals had to overcome. Consider the case of Hatshepsut, the eldest daughter of ancient Egyptian King Thutmose I and his queen, Ahmose. After her father and half brother died, Hatshepsut was allowed to assume the role of regent only because the rightful heir, her son, was an infant. She took full advantage of the situation, essentially claiming the throne for herself while nominally coruling with her son. For a woman, Hatshepsut wielded unprecedented power. Court artists, unfamiliar with representations of a queen in such firm control, took to depicting her as a man, full beard and all.

Another ruler of Egypt, Cleopatra, rose to power when she was 18 years old, coruling with her brother, Ptolemy XIII. As the eldest sibling by eight years, Cleopatra quickly became the dominant ruler, much to Ptolemy XIII's displeasure. It did not take long for Ptolemy to forcibly remove Cleopatra from her position. The young queen did not take this coup lying down. She fled to Syria, where she promptly gathered an army and returned to confront her brother in a successful attempt to reclaim the throne.

Restored to power after forcing Ptolemy to flee Alexandria, Cleopatra fortified her position through clever political and romantic alliances with future emperor Julius Caesar and the Roman general Mark Antony. Although forced to share power with first her brothers, then her son (allegedly fathered by Caesar), Cleopatra proved to be the true driving force behind the Egyptian throne for 22 years.

Other women became influential rulers directly through marriage or by giving birth. Eleanor of Aquitaine, for example, had considerable power as the wife and mother of several reigning kings of France and England. As the daughter of William X, the duke of Aquitaine, Eleanor inherited a large portion of western France upon his death. In 1137, she married the heir to the throne of France, Louis VII, and became queen of France. When the marriage was annulled in 1152, she married the heir to the throne of England, Henry II, and became queen of England. She and Louis had two daughters, but she and Henry produced three daughters and five sons, including Richard the Lion-Heart, and John, both of whom would become kings of England. Her daughters also married into the royal families of Bavaria, Castile, and Sicily.

The women of England were not always relegated to the role of wife and mother of kings. Some of them ruled the country on their own. The first English queen to rule in her own right was Mary I, daughter of Henry VIII and his first wife, Catherine of Aragon. Mary is better known by the nickname "Bloody Mary," a moniker she earned while trying desperately to suppress a Protestant uprising and restore Roman Catholicism to England. Hundreds of people died during this three-year, ultimately unsuccessful, battle.

After the death of her half-sister Mary, Elizabeth ascended the throne and became the queen of England at the age of 25. Religious and political strife did not disappear under her rule, yet England did emerge as a more powerful country on the world's stage by its end. Remembered far more fondly than "Bloody Mary," Elizabeth I ruled for 45 years. Her reign, though, was not the longest in the history. That honour goes to Queen Victoria I, who ruled the United Kingdom for almost sixty-four years. So influential was she during her lengthy reign that she has been immortalized by having an epoch named after her—the Victorian Age.

Even today, the United Kingdom is ruled by a woman. Like the first Queen Elizabeth, Elizabeth II came to the throne when she was 25 years old. Through her son and heir apparent, Prince Charles, Elizabeth is connected to another notable women profiled in this book, Diana, Princess of Wales. Diana's personality, beauty, and unwavering support of the arts, children's issues, and AIDS relief quickly made her a popular public figure all over the world. Her untimely death in 1997 at the age of 36 was mourned by many.

Other countries around the world also have been led by women in the modern age. The first female prime minister in history was Sirimavo Bandaranaike, elected to lead Sri Lanka in 1960. She would ultimately go on to serve three terms in that office, remaining an important part of Sri Lankan politics until her death in 2000. Six years later, Indira Gandhi became the first female prime minister of India. She served four terms before being assassinated in 1984. Ireland elected its first female president, Mary Robinson, in 1990, and in 2006, Ellen Johnson-Sirleaf became the first woman to be head of state in an African country when she was elected president of Liberia.

While the United States has yet to elect a woman president, there have been women who have achieved high political office. Among them is Hillary Rodham Clinton, who made political history as the first American first lady to win an elective office when she became a United States senator in 2001. Although her bid for president failed, Clinton earned her way back into the White House as secretary of state in Barack Obama's administration.

Rather than wield power themselves, some of the individuals featured in this title came to the fore by helping to empower other women. In the United States, Susan B. Anthony and Elizabeth Cady Stanton struggled to win for women in America the right to vote. In 1920, their work culminated in the 19th amendment of the United States Constitution, which granted women this right. Emmeline Pankhurst and her daughter Christabel did much the same thing in England. In 1928, these suffragists saw the passage of the Representation of the People Act giving women and men equal voting rights in England.

Still others fought for the rights of other marginalized groups. In the 1800s, Harriet Tubman fought to see African American men and women treated as equal in American society. An escaped slave, Tubman helped countless others fleeing for freedom on the Underground Railroad. Sojourner Truth, another former slave, also spoke out against slavery as well as for equal rights for women in the 1800s.

Another woman who worked tirelessly on behalf of others was Eleanor Roosevelt. One of the most admired women of the 20th century, Roosevelt used her position as first lady to help African Americans, children, and the poor. Active in the Women's Trade Union League and the League of Women Voters, and, in later years, as chair of Pres. John F. Kennedy's Commission on the Status of Women, she also helped pave the way for American women to make a difference in politics and other fields.

Activism isn't the only means by which women have been able to help scores of people at once. The medical professionals among the elite individuals featured in this book impacted the masses by not only their service but by advancing the field of health care as well. Florence Nightingale, fondly remembered primarily as a nurse, was also a tireless social reformer who was instrumental in overhauling military medical and purveyance systems. She also devised models for the practice of nursing that are used to this day.

Around the same time as Nightingale was staging her renaissance of nursing, Elizabeth Blackwell was blazing a trail that would eventually allow women to become physicians. Regarded as the first woman doctor in modern times, Blackwell opened a medical college for women in New York City. Women's Medical College was instituted to help others bypass the difficulties and prejudice Blackwell herself had endured when she enrolled in medical school.

Women of science made great strides toward helping humanity, too. Elizabeth Stern conducted pioneering research into the risk factors for, and the causes and progression of, cervical cancer. Early detection and highly successful treatment measures for this particular disease were made possible because of Stern's findings. Margaret Sanger's promotion of birth control did more than give women choices when it came to procreation. Her advocacy helped lower the high rates of infant and maternal mortality prevalent in early 20th-century America. And although her work was largely uncredited, Rosalind Franklin played a vital role in unraveling the mystery of DNA.

Then there are the women who have left their mark on humankind's collective creative history. Several distinguished and talented women have entertained and enlightened the public through their art. Sarah Bernhardt and Marlene Dietrich, for example, are grand dames of stage and screen, respectively. Their performances became the watermark by which other actresses have measured their own careers.

A star of stage and screen in her own right, Lucille Ball is perhaps best known as the star of the *I Love Lucy* television program. The show revolutionized TV sitcoms by utilizing a three-camera setup, as opposed to the one static camera, to capture the action. Other shows quickly followed suit. Today, the multicamera format is the standard for television comedies. Ball made us laugh as one of the world's greatest comic actors. More than that, she was a shrewd businessperson who became one of the first women to run a major Hollywood production company, paving the way for future generations of female producers and studio heads.

Other women chose to sway public opinion with the written word. The world's first novel, *The Tale of Genji*, was written by a woman, the Japanese author Murasaki Shikibu. Joining Homer in the panoply of great poets of ancient Greece is Sappho, who wrote about love, passion, and the education of young women in the "nuptial arts." In England, novelist Jane Austen and, later, the Brontë sisters, Charlotte and Emily, were weaving tales that would eventually become classics. Charlotte's *Jane Eyre* was an immediate hit with critics and readers when it was first published, while the dramatic and poetic nature of Emily's *Wuthering Heights* wasn't fully appreciated until years later. Regardless, both novels are considered prime examples of superb English literature—as is Austen's entire oeuvre.

Another book that still has the power to touch people today is not a novel, but a memoir. *The Diary of a Young Girl* portrays the short life of Anne Frank, one of the millions of Jewish victims of the Holocaust. More than a classic of war literature, Anne Frank's diary puts a human face on an unimaginable tragedy, and serves as a beacon of hope to all young women who face adversity.

The influence of these women, and the others profiled in this book, reverberates throughout the ages. Their leadership, scientific research, and artistic vision have served to enrich, enlighten, and shape modern society. These amazing and influential individuals have given all of us, men and women alike, something to admire and strive for in our own lives.

HATSHEPSUT

(fl. 15th century BCE)

The most famous female king of Egypt was Hatshepsut (Hatchepsut), who reigned in her own right *c.* 1473–58 BCE. She attained unprecedented power for a woman, adopting the full titles and regalia of a pharaoh.

Hatshepsut was the elder daughter of the 18th-dynasty king Thutmose I and his consort Ahmose, and she was married to her half brother Thutmose II, son of the lady Mutnofret. Since three of Mutnofret's older sons had died prematurely, Thutmose II inherited his father's throne about 1492 BCE, with Hatshepsut as his consort. Hatshepsut bore one daughter, Neferure, but no son. When her husband died about 1479 BCE, the throne passed to his son Thutmose III, born to Isis, a lesser harem queen. As Thutmose III was an infant, Hatshepsut acted as regent for the young king.

For the first few years of her stepson's reign, Hatshepsut was an entirely conventional regent. But by the end of his seventh regnal year, she had assumed the kingship and adopted a full royal titulary (the royal protocol adopted by Egyptian sovereigns). Hatshepsut and Thutmose III were now corulers of Egypt, with Hatshepsut very much the dominant king. Hitherto Hatshepsut had been depicted as a typical queen, with a female body and appropriately feminine garments. But now, after a brief period of experimentation that involved combining a female body with kingly (male) regalia, her formal portraits began to show Hatshepsut with a male body, wearing the traditional regalia of kilt, crown or head-cloth, and false beard. To dismiss this as a serious attempt to pass herself off as a man is to misunderstand Egyptian artistic convention, which showed things not as they were but as they should be. In causing herself to be depicted as a traditional king, Hatshepsut ensured that this is what she would become.

In styling herself as a king, Hatshepsut avoided the epithet "mighty bull," regularly employed by other kings. Although in her reliefs she was depicted as a male, pronominal references in the texts usually reflect her womanhood. Similarly, much of her statuary shows her in male form, but there are rarer examples that render her as a woman. In less formal documents she was referred to as "King's Great Wife"—that is, "Queen"—while Thutmose III was "King." There is thus a certain ambiguity in the treatment of Hatshepsut as king.

Hatshepsut never explained why she took the throne or how she persuaded Egypt's elite to accept her new position. However, an essential element of her success was a group of loyal officials, many handpicked, who controlled all the key positions in her government. Most prominent amongst these was Senenmut, overseer of all royal works and tutor to Neferure.

Traditionally, Egyptian kings defended their land against the enemies who lurked at Egypt's borders. Hatshepsut's reign was essentially a peaceful one, and her foreign policy was based on trade rather than war. But scenes on the walls of her Dayr al-Baḥrī temple, in western Thebes, suggest that she began with a short, successful military campaign in Nubia. More complete scenes show Hatshepsut's seaborne trading expedition to Punt, a trading centre (since vanished) on the East African coast beyond the southernmost end of the Red Sea. Gold, ebony, animal skins, baboons, processed myrrh, and living myrrh trees were brought back to Egypt, and the trees were planted in the gardens of Dayr al-Baḥrī.

Restoration and building were important royal duties. Hatshepsut claimed, falsely, to have restored the damage wrought by the Hyksos (Asian) kings during their rule in Egypt. She undertook an extensive building program. In

Thebes this focused on the temples of her divine father, the national god Amon-Re. At the Karnak temple complex, she remodeled her earthly father's hypostyle hall, added a barque shrine (the Red Chapel), and introduced two pairs of obelisks. At Beni Hasan in Middle Egypt, she built a rock-cut temple known in Greek as Speos Artemidos. Her supreme achievement was her Dayr al-Baḥrī temple; designed as a funerary monument for Hatshepsut, it was dedicated to Amon-Re and included a series of chapels dedicated to the gods Osiris, Re, Hathor, and Anubis and to the royal ancestors. Hatshepsut was to be interred in the Valley of the Kings, where she extended her father's tomb so that she could be buried with him.

Toward the end of her reign, Hatshepsut allowed Thutmose to play an increasingly prominent role in state affairs; following her death, Thutmose III ruled Egypt alone for 33 years. At the end of his reign, an attempt was made to remove all traces of Hatshepsut's rule. Her statues were torn down, her monuments were defaced, and her name was removed from the official king list. Early scholars interpreted this as an act of vengeance, but it seems that Thutmose was ensuring that the succession would run from Thutmose I through Thutmose II to Thutmose III without female interruption. Hatshepsut sank into obscurity until 1822, when the decoding of hieroglyphic script allowed archaeologists to read the Dayr al-Baḥrī inscriptions. Initially the discrepancy between the female name and the male image caused confusion, but today the Thutmoside succession is well understood.

NEFERTITI

(fl. 14th century BCE)

Nefertiti, also called Neferneferuaten-Nefertiti, was the queen of Egypt and wife of King Akhenaton (formerly Amenhotep IV; reigned *c.* 1353–36 BCE), and she played a prominent role in the cult of the sun god (Aton, or Aten) that he established.

Nefertiti's parentage is unrecorded, but, as her name translates as "A Beautiful Woman Has Come," early Egyptologists believed that she must have been a princess from Mitanni (Syria). There is strong circumstantial evidence, however, to suggest that she was the Egyptian-born daughter of the courtier Ay, brother of Akhenaton's mother, Tiy. In any case, it is known that she had a younger sister, Mutnodjmet. Married to him before her husband's accession, Nefertiti bore six daughters within 10 years of her marriage, the elder three being born at Thebes, the younger three at Tell el-Amarna. Two of her daughters became queens of Egypt.

The earliest images of Nefertiti come from the Theban tombs of the royal butler Parennefer and the vizier Ramose, where she is shown accompanying her husband. In the Theban temple known as Hwt-Benben ("Mansion of the Benben Stone"; the benben was a cult object

Nefertiti, painted limestone bust, about 1350 BC; in the Egyptian Museum, Berlin. Bildarchiv Preussischer Kulturbesitz, Ägyptisches Museum, Staatliche Museen zu Berlin/Preussischer Kulturbesitz, Berlin; photograph, Jurgen Liepe

associated with solar ritual), Nefertiti played a more prominent role, usurping kingly privileges in order to serve as a priest and offer to the Aton, represented by the sun's disk. A group of blocks recovered from Karnak (Luxor) and Hermopolis Magna (Al-Ashmunayn) shows Nefertiti participating in the ritual smiting of the female enemies of Egypt. She wears her own unique headdress — a tall, straight-edged, flat-topped blue crown.

By the end of Akhenaton's fifth regnal year, the Aton had become Egypt's dominant national god. The old state temples were closed and the court transferred to a purpose-built capital city, Akhetaton (Amarna). Here Nefertiti continued to play an important religious role, worshipping alongside her husband and serving as the female element in the divine triad formed by the god Aton, the king Akhenaton, and his queen. Her sexuality, emphasized by her exaggeratedly feminine body shape and her fine linen garments, and her fertility, emphasized by the constant appearance of the six princesses, indicate that she was considered a living fertility goddess. Nefertiti and the royal family appeared on private devotional stelae and on the walls of nonroyal tombs, and images of Nefertiti stood at the four corners of her husband's sarcophagus.

Some historians, having considered her reliefs and statuary, believe that Nefertiti may have acted as queen regnant—her husband's coruler rather than his consort. However, the evidence is by no means conclusive, and there is no written evidence to confirm her political status.

Soon after Akhenaton's 12th regnal year, one of the princesses died, three disappeared (and are also presumed to have died), and Nefertiti vanished. The simplest inference is that Nefertiti also died, but there is no record of her death and no evidence that she was ever buried in the Amarna royal tomb. Early Egyptologists, misunderstanding the textual evidence recovered from the Maru-Aten sun temple at Amarna, deduced that Nefertiti had separated from Akhenaton and had retired to live either in the north palace at Amarna or in Thebes. This theory is now discredited. Others have suggested that she outlived her husband, took the name Smenkhkare, and ruled alone as female king before handing the throne to Tutankhamen. There is good evidence for a King Smenkhkare, but the identification in the 20th century of a male body buried in the Valley of the Kings as Tutankhamen's brother makes it unlikely that Nefertiti and Smenkhkare were the same person.

Nefertiti's body has never been discovered. Had she died at Amarna, it seems inconceivable that she would not have been buried in the Amarna royal tomb. But the burial in the Valley of the Kings confirms that at least one of the Amarna burials was reinterred at Thebes during Tutankhamen's reign. Egyptologists have therefore speculated that Nefertiti may be one of the unidentified bodies recovered from the caches of royal mummies in the Valley of the Kings. In the early 21st century attention focused on the "Younger Lady" found in the tomb of Amenhotep II, although it is now accepted that this body is almost certainly too young to be Nefertiti.

Amarna was abandoned soon after Akhenaton's death, and Nefertiti was forgotten until, in 1912, a German archaeological mission led by Ludwig Borchardt discovered a portrait bust of Nefertiti lying in the ruins of the Amarna workshop of the sculptor Thutmose. The bust went on display at the Egyptian Museum in Berlin in the 1920s and immediately attracted worldwide attention, causing Nefertiti to become one of the most recognizable and, despite a missing left eye, most beautiful female figures from the ancient world.

SAPPHO

(b. *c.* 610 BCE, Lesbos [Greece] — d. *c.* 570 BCE)

The Greek lyric poet Sappho (or Psappho, as her name is given in the Aeolic dialect spoken by the poet) has been greatly admired in all ages for the beauty of her writing style. She ranks with Archilochus and Alcaeus, among Greek poets, for her ability to impress readers with a lively sense of her personality. Her language contains elements from Aeolic vernacular speech and Aeolic poetic tradition, with traces of epic vocabulary familiar to readers of Homer. Her phrasing is concise, direct, and picturesque. She has the ability to stand aloof and judge critically her own ecstasies and grief, and her emotions lose nothing of their force by being recollected in tranquillity.

Legends about Sappho abound, many having been repeated for centuries. She is said, for example, to have been married to Cercylas, a wealthy man from the island of Andros. But many scholars challenge this claim, finding evidence in the Greek words of the bawdry of later comic poets. Most modern critics also consider it legend that Sappho leaped from the Leucadian rock to certain death in the sea because of her unrequited love of Phaon, a younger man and a sailor. She had at least two brothers, Larichus and Charaxus, and may have had a third. A fragment from Sappho that is dedicated to Charaxus has survived. One of her poems mentions a daughter named Cleis or Claïs. The tradition that she fled the island or was banished and went to Sicily may be true, but she lived most of her life in her hometown of Mytilene on Lesbos.

Sappho's work contains only a few apparent allusions to the political disturbances of the time, which are so frequently reflected in the verse of her contemporary Alcaeus. Her themes are invariably personal—primarily concerned with her *thiasos*, the usual term (not found in Sappho's extant writings) for the female community, with a religious and educational background, that met under her leadership. Sappho herself attacks in her poems other *thiasoi* directed by other women.

The goal of the Sapphic *thiasos* is the education of young women, especially for marriage. Aphrodite is the group's tutelary divinity and inspiration. Sappho is the intimate and servant of the goddess and her intermediary with the girls. In the ode to Aphrodite, the poet invokes the goddess to appear, as she has in the past, and to be her ally in persuading a girl she desires to love her. Frequent images in Sappho's poetry include flowers, bright garlands, naturalistic outdoor scenes, altars smoking with incense, perfumed unguents to sprinkle on the body and bathe the hair—that is, all the elements of Aphrodite's rituals. In the *thiasos* the girls were educated and initiated into grace and elegance for seduction and love. Singing, dancing, and poetry played a central role in this educational process and other cultural occasions. As was true for other female communities, including the Spartan, and for the corresponding masculine institutions, the practice of homoeroticism within the *thiasos* played a role in the context of initiation and education.

In Sappho's poetry, love is passion, an inescapable power that moves at the will of the goddess. It is desire and sensual emotion, nostalgia and memory of affections that are now distant but shared by the community of the *thiasos*. There is a personal poetic dimension, which is also collective because all the girls of the group recognize themselves in it. An important part of Sappho's poetic oeuvre is occupied by epithalamia, or nuptial songs.

It is not known how her poems were published and circulated in her own lifetime and for the following three or four centuries. In the era of Alexandrian scholarship

(3rd and 2nd centuries BCE), what survived of her work was collected and published in a standard edition of nine books of lyrical verse, divided according to metre. This edition did not endure beyond the early Middle Ages. By the 8th or 9th century CE, Sappho was represented only by quotations in other authors. Only the ode to Aphrodite, which is 28 lines long, is complete. The next longest fragment is 16 lines long. Since 1898 these fragments have been greatly increased by papyrus finds, though, in the opinion of some scholars, nothing equal in quality to the two longer poems.

CLEOPATRA

(b. 70/69 BCE — d. August of 30 BCE, Alexandria, Egypt)

Noted in history and drama as the lover of Julius Caesar and later the wife of Mark Antony, Cleopatra became queen on the death of her father, Ptolemy XII Auletes, in 51 BCE. She ruled successively with her two brothers, Ptolemy XIII (51–47) and Ptolemy XIV (47–44), and her son Ptolemy XV Caesar (44–30). Cleopatra actively influenced Roman politics at a crucial period, and she came to represent, as did no other woman of antiquity, the prototype of the romantic femme fatale.

EARLY LIFE AND REIGN

The Greek name Cleopatra means "Famous in Her Father," and her full regnal name is Cleopatra VII Thea Philopator ("Cleopatra the Father-Loving Goddess"). She was destined to become the last queen of the Macedonian dynasty that ruled Egypt between the death of Alexander the Great in 323 BCE and its annexation by Rome in 30 BCE. The line had been founded by Alexander's general Ptolemy, who became King Ptolemy I Soter of Egypt. Cleopatra was of Macedonian descent and had little, if any, Egyptian blood, although the Classical author Plutarch wrote that she alone of her house took the trouble to learn Egyptian and, for political reasons, styled herself as the new Isis, a title that distinguished her from the earlier Ptolemaic queen Cleopatra III, who had also claimed to be the living embodiment of the goddess Isis. Coin portraits of Cleopatra show a countenance alive rather than beautiful, with a sensitive mouth, firm chin, liquid eyes, broad forehead, and prominent nose.

When Ptolemy XII died in 51 BCE, the throne passed to his young son, Ptolemy XIII, and daughter, Cleopatra VII. It is likely, but not proven, that the two married soon after their father's death, a practice common among royalty. The 18-year-old Cleopatra, older than her brother by about eight years, became the dominant ruler. Evidence shows that the first decree in which Ptolemy's name precedes Cleopatra's was in October of 50 BCE. Soon after, Cleopatra was forced to flee Egypt for Syria, where she raised an army and in 48 BCE returned to face her brother at Pelusium, on Egypt's eastern border. The murder of the Roman general Pompey, who had sought refuge from Ptolemy XIII at Pelusium, and the arrival of Julius Caesar brought temporary peace.

A Powerful Alliance

Cleopatra realized that she needed Roman support, or, more specifically, Caesar's support, if she was to regain her throne. Each was determined to use the other. Caesar sought money for repayment of the debts incurred by Cleopatra's father, Auletes, as he struggled to retain his throne. Cleopatra was determined to keep her throne and, if possible, to restore the glories of the first Ptolemies and recover as much as possible of their dominions, which had included southern Syria and Palestine.

Caesar and Cleopatra became lovers and spent the winter besieged in Alexandria. Roman reinforcements arrived the following spring, and Ptolemy XIII fled and drowned in the Nile. Cleopatra, now married to her brother Ptolemy XIV, was restored to her throne. In June 47 BCE she gave birth to Ptolemy Caesar (known to the people of Alexandria as Caesarion, or "little Caesar"). Whether Caesar was the father of Caesarion, as his name implies, cannot now be known.

It took Caesar two years to extinguish the last flames of Pompeian opposition. As soon as he returned to Rome, in 46 BCE, he celebrated a four-day triumph—the ceremonial in honour of a general after his victory over a foreign enemy—in which Arsinoe, Cleopatra's younger and hostile sister, was paraded. Cleopatra paid at least one state visit to Rome, accompanied by her husband-brother and son. She was accommodated in Caesar's private villa beyond the Tiber River and may have been present to witness the dedication of a golden statue of herself in the temple of Venus Genetrix, the ancestress of the Julian family to which Caesar belonged. Cleopatra was in Rome when Caesar was murdered in 44 BCE.

ANTONY AND CLEOPATRA

Soon after her return to Alexandria, in 44 BCE, Cleopatra's coruler, Ptolemy XIV, died. Cleopatra now ruled with her infant son, Ptolemy XV Caesar. When, at the Battle of Philippi in 42 BCE, Caesar's assassins were routed, Mark Antony became the heir apparent of Caesar's authority—or so it seemed, for Caesar's great-nephew and personal heir, Octavian, was but a sickly boy. Antony, now controller of Rome's eastern territories, sent for Cleopatra so that she might explain her role in the aftermath of Caesar's assassination. She set out for Tarsus in Asia Minor loaded with gifts, having delayed her departure to heighten Antony's expectation. She entered the city by sailing up the Cydnus River in a barge while dressed in the robes of the new Isis. Antony, who equated himself with the god Dionysus, was captivated. Forgetting his wife, Fulvia, who in Italy was doing her best to maintain her husband's interests against the growing menace of young Octavian, Antony returned to Alexandria, where he treated Cleopatra not as a "protected" sovereign but as an independent monarch.

In Alexandria, Cleopatra and Antony formed a society of "inimitable livers" whose members lived what some historians have interpreted as a life of debauchery and folly and others have interpreted as lives dedicated to the cult of the mystical god Dionysus.

In 40 BCE Cleopatra gave birth to twins, whom she named Alexander Helios and Cleopatra Selene. Antony had already left Alexandria to return to Italy, where he was forced to conclude a temporary settlement with Octavian. As part of this settlement, he married Octavian's sister, Octavia (Fulvia having died). Three years later Antony was convinced that he and Octavian could never come to terms. His marriage to Octavia now an irrelevance, he returned to the east and reunited with Cleopatra. Antony needed Cleopatra's financial support for his postponed Parthian campaign. In return, Cleopatra requested the return of much of Egypt's eastern empire, including large portions of Syria and Lebanon and even the rich balsam groves of Jericho.

The Parthian campaign was a costly failure, as was the temporary conquest of Armenia. Nevertheless, in 34 BCE Antony celebrated a triumphal return to Alexandria. This was followed by a celebration known as "the Donations of Alexandria." Crowds flocked to the Gymnasium to see Cleopatra and Antony seated on golden thrones on a silver platform with their children sitting on slightly lower thrones beside them. Antony proclaimed Caesarion to be Caesar's son—thus relegating Octavian, who had been adopted by Caesar as his son and heir, to legal bastardy. Cleopatra was hailed as queen of kings, Caesarion as king of kings. Alexander Helios was awarded Armenia and the territory beyond the Euphrates, his infant brother Ptolemy the lands to the west of it. The boys' sister, Cleopatra Selene, was to be ruler of Cyrene. It was clear to Octavian, watching from Rome, that Antony intended his extended family to rule the civilized world. A propaganda war erupted. Octavian seized Antony's will (or what he claimed to be Antony's will) from the temple of the Vestal Virgins, to whom it had been entrusted, and revealed to the Roman people that not only had Antony bestowed Roman possessions on a foreign woman but intended to be buried beside her in Egypt. The rumour quickly spread that Antony also intended to transfer the capital from Rome to Alexandria.

Antony and Cleopatra spent the winter of 32–31 BCE in Greece. The Roman Senate deprived Antony of his prospective consulate for the following year, and it then declared war against Cleopatra. The naval Battle of Actium, in which Octavian faced the combined forces of Antony and Cleopatra on Sept. 2, 31 BCE, was a disaster for the Egyptians. Antony and Cleopatra fled to Egypt, and Cleopatra retired to her mausoleum as Antony went off to fight his last battle. Receiving the false news that Cleopatra had died, Antony fell on his sword. In a last excess of devotion, he had himself carried to Cleopatra's retreat and there died, after bidding her to make her peace with Octavian.

Cleopatra buried Antony and then committed suicide. The means of her death is uncertain, though Classical writers came to believe that she had killed herself by means of an asp, symbol of divine royalty. She was 39 and had been a queen for 22 years and Antony's partner for 11. They were buried together, as both of them had wished, and with them was buried the Roman Republic.

CLEOPATRA THROUGH THE AGES

The vast majority of Egypt's many hundreds of queens, although famed throughout their own land, were more or less unknown in the outside world. As the dynastic age ended and the hieroglyphic script was lost, the queens' stories were forgotten and their monuments buried under Egypt's sands. But Cleopatra had lived in a highly literate age, and her actions had influenced the formation of the Roman Empire; her story could not be forgotten. Octavian (the future emperor Augustus) was determined that Roman history should be recorded in a way that confirmed his right to rule. To achieve this, he published his own autobiography and censored Rome's official records. As Cleopatra had played a key role in his struggle to power, her story was preserved as an integral part of his, but it was diminished to just two episodes: her relationships with Julius Caesar and Mark Antony. Cleopatra, stripped of any political validity, was to be remembered as an immoral foreign woman who tempted upright Roman men. As such, she became a useful enemy for Octavian, who preferred to be remembered for fighting against foreigners rather than against his fellow Romans.

This official Roman version of a predatory, immoral Cleopatra passed into Western culture, where it was retold and reinterpreted as the years passed, until it evolved into a story of a wicked life made good by an honourable death. Meanwhile, Muslim scholars, writing after the Arab conquest of Egypt about 640 CE, developed their own version of the queen. Their Cleopatra was first and foremost a scholar and a scientist, a gifted philosopher and a chemist.

Plutarch's *Parallel Lives*, translated from the Greek into French by Jacques Amyot (1559) and then from the French into English by Sir Thomas North (1579), served as the inspiration behind Shakespeare's play *Antony and Cleopatra* (1606–07). Shakespeare dropped some of Plutarch's disapproval and allowed his queen to become a true heroine. His was by no means the first revision of Cleopatra, nor was it to be the last, but his is the Cleopatra that has lingered longest in the public imagination. From Shakespeare stems a wealth of Cleopatra-themed art—plays, poetry, paintings, and operas.

In the 20th century Cleopatra's story was preserved and further developed through film. Many actresses, including Theda Bara (1917), Claudette Colbert (1934), and Elizabeth Taylor (1963), have played the queen, typically in expensive, exotic films that concentrate on the queen's love life rather than her politics. Meanwhile, Cleopatra's seductive beauty—a seductive beauty that is not supported by the queen's contemporary portraiture—has been used to sell a wide range of products, from cosmetics to cigarettes. In the late 20th century Cleopatra's racial heritage became a subject of intense academic debate, with some African American scholars embracing Cleopatra as a black African heroine.

MARY

(fl. beginning of the Christian, or Common, Era)

The Virgin Mary and Saint Mary are among the many names by which Mary, the mother of Jesus, is known. She has been an object of veneration in the Christian church since the apostolic age and a favourite subject in Western art, music, and literature. Mary is known from biblical references, which are, however, too sparse to construct a coherent biography. The development of the doctrine of

The Virgin Adoring the Child, *oil on wood panel by Fra Filippo Lippi*, c. *1460; in the Staatliche Museen Preussischer Kulturbesitz, Berlin.* Staatliche Museen Preussischer Kulturbesitz, Berlin

Mary can be traced through titles that have been ascribed to her in the history of the Christian communions—guarantee of the incarnation, virgin mother, second Eve, mother of God, ever virgin, immaculate, and assumed into heaven.

The New Testament account of her humility and obedience to the message of God have made her an exemplar for all ages of Christians. Out of the details supplied in the New Testament by the Gospels about the maid of Galilee, Christian piety and theology have constructed a picture of Mary that fulfills the prediction ascribed to her in the Magnificat (Luke 1:48): "Henceforth all generations will call me blessed."

The first mention of Mary is the story of the Annunciation, which reports that she was living in Nazareth and was betrothed to Joseph (Luke 1:26 ff.); the last mention of her (Acts 1:14) includes her in the company of those who devoted themselves to prayer after the ascension of Jesus into heaven. Other stories about her recount her visit with Elizabeth, her kinswoman and the mother of John the Baptist, the precursor of Jesus (Luke 1:39 ff.); the birth of Jesus and the presentation of him in the Temple (Luke 2:1 ff.); the coming of the Magi and the flight to Egypt (Matthew 2:1 ff.); the Passover visit to Jerusalem when Jesus was 12 years old (Luke 2:41 ff.); the marriage at Cana in Galilee, although her name is not used (John 2:1 ff.); the attempt to see Jesus while he was teaching (Mark 3:31 ff.); and the station at the cross, where, apparently widowed, she was entrusted to the disciple John (John 19:26 ff.). Even if one takes these scenes as literal historical accounts, they do not add up to an integrated portrait of Mary. Only in the narratives of the Nativity and the Passion of Christ is her place a significant one. In contrast, her acceptance of the privilege conferred on her in the Annunciation is the solemn prologue to the Christmas story. Not only does she stand at the foot of the Cross, but in the Easter story, "the other

Mary" who came to the tomb of Jesus (Matthew 28:1) is not she; according to traditional interpretations, she knew that the body of Jesus would not be there. On the other hand, the incidents that belong to the life of Jesus contain elements of a pronouncedly human character, perhaps even the suggestion that she did not fully understand Jesus' true mission.

Since the early days of Christianity, however, the themes that these scenes symbolize have been the basis for thought and contemplation about Mary. Christian communions and theologians differ from one another in their interpretations of Mary principally on the basis of where they set the terminal point for such development and expansion—that is, where they maintain that the legitimate development of doctrine may be said to have ended.

Mary has achieved great cultural importance. Popular devotion to Mary—in such forms as feasts, devotional services, and the rosary—has played a tremendously important role in the lives of Roman Catholics and the Orthodox; at times, this devotion has pushed other doctrines into the background. Modern Roman Catholicism has emphasized that the doctrine of Mary is not an isolated belief but must be seen in the context of two other Christian doctrines: the doctrine of Christ and the doctrine of the church. What is said of Mary is derived from what is said of Jesus: this was the basic meaning of Theotokos. She has also been known as "the first believer" and as the one in whom the humanity of the church was representatively embodied.

HYPATIA

(b. c. 370, Alexandria, Egypt—d. March 415, Alexandria)

The Egyptian Neoplatonist philosopher Hypatia was also the first notable woman in the field of mathematics.

The daughter of Theon, also a notable mathematician and philosopher, Hypatia became the recognized head of the Neoplatonist school of philosophy at Alexandria about 400, and her eloquence, modesty, and beauty, combined with her remarkable intellectual gifts, attracted a large number of pupils. Among them was Synesius of Cyrene, afterward bishop of Ptolemais (*c.* 410), several of whose letters to her are still extant.

Hypatia lectured on mathematics and on the philosophical teachings of two Neoplatonists: Plotinus (*c.* 205–270 CE), the founder of Neoplatonism, and Iamblichus (*c.* 250–330 CE), the founder of the Syrian branch of Neoplatonism. She symbolized learning and science, which at that time in Western history were largely identified with paganism.

This left Hypatia in a precarious situation. Theodosius I, Roman emperor in the East from 379 to 392 and then emperor in both the East and West until 395, initiated an official policy of intolerance to paganism and Arianism in 380. In 391, in reply to Theophilus, the bishop of Alexandria, he gave permission to destroy Egyptian religious institutions. Christian mobs obliged by destroying the Library of Alexandria, the Temple of Serapis, and other pagan monuments. Although legislation in 393 sought to curb violence, particularly the looting and destruction of Jewish synagogues, a renewal of disturbances occurred after the accession of Cyril to the patriarchate of Alexandria in 412. Tension culminated in the forced, albeit illegal, expulsion of Alexandrian Jews in 414 and the murder of Hypatia, the most prominent Alexandrian pagan, by a fanatical mob of Christians in 415. The departure soon afterward of many scholars marked the beginning of the decline of Alexandria as a major centre of ancient learning.

According to the *Suda Lexicon*, a 10th-century encyclopedia, Hypatia wrote commentaries on the *Arithmetica* of

Diophantus of Alexandria, on the *Conics* of Apollonius of Perga, and on an astronomical canon (presumably Ptolemy's *Almagest*). We have it on the authority of her father, Theon, that she revised Book III of his commentary on the *Almagest*. All of these works are lost, although some may survive as parts of the extant Arabic versions of the *Arithmetica*. The known titles of her works, combined with the letters of Synesius who consulted her about the construction of an astrolabe and a hydroscope (identified in the 17th century by Pierre de Fermat as a hydrometer), indicate that she devoted herself particularly to astronomy and mathematics. The existence of any strictly philosophical works by her is unknown. Indeed, her philosophy was more scholarly and scientific in its interest and less mystical and intransigently pagan than the Neoplatonism taught in other schools. Nevertheless, statements attributed to her, such as "Reserve your right to think, for even to think wrongly is better than not to think at all" and "To teach superstitions as truth is a most terrible thing," must have incensed Cyril, who in turn incensed the mob.

Hypatia's reputation as a learned and beautiful female philosopher, combined with the dramatic details of her grisly death, have inspired the imaginations of numerous writers, inspiring works such as Charles Kingsley's novel *Hypatia: New Foes with an Old Face* (1852).

THEODORA

(b. *c.* 497 —d. June 28, 548, Constantinople [now Istanbul, Turkey])

The Byzantine empress Theodora was the wife of the emperor Justinian I (reigned 527–565) and probably the most powerful woman in Byzantine history. Her intelligence and political acumen made her Justinian's most trusted adviser and enabled her to use the power and influence of her office to promote religious and social policies that favoured her interests.

Little is known of Theodora's early life, but a combination of the official version with that found in the highly coloured *Secret History of Procopius of Caesarea* probably provides the best explanation. Her father was a bear keeper at the Hippodrome (circus) in Constantinople. She became an actress while still young, leading an unconventional life that included giving birth to at least one child out of wedlock. For a time, she made her living as a wool spinner. When Justinian met her, she had been converted to monophysitism, a nonorthodox doctrine. Attracted by her beauty and intelligence, he made her his mistress, raised her to the rank of patrician, and in 525 married her. When Justinian succeeded to the throne in 527, she was proclaimed Augusta.

Theodora exercised considerable influence, and though she was never coregent, her superior intelligence and deft handling of political affairs caused many to think that it was she, rather than Justinian, who ruled Byzantium. Her name is mentioned in nearly all the laws passed during that period. She received foreign envoys and corresponded with foreign rulers, functions usually reserved for the emperor. Her influence in political affairs was decisive, as illustrated in the Nika revolt of January 532. The two political factions in Constantinople, the Blues and the Greens, united in their opposition to the government and set up a rival emperor. Justinian's advisers urged him to flee, but Theodora advised him to stay and save his empire, whereupon Justinian's general, Belisarius, herded the rioters into the Hippodrome and cut them to pieces.

Theodora is remembered as one of the first rulers to recognize the rights of women, passing strict laws to prohibit the traffic in young girls and altering the divorce laws to give greater benefits to women. She spent much of her reign trying to mitigate the laws against the monophysites. Though she succeeded in ending their persecution in 533, she never succeeded in changing Justinian's religious policy from its emphasis on orthodoxy and friendship with Rome.

The best-known representation of Theodora is the mosaic portrait in the Church of San Vitale in Ravenna. Her death, possibly from cancer or gangrene, was a severe blow to Justinian. Her importance in Byzantine political life is shown by the fact that little significant legislation dates from the period between her death and that of Justinian (565).

WUHOU

(b. 624, Wenshui [now in Shanxi province], China—d. Dec. 16, 705, Luoyang)

Wuhou is the posthumous name (*shi*) of the woman who rose from concubinage to become empress of China during the Tang dynasty (618–907). She ruled effectively for many years, the last 15 (690–705) in her own name. During her reign, Tang rule was consolidated, and the empire was unified.

Wu Zhao, also called Wu Zetian, entered the palace of the Tang emperor Taizong (ruled 626–649) in 638, at age 14, as a junior concubine. By that time, the Tang dynasty had recently reunited China, largely through the efforts of Taizong. Little is known of Wu's life as a concubine of Taizong, but, on his death in 649, she is traditionally said to have already entered into intimate relations with his heir, the Gaozong emperor. Relegated to a Buddhist convent on the death of Taizong, as custom required, the future empress Wuhou was visited there by the new emperor, who had her brought back to the palace to be his own favourite concubine. She first eliminated her female rivals within the palace—the existing empress and leading concubines—and in 655 gained the position of empress for herself, eventually bearing Gaozong four sons and one daughter.

Wuhou used her authority to bring about the fall of the elder statesmen, all of whom had served Taizong and still exercised great influence over the government. These men opposed her elevation to the position of empress, mainly because, although she was the daughter of a relatively senior officer, her family was not one of the great aristocratic clans. They also objected to the nature of her relationship with Gaozong, on the grounds that as she had been a concubine of Taizong, it was incestuous. By 660 the empress had triumphed over all opponents, who had been dismissed, exiled, and, in many instances, finally executed. Even the emperor's uncle, the head of the great family of the Changsun, of imperial descent, was hounded to death, and his relatives were exiled or ruined.

Virtually supreme power was now exercised by the Wuhou empress in the name of the sickly Gaozong, who was often too ill to attend to state affairs for long periods. The emperor, who was weak in character, relied on her entirely, and for the last 23 years of his life, the empress was the real ruler of China. She continued to eliminate potential rivals, even when these were her own relatives, but she governed the empire with great efficiency, employing able men who clearly felt loyalty to her and stood by her when she was challenged. Her great ability as an administrator, her courage, decisive character, and readiness to use ruthless means against any opponent, however highly placed, won her the respect, if not the love, of the court.

In the years between 655 and 675, the Tang empire conquered Korea under military leaders who were picked and promoted by the empress. When Gaozong died in

683, he was succeeded by his son Li Xian (by Wuhou), known as the Zhongzong emperor. The new emperor had been married to a woman of the Wei family, who now sought to put herself in the same position of authority as that of Wuhou, for Zhongzong was as weak and incompetent as his father. After one month Wuhou deposed her son, exiled him, and installed as emperor her second son, Li Dan (the Ruizong emperor), whose authority was purely nominal. A revolt was raised by Tang loyalists and ambitious young officials in the south. It was crushed within weeks with the loyal cooperation of the main armies of the throne. This demonstration of the support she commanded in the public service made the position of the empress unshakable.

Six years later, in 690, at age 65, the empress usurped the throne itself. Accepted without revolt, she ruled for 15 years. During that period the question of the succession began to assume great urgency. Her own nephews of the Wu family had hoped that as she had already changed the name of the dynasty to Zhou, she would also displace the Tang heirs of the Li family and leave the throne to one of the Wu nephews. Neither of them nor their sons was popular or unusually capable; on the other hand, Wuhou's own sons, the two former emperors Zhongzong and Ruizong, had little support and less ability. But, even among her loyal supporters, there was a growing hope that the Tang family of Li would not be discarded. In 698 the empress decided to accede to these views; the exiled Zhongzong was recalled to court and made crown prince. The empress showed her remarkable quality in this decision; she did not place her own family in the line of succession or designate one of her nephews as her heir. She seems to have had no ambition on behalf of her own family, only a determination to retain power for herself to the end.

In the last years of her life, from 699, the empress gave her favour to the Zhang brothers, artistic but depraved courtiers who engaged her affection by elaborate entertainments and skillful flattery. They were intensely resented by the court and senior officials, many of whom had the temerity—and courage—to warn the empress of their pernicious activity. She did not heed these warnings and, as she gradually fell into ill health, depended increasingly on the care of the Zhang brothers. In February 705 a conspiracy formed among the leading ministers and generals, who seized the palace, executed the Zhang brothers, and compelled the empress, old and ill, to yield power to Zhongzong, who reigned until 710. She retired to another palace and died there in December of that year.

The Wuhou empress was a highly competent ruler, using men of her own choice, regardless of their social standing. Although her motives were to secure her own authority, the consequences of her policies were to be of great historical importance. The transformation of Chinese society in the Tang period from one dominated by a military and political aristocracy to one governed by a scholarly bureaucracy drawn from the gentry was promoted by her policy. The significance of this aspect of her rule was long obscured by the prejudice of Chinese historians against an usurping empress and her many acts of cruelty toward opponents. She established the new unified empire on a lasting basis and brought about needed social changes that stabilized the dynasty and ushered in one of the most fruitful ages of Chinese civilization.

IRENE

(b. *c.* 752, Athens [Greece]—d. Aug. 9, 803, Lesbos)

Irene was a Byzantine ruler and saint of the Greek Orthodox Church who was instrumental in restoring the use of icons in the Eastern Roman Empire.

The wife of the Byzantine emperor Leo IV, Irene became, on her husband's death in September 780, guardian of their 10-year-old son, Constantine VI, and co-emperor with him. Later in that year she crushed what seems to have been a plot by the Iconoclasts (opposers of the use of icons) to put Leo's half brother, Nicephorus, on the throne.

Irene favoured the restoration of the use of icons, which had been prohibited in 730. She had Tarasius, one of her supporters, elected patriarch of Constantinople and then summoned a general church council on the subject. When it met in Constantinople in 786, it was broken up by Iconoclast soldiers stationed in that city. Another council, which is recognized by both the Roman Catholic and Eastern Orthodox churches as the Seventh Ecumenical Council, met at Nicaea in 787 and restored the cult of images.

As Constantine approached maturity, he grew resentful of his mother's controlling influence in the empire. An attempt to seize power was crushed by the empress, who demanded that the military oath of fidelity should recognize her as senior ruler. Anger at the demand prompted the themes (administrative divisions) of Asia Minor to open resistance in 790. Constantine VI was proclaimed sole ruler and his mother banished from court. In January 792, however, Irene was allowed to return to court and even to resume her position as coruler. By skillful intrigues with the bishops and courtiers she organized a conspiracy against Constantine, who was arrested and blinded at his mother's orders (797).

Irene then reigned alone as emperor (not empress) for five years. In 798 she opened diplomatic relations with the Western emperor Charlemagne, and in 802 a marriage between her and Charlemagne was reportedly contemplated. According to the contemporary Byzantine historian Theophanes, the scheme was frustrated by one of Irene's favourites. In 802 a conspiracy of officials and generals deposed her and placed on the throne Nicephorus, the minister of finance. She was exiled, first to the island of Prinkipo (now Büyükada) and then to Lesbos.

Irene's zeal in restoring icons and her patronage of monasteries ensured her a place among the saints of the Greek Orthodox Church. Her feast day is August 9.

MURASAKI SHIKIBU

(b. *c.* 978, Kyōto, Japan—d. *c.* 1014, Kyōto)

The court lady known as Murasaki Shikibu was the author of the *Genji monogatari* (*The Tale of Genji*), generally considered the greatest work of Japanese literature and thought to be the world's oldest full novel.

The author's real name is unknown; it is conjectured that she acquired the sobriquet of Murasaki from the name of the heroine of her novel, and the name Shikibu reflects her father's position at the Bureau of Rites. She was born into a lesser branch of the noble and highly influential Fujiwara family and was well educated, having learned Chinese (generally the exclusive sphere of males). She married a much older distant cousin, Fujiwara Nobutaka, and bore him a daughter, but after two years of marriage he died.

Some critics believe that she wrote the entire *Tale of Genji* between 1001 (the year her husband died) and 1005, the year in which she was summoned to serve at court (for reasons unknown). It is more likely that the composition of her extremely long and complex novel extended over a much greater period; her new position within what was then a leading literary centre likely enabled her to produce a story that was not finished until about 1010. In any case this work is the main source of knowledge about her life. It possesses considerable interest for the delightful

Murasaki Shikibu confers with wise men and fellow poets in this detail of a woodcut by Kitigawa Utamaro. She is credited with writing one of the greatest works of Japanese literature. Library of Congress Prints and Photographs Division

glimpses it affords of life at the court of the empress Jōtō mon'in, whom Murasaki Shikibu served.

The Tale of Genji captures the image of a unique society of ultrarefined and elegant aristocrats, whose indispensable accomplishments were skill in poetry, music, calligraphy, and courtship. Much of it is concerned with the loves of Prince Genji and the different women in his life, all of whom are exquisitely delineated. Although the novel does not contain scenes of powerful action, it is permeated with a sensitivity to human emotions and to the beauties of nature hardly paralleled elsewhere. The tone of the novel darkens as it progresses, indicating perhaps a deepening of Murasaki Shikibu's Buddhist conviction of the vanity of the world. Some, however, believe that its last 14 chapters were written by another author.

Arthur Waley was the first to translate *The Tale of Genji* into English (6 vol., 1925–33). Waley's translation is beautiful and inspiring, a classic of English literature, but also very free. Edward Seidensticker's translation (1976) is true to the original in both content and tone, but its notes and reader aids are sparse, unlike the translation published by Royall Tyler in 2001. Murasaki Shikibu's diary is included in *Diaries of Court Ladies of Old Japan* (1935), translated by Annie Shepley Ōmori and Kōchi Doi.

HILDEGARD

(b. 1098, Böckelheim, West Franconia [Germany] — d. Sept. 17, 1179, Rupertsberg, near Bingen; traditional feast day September 17)

Hildegard, also called Hildegard von Bingen and the Sibyl of the Rhine, was a German abbess, visionary mystic, and composer. Born of noble parents, Hildegard was educated at the Benedictine cloister of Disibodenberg by Jutta, an anchorite and sister of the count of Spanheim.

Hildegard was 15 years old when she began wearing the Benedictine habit and pursuing a religious life. She succeeded Jutta as prioress in 1136.

Having experienced visions since she was a child, at age 43 she consulted her confessor, who in turn reported the matter to the archbishop of Mainz. A committee of theologians subsequently confirmed the authenticity of Hildegard's visions, and a monk was appointed to help her record them in writing. The finished work, *Scivias* (1141–52), consists of 26 visions that are prophetic and apocalyptic in form and in their treatment of such topics as the church, the relationship between God and man, and redemption. About 1147 Hildegard left Disibodenberg with several nuns to found a new convent at Rupertsberg, where she continued to exercise the gift of prophecy and to record her visions in writing.

A talented poet and composer, Hildegard collected 77 of her lyric poems, each with a musical setting composed by her, in *Symphonia armonie celestium revelationum*. Her numerous other writings include lives of saints; two treatises on medicine and natural history, reflecting a quality of scientific observation rare at that period; and extensive correspondence, in which are to be found further prophecies and allegorical treatises. She also for amusement contrived her own language. She traveled widely throughout Germany, evangelizing to large groups of people about her visions and religious insights. Though her earliest biographer proclaimed her a saint and miracles were reported during her life and at her tomb, she was never formally canonized. She is, however, listed as a saint in the Roman Martyrology and is honoured on her feast day in certain German dioceses.

As one of the few prominent women in medieval church history, Hildegard became the subject of increasing interest in the latter half of the 20th century. Her writings were widely translated into English; several recordings of her music were made available; and works of fiction, including Barbara Lachman's *The Journal of Hildegard of Bingen* (1993) and Joan Ohanneson's *Scarlet Music: A Life of Hildegard of Bingen* (1997), were published.

ELEANOR OF AQUITAINE

(b. *c.* 1122 — d. April 1, 1204, Fontevrault, Anjou, France)

The queen consort of both Louis VII of France (1137–52) and Henry II of England (1152–1204), Eleanor of Aquitaine (also called Eleanor of Guyenne) was the mother of Richard the Lion-Heart and John of England. She was perhaps the most powerful woman in 12th-century Europe.

Eleanor (French: Éléonore, or Aliénor, d'Aquitaine [or de Guyenne]) was the daughter and heiress of William X, duke of Aquitaine and count of Poitiers, who possessed one of the largest domains in France — larger, in fact, than those held by the French king. Upon William's death in 1137 she inherited the duchy of Aquitaine and in July 1137 married the heir to the French throne, who succeeded his father, Louis VI, the following month. Eleanor became queen of France, a title she held for the next 15 years. Beautiful, capricious, and adored by Louis, Eleanor exerted considerable influence over him, often goading him into undertaking perilous ventures.

From 1147 to 1149 Eleanor accompanied Louis on the Second Crusade to protect the fragile Latin kingdom of Jerusalem, founded after the First Crusade only 50 years before, from Turkish assault. Eleanor's conduct during this expedition, especially at the court of her uncle Raymond of Poitiers at Antioch, aroused Louis's jealousy and marked the beginning of their estrangement. After their return to France and a short-lived reconciliation,

Eleanor of Aquitaine marrying Louis VII in 1137 (left scene) *and Louis VII departing on the Second Crusade (1147), drawing from* Les Chroniques de Saint-Denis, *late 14th century.* © Photos.com/Jupiterimages

their marriage was annulled in March 1152. According to feudal customs, Eleanor then regained possession of Aquitaine, and two months later she married the grandson of Henry I of England, Henry Plantagenet, count of Anjou and duke of Normandy. In 1154 he became, as Henry II, king of England, with the result that England, Normandy, and the west of France were united under his rule.

Eleanor had only two daughters by Louis VII; to her new husband she bore five sons and three daughters. The sons were William, who died at the age of three; Henry; Richard, the Lion-Heart; Geoffrey, duke of Brittany; and John, surnamed Lackland until, having outlived all his brothers, he inherited, in 1199, the crown of England. The daughters were Matilda, who married Henry the Lion, duke of Saxony and Bavaria; Eleanor, who married Alfonso VIII, king of Castile; and Joan, who married successively William II, king of Sicily, and Raymond VI, count of Toulouse. Eleanor would well have deserved to be named the "grandmother of Europe."

During her childbearing years, she participated actively in the administration of the realm and even more actively in the management of her own domains. She was instrumental in turning the court of Poitiers, then frequented by the most famous troubadours of the time, into a centre of poetry and a model of courtly life and manners. She was the great patron of the two dominant poetic movements of the time: the courtly love tradition, conveyed in the romantic songs of the troubadours, and the historical *matière de Bretagne*, or "legends of Brittany," which originated in Celtic traditions and in the *Historia regum Britanniae*, written by the chronicler Geoffrey of Monmouth sometime between 1135 and 1138.

The revolt of her sons against her husband in 1173 put her cultural activities to a brutal end. Since Eleanor, 11 years her husband's senior, had long resented his infidelities, the revolt may have been instigated by her; in any case, she gave her sons considerable military support. The revolt failed, and Eleanor was captured while seeking refuge in the kingdom of her first husband, Louis VII. Her semi-imprisonment in England ended only with the death of Henry II in 1189. On her release, Eleanor played a greater political role than ever before. She actively prepared for Richard's coronation as king, was administrator of the realm during his Crusade to the Holy Land, and, after his capture by the duke of Austria on Richard's return from the East, collected his ransom and went in person to escort him to England. During Richard's absence, she succeeded in keeping his kingdom intact and in thwarting the intrigues of his brother John Lackland and Philip II Augustus, king of France, against him.

In 1199 Richard died without leaving an heir to the throne, and John was crowned king. Eleanor, nearly 80 years old, fearing the disintegration of the Plantagenet domain, crossed the Pyrenees in 1200 in order to fetch her granddaughter Blanche from the court of Castile and marry her to the son of the French king. By this marriage she hoped to ensure peace between the Plantagenets of England and the Capetian kings of France. In the same year she helped to defend Anjou and Aquitaine against her grandson Arthur of Brittany, thus securing John's French possessions. In 1202 John was again in her debt for holding Mirebeau against Arthur, until John, coming to her relief, was able to take him prisoner. John's only victories on the Continent, therefore, were due to Eleanor. She died in 1204 at the monastery at Fontevrault, Anjou, where she had retired after the campaign at Mirebeau.

Her contribution to England extended beyond her own lifetime. After the loss of Normandy (1204), it was her own ancestral lands and not the old Norman territories that remained loyal to England. She has been misjudged by many French historians who have noted only her youthful frivolity, ignoring the tenacity, political wisdom, and energy that characterized the years of her maturity. "She was beautiful and just, imposing and modest, humble and elegant"; and, as the nuns of Fontevrault wrote in their necrology, a queen "who surpassed almost all the queens of the world."

MARGARET I

(b. 1353, Søborg, Den.—d. Oct. 28, 1412, Flensburg)

As the regent of Denmark (from 1375), of Norway (from 1380), and of Sweden (from 1389), Margaret I, by diplomacy and war, pursued dynastic policies that led to the Kalmar Union (1397), which united Denmark, Norway, and Sweden until 1523 and Denmark and Norway until 1814.

The daughter of King Valdemar IV of Denmark, Margaret was only six years old when she was betrothed to Haakon, king of Norway and son of King Magnus Eriksson of Sweden and Norway. The betrothal, intended to counter the dynastic claims to the Scandinavian thrones by the dukes of Mecklenburg and the intrigues of certain aristocratic factions within the Scandinavian countries, was imperilled by the renewal in 1360 of the old struggle between Valdemar of Denmark and Magnus of Sweden. But military reverses and the opposition of his own nobility forced Magnus to suspend hostilities in 1363. The wedding of Margaret and Haakon took place in Copenhagen in the same year.

Haakon's aspirations to become king of Sweden were thwarted when he and his father were defeated soon afterward by Albert of Mecklenburg, who bore the Swedish crown from 1364 to 1389. Haakon, however, succeeded in keeping his Norwegian kingdom, and it was there that Margaret spent her youth, under the tutelage of Märta Ulfsdotter, a daughter of the Swedish saint, Bridget. Margaret early displayed her talent as a ruler: she soon overshadowed her husband and appears to have exercised the real power. The couple's only child, Olaf, was born in 1370.

After her father's death in 1375, Margaret—over the objections of the Mecklenburgian claimants—was successful in getting Olaf elected to the Danish throne. Following Haakon's death in 1380, Margaret also ruled Norway in her son's name. Thus began the Danish-Norwegian union that lasted until 1814. Margaret secured and extended her sovereignty: in 1385 she won back the economically important strongholds on the west coast of Scandia from the Hanseatic League, and for a time she was also able to safeguard Denmark's southern borders by agreement with the counts of Holstein.

Margaret and Olaf, who came of age in 1385, were on the point of making war on Albert to enforce their claims to the Swedish throne when Olaf died unexpectedly in 1387. Deploying all her diplomatic skill, Margaret consolidated her position, becoming regent of both Norway and Denmark and, in the absence of an heir, adopting her six-year-old nephew, Erik of Pomerania. She then joined forces with the Swedish nobles, who had risen against the unpopular king Albert in a dispute over the will disposing of the lands of Bo Jonsson Grip, the powerful chancellor. By the Treaty of Dalaborg of 1388, the nobles proclaimed Margaret Sweden's "sovereign lady and rightful ruler" and granted her the main portion of Bo Jonsson Grip's vast domains.

Defeating Albert in 1389, Margaret took him captive and released him only after the conclusion of peace six years later. His supporters, who had allied themselves with pirate bands in the Baltic Sea, did not surrender Stockholm until 1398.

Margaret was now the undisputed ruler of the three Scandinavian states. Her heir, Erik of Pomerania, was proclaimed hereditary king of Norway in 1389 and was elected king of Denmark and Sweden (which also included Finland) in 1396. His coronation took place the following year in the southern Swedish town of Kalmar, in the presence of the leading figures of all the Scandinavian countries.

At Kalmar the nobility manifested its opposition to Margaret's increasing exercise of absolute power. The two extant documents disclose traces of the struggle between two political principles: the principle of absolute hereditary monarchy, as expressed in the so-called coronation act, and the constitutional elective kingship preferred by some nobles, as expressed in the so-called union act. The Kalmar assembly was a victory for Margaret and absolutism; the union act—perhaps the medieval Scandinavian document most debated by historians—denoted a plan that failed.

Despite Erik's coronation, Margaret remained Scandinavia's actual ruler until her death. Her aim was to further develop a strong royal central power and to foster the growth of a united Scandinavian state with its centre of gravity located in Denmark, her old hereditary dominion. She succeeded in eliminating the opposition of the nobility, in curbing the powers of the council of state, and in consolidating the administration through a network of royal sheriffs. In order to secure her position economically, she levied heavy taxes and confiscated church estates and lands exempt from dues to the crown. That such a policy succeeded without fatal strife to the union testifies to her strong political position as well as to her diplomatic skills and her ruthlessness. By adroitly using her relations to the Holy See, she was able to strengthen her influence over the church and on the politically important episcopal elections.

Margaret's political acumen was also evident in foreign affairs. Her main goals were to put an end to German expansion to the north and to extend and secure Denmark's southern borders, goals she tried to achieve through diplomatic means. An armed conflict did, however, break out with Holstein, and during the war Margaret died unexpectedly in 1412.

One of Scandinavia's most eminent monarchs, Margaret was able not only to establish peace in her realms but also to maintain her authority against the aspirations of German princes and against the superior economic power of the Hanseatic League. The united kingdom that she created and left as a legacy, whose cementing factor was a strong monarchy, remained in existence until 1523, albeit not without interruptions.

CHRISTINE DE PISAN
(b. 1364, Venice [Italy]—d. c. 1430)

One of the earliest feminists, Christine de Pisan was a prolific and versatile French poet and author whose diverse writings include numerous poems of courtly love, a biography of Charles V of France, and several works championing women.

Christine's Italian father was astrologer to Charles V, and she spent a pleasant, studious childhood at the French court. At 15 she married Estienne de Castel, who became court secretary. Widowed after 10 years of marriage, she took up writing in order to support herself and her three young children. Her first poems were ballades of lost love written to the memory of her husband. These verses met with success, and she continued writing ballads, rondeaux, lays, and complaints in which she expressed her feelings with grace and sincerity. Among her patrons were Louis I, the duke d'Orléans, the duke de Berry, Philip II the Bold of Burgundy, Queen Isabella of Bavaria, and, in England, the 4th earl of Salisbury. In all, she wrote 10 volumes in verse, including *L'Épistre au Dieu d'amours* (1399; "Letter to the God of Loves"), in which she defended women against the satire of Jean de Meun in the *Roman de la rose*.

Christine's prose works include *Le Livre de la cité des dames* (1405; *The Book of the City of Ladies*), in which she wrote of women known for their heroism and virtue, and *Le Livre des trois vertus* (1405; "Book of Three Virtues"), a sequel comprising a classification of women's roles in medieval society and a collection of moral instructions for women in the various social spheres. The story of her life, *L'Avision de Christine* (1405), told in an allegorical manner, was a reply to her detractors. At the request of the regent, Philip the Bold of Burgundy, Christine wrote the life of the deceased king, Charles — *Le Livre des fais et bonnes meurs du sage roy Charles V* (1404; "Book of the Deeds and Good Morals of the Wise King Charles V"), a firsthand picture of Charles V and his court. Her eight additional prose works reveal her remarkable breadth of knowledge.

After the disastrous Battle of Agincourt in 1415, she retired to a convent. Her last work, *Le Ditié de Jehanne d'Arc* (written in 1429), is a lyrical, joyous outburst inspired by the early victories of Joan of Arc; it is the only such French-language work written during Joan's lifetime.

JOAN OF ARC

(b. *c.* 1412, Domrémy, Bar, France — d. May 30, 1431, Rouen; canonized May 16, 1920; feast day May 30; French national holiday, second Sunday in May)

Joan of Arc (French: Jeanne d'Arc) is a national heroine of France, perhaps more significant for her contribution to the history of human courage than to the political and military history of France. She was a peasant girl who, believing that she was acting under divine guidance, led the French army in a momentous victory at Orléans that repulsed an English attempt to conquer France during the Hundred Years' War. Captured a year afterward, Joan was

In 1429, Joan of Arc celebrated the defeat of British troops in Orleans with a triumphant ride through the city. Two years later, she was captured and burned at the stake. Hulton Archive/Getty Images

burned by the English and their French collaborators as a heretic. She became the greatest national heroine of her compatriots. Her achievement was a decisive factor in the later awakening of French national consciousness.

Joan was the daughter of a tenant farmer. In her mission of expelling the English and their Burgundian allies from the Valois kingdom of France, she felt herself to be guided by the "voices" of St. Michael, St. Catherine, and St. Margaret. She possessed many attributes characteristic of the female visionaries who were a noted feature of her time. These qualities included extreme personal piety, a claim to direct communication with the saints, and a consequent reliance upon individual experience of God's presence beyond the ministrations of the priesthood and the confines of the institutional church. But to these were added remarkable mental and physical courage, as well as a robust common sense. Known as La Pucelle, or the Maid, of Orléans, Joan became in the following centuries a focus of unity for the French people, especially at times of crisis.

JOAN'S MISSION

The crown of France at the time was in dispute between the dauphin Charles (later Charles VII), son and heir of the Valois king Charles VI, and the Lancastrian English king Henry VI. Henry's armies were in alliance with those of Philip the Good, duke of Burgundy (whose father, John the Fearless, had been assassinated in 1419 by partisans of the Dauphin), and were occupying much of the northern part of the kingdom. The apparent hopelessness of the Dauphin's cause at the end of 1427 was increased by the fact that, five years after his father's death, he still had not been crowned. Reims, the traditional place for the investiture of French kings, was well within the territory held by his enemies. As long as the Dauphin remained unconsecrated, the rightfulness of his claim to be king of France was open to challenge.

Joan's village of Domrémy was on the frontier between the France of the Anglo-Burgundians and that of the Dauphin. The villagers had already had to abandon their homes before Burgundian threats. Led by her voices, Joan traveled in May 1428 from Domrémy to Vaucouleurs, the nearest stronghold still loyal to the Dauphin, where she asked the captain of the garrison, Robert de Baudricourt, for permission to join the Dauphin. He did not take the 16-year-old girl and her visions seriously, and she returned home. Joan went to Vaucouleurs again in January 1429. This time her quiet firmness and piety gained her the respect of the people, and the captain, persuaded that she was neither a witch nor feebleminded, allowed her to go to the Dauphin at Chinon.

She left Vaucouleurs about February 13, dressed in men's clothes and accompanied by six men-at-arms. Crossing territory held by the enemy, and traveling for 11 days, she reached Chinon.

Joan went at once to the castle occupied by the Dauphin Charles. He was uncertain whether to receive her, but two days later he granted her an audience. Charles had hidden himself among his courtiers, but Joan made straight for him and told him that she wished to go to battle against the English and that she would have him crowned at Reims. On the Dauphin's orders she was immediately interrogated by ecclesiastical authorities in the presence of Jean, duc d'Alençon, a relative of Charles, who showed himself well-disposed toward her. For three weeks she was further questioned at Poitiers by eminent theologians who were allied to the Dauphin's cause. These examinations, the record of which has not survived, were occasioned by the ever-present fear of heresy following the end of the Great Schism in 1417. Joan told the ecclesiastics that it was not at Poitiers but at Orléans that she would give proof of her mission; forthwith, on March 22, she dictated letters of defiance to the English. In their report the churchmen suggested that in view of the desperate situation of Orléans, which had been under English siege for months, the Dauphin would be well-advised to make use of her.

Joan returned to Chinon. At Tours, during April, the Dauphin provided her with a military household of several men; Jean d'Aulon became her squire, and she was joined by her brothers Jean and Pierre. She had her standard painted with an image of Christ in Judgment and a banner made bearing the name of Jesus. When the question of a sword was brought up, she declared that it would be found in the church of Sainte-Catherine-de-Fierbois, and one was in fact discovered there.

ACTION AT ORLÉANS

Troops numbering several hundred men were mustered at Blois, and on April 27 they set out for Orléans. The city, besieged since Oct. 12, 1428, was almost totally surrounded by a ring of English strongholds. When Joan and one of the French commanders, La Hire, entered with supplies on April 29, she was told that action must be deferred until further reinforcements could be brought in.

On the evening of May 4, when Joan was resting, she suddenly sprang up, apparently inspired, and announced that she must go and attack the English. Having herself armed, she hurried out to the east of the city toward an English fort where, indeed, an engagement of which she had not been told was taking place. Her arrival roused the French, and they took the fort. The next day Joan addressed another of her letters of defiance to the English.

On the morning of May 6 she crossed to the south bank of the river and advanced toward another fort. The English immediately evacuated it in order to defend a stronger position nearby, but Joan and La Hire attacked them there and took it by storm. Very early on May 7 the French advanced against the fort of Les Tourelles. Joan was wounded but quickly returned to the fight; it was thanks in part to her example that the French commanders maintained the attack until the English capitulated. Next day the English were seen to be retreating, but, because it was a Sunday, Joan refused to allow any pursuit.

VICTORIES AND CORONATION

Joan left Orléans on May 9 and met Charles at Tours. She urged him to make haste to Reims to be crowned. Though he hesitated because some of his more prudent counselors were advising him to undertake the conquest of Normandy, Joan's importunity ultimately carried the day. It was decided, however, first to clear the English out of the other towns along the Loire River. Joan met her friend the duc d'Alençon, who had been made lieutenant general of the French armies, and they moved off together, taking a town and an important bridge. They next attacked Beaugency, whereupon the English retreated into the castle. Then, notwithstanding the opposition of the Dauphin and Georges de La Trémoille, one of his favourites, and despite the reserve of Alençon, Joan received the Constable de Richemont, who was under suspicion at the French court. After making him swear fidelity, she accepted his help. Shortly thereafter the castle of Beaugency was surrendered.

The French and English armies came face to face at Patay on June 18, 1429. Joan promised success to the French, saying that Charles would win a greater victory that day than any he had won so far. The victory was indeed complete; the English army was routed and with it, finally, its reputation for invincibility.

Instead of pressing home their advantage by a bold attack upon Paris, Joan and the French commanders turned back to rejoin the Dauphin, who was staying with La Trémoille at Sully-sur-Loire. Again Joan urged upon Charles the need to go on swiftly to Reims. He vacillated, however; and as he meandered through the towns along the Loire, Joan accompanied him, arguing all the while in an attempt to vanquish his hesitancy and prevail over the counselors who advised delay. She was not unaware of the dangers and difficulties involved but declared them of no account. Finally she won Charles to her view.

From Gien, where the army began to assemble, the Dauphin sent out the customary letters of summons to the coronation. Joan wrote two letters: one of exhortation to the people of Tournai, always loyal to Charles, the other a challenge to Philip the Good, duke of Burgundy. She and the Dauphin set out on the march to Reims on June 29. Before arriving at Troyes, Joan wrote to the inhabitants, promising them pardon if they would submit. They countered by sending a friar, the popular preacher Brother Richard to take stock of her. Though he returned full of enthusiasm for the Maid and her mission, the townsfolk decided after all to remain loyal to the Anglo-Burgundian regime. The Dauphin held a council, and Joan proposed that the town be attacked. The next morning she began the assault, and the citizens at once asked for terms.

The royal army then marched on to Châlons. Despite an earlier decision to resist, the Count-Bishop handed the keys of the town to Charles. On July 16 the royal army reached Reims, which opened its gates. The coronation took place on July 17, 1429. Joan was present at the consecration, standing with her banner not far from the altar. After the ceremony she knelt before Charles, calling him her king for the first time. That same day she wrote to the duke of Burgundy, adjuring him to make peace with the king and to withdraw his garrisons from the royal fortresses.

Ambitions for Paris

Charles VII left Reims on July 20, and for a month the army paraded through Champagne and the Île-de-France. On August 2 the king decided on a retreat from Provins to the Loire, a move that implied abandoning any plan to attack Paris. The loyal towns that would thus have been left to the enemy's mercy expressed some alarm. Joan, who was opposed to Charles's decision, wrote to reassure the citizens of Reims on August 5, saying that the duke of Burgundy, then in possession of Paris, had made a fortnight's truce, after which it was hoped that he would yield Paris to the king. In fact, on August 6, English troops prevented the royal army from crossing the Seine at Bray, much to the delight of Joan and the commanders, who hoped that Charles would attack Paris. Everywhere acclaimed, Joan was now, according to a 15th-century chronicler, the idol of the French. She herself felt that the purpose of her mission had been achieved.

Near Senlis, on August 14, the French and English armies again confronted each other. This time only skirmishes took place, neither side daring to start a battle, though Joan carried her standard up to the enemy's earthworks and openly challenged them. Meanwhile Compiègne, Beauvais, Senlis, and other towns north of Paris surrendered to the king. Soon afterward, on August 28, a four months' truce for all the territory north of the Seine was concluded with the Burgundians.

Joan, however, was becoming more and more impatient; she thought it essential to take Paris. She and Alençon were at Saint-Denis on the northern outskirts of Paris on August 26, and the Parisians began to organize their defenses. Charles arrived on September 7, and an attack was launched on September 8, directed between the gates of Saint-Honoré and Saint-Denis. The Parisians could be in no doubt of Joan's presence among the besiegers; she stood forward on the earthworks, calling on them to surrender their city to the king of France. Wounded, she continued to encourage the soldiers until she had to abandon the attack. Though the next day she and Alençon sought to renew the assault, they were ordered by Charles's council to retreat.

FURTHER STRUGGLE

Charles VII retired to the Loire, Joan following him. At Gien, which they reached on September 22, the army was disbanded. Alençon and the other captains went home; only Joan remained with the king. Later, when Alençon was planning a campaign in Normandy, he asked the king to let Joan rejoin him, but La Trémoille and other courtiers dissuaded him. Joan went with the king to Bourges. In October she was sent against Saint-Pierre-le-Moûtier; through her courageous assault, with only a few men, the town was taken. Joan's army then laid siege to La Charité-sur-Loire; short of munitions, they appealed to neighbouring towns for help. The supplies arrived too late, and after a month they had to withdraw.

Joan then rejoined the king, who was spending the winter in towns along the Loire. Late in December 1429 Charles issued letters ennobling Joan, her parents, and her brothers. Early in 1430 the duke of Burgundy began to threaten Brie and Champagne. The inhabitants of Reims became alarmed, and Joan wrote in March to assure them of the king's concern and to promise that she would come to their defense. When the duke moved up to attack Compiègne, the townsfolk determined to resist, and in late March or early April Joan left the king and set out to their aid, accompanied only by her brother Pierre, her squire Jean d'Aulon, and a small troop of men-at-arms. She arrived at Melun in the middle of April, and it was no doubt her presence that prompted the citizens there to declare themselves for Charles VII.

Joan was at Compiègne by May 14, 1430. There she found Renaud de Chartres, archbishop of Reims, and Louis I de Bourbon, comte de Vendôme, a relative of the king. With them she went on to Soissons, where the townspeople refused them entry. Renaud and Vendôme therefore decided to return south of the Marne and Seine rivers; but Joan refused to accompany them, preferring to return to her "good friends" in Compiègne.

Capture, Trial, and Execution

On her way back Joan heard that John of Luxembourg, the captain of a Burgundian company, had laid siege to Compiègne. Hurrying on, she entered Compiègne under cover of darkness. The next afternoon, May 23, she led a sortie and twice repelled the Burgundians but was eventually outflanked by English reinforcements and compelled to retreat. Remaining until the last to protect the rear guard while they crossed the Oise River, she was unhorsed and could not remount. She gave herself up and, with her brother Pierre and Jean d'Aulon, was taken to Margny, where the duke of Burgundy came to see her. In telling the people of Reims of Joan's capture, Renaud de Chartres accused her of rejecting all counsel and acting willfully. Charles, who was working toward a truce with the duke of Burgundy, made no attempts to save her.

John of Luxembourg sent Joan and Jean d'Aulon to his castle in Vermandois. When she tried to escape in order to return to Compiègne, he sent her to one of his more distant castles. There, though she was treated kindly, she became more and more distressed at the predicament of Compiègne. Her desire to escape became so great that she jumped from the top of a tower, falling unconscious into the moat. She was not seriously hurt, and when she had recovered, she was taken to Arras, a town adhering to the duke of Burgundy.

News of her capture had reached Paris on May 25. The next day the theology faculty of the University of Paris, which had taken the English side, requested the duke of Burgundy to turn her over for judgment either to the chief inquisitor or to the bishop of Beauvais, Pierre Cauchon, in whose diocese she had been seized. The university wrote also, to the same effect, to John of Luxembourg; and on July 14 the Bishop of Beauvais presented himself before the duke of Burgundy asking, on his own behalf and in the name of the English king, that the Maid be handed over in return for a payment of 10,000 francs. The duke passed on the demand to John of Luxembourg, and by Jan. 3, 1431, she was in the bishop's hands.

The trial was fixed to take place at Rouen. Joan was moved to a tower in the castle of Bouvreuil, which was occupied by the earl of Warwick, the English commander at Rouen. Though her offenses against the Lancastrian monarchy were common knowledge, Joan was brought to trial before a church court because the theologists at the University of Paris, as arbiter in matters concerning the faith, insisted that she be tried as a heretic. Her beliefs were not strictly orthodox, according to the criteria for orthodoxy laid down by many theologians of the period.

She was no friend of the church militant on Earth (which perceived itself as in spiritual combat with the forces of evil), and she threatened its hierarchy through her claim that she communicated directly with God by means of visions or voices. Further, her trial might serve to discredit Charles VII by demonstrating that he owed his coronation to a witch, or at least a heretic. Her two judges were to be Cauchon, bishop of Beauvais, and Jean Lemaître, the vice-inquisitor of France.

THE TRIAL

Beginning Jan. 13, 1431, statements taken in Lorraine and elsewhere were read before the Bishop and his assessors; they were to provide the framework for Joan's interrogation. Summoned to appear before her judges on February 21, Joan asked for permission to attend mass beforehand, but it was refused on account of the gravity of the crimes with which she was charged, including attempted suicide in having jumped into the moat. She was ordered to swear to tell the truth and did so swear, but she always refused to reveal the things she had said to Charles. Cauchon forbade her to leave her prison, but Joan insisted that she was morally free to attempt escape. Guards were then assigned to remain always inside the cell with her, and she was chained to a wooden block and sometimes put in irons.

Between February 21 and March 24 she was interrogated nearly a dozen times. On every occasion she was required to swear anew to tell the truth, but she always made it clear that she would not necessarily divulge everything to her judges since they were enemies of King Charles. The report of this preliminary questioning was read to her on March 24, and apart from two points she admitted its accuracy.

When the trial proper began a day or so later, it took two days for Joan to answer the 70 charges that had been drawn up against her. These were based mainly on the contention that her whole attitude and behaviour showed blasphemous presumption: in particular, that she claimed for her pronouncements the authority of divine revelation; prophesied the future; endorsed her letters with the names of Jesus and Mary, thereby identifying herself with the novel and suspect cult of the Name of Jesus; professed to be assured of salvation; and wore men's clothing. Perhaps the most serious charge was of preferring what she believed to be the direct commands of God to those of the church.

On March 31 she was questioned again on several points about which she had been evasive, notably on the question of her submission to the church. In her position, obedience to the court that was trying her was inevitably made a test of such submission. She did her best to avoid this trap, saying she knew well that the church militant could not err, but it was to God and to her saints that she held herself answerable for her words and actions. The trial continued, and the 70 charges were reduced to 12, which were sent for consideration to many eminent theologians in both Rouen and Paris.

Meanwhile, Joan fell sick in prison and was attended by two doctors. She received a visit on April 18 from Cauchon and his assistants, who exhorted her to submit to the church. Joan, who was seriously ill and obviously thought she was dying, begged to be allowed to go to confession and receive Holy Communion and to be buried in consecrated ground. But they continued to badger her, receiving only her constant response "I am relying on our Lord, I hold to what I have already said." They became more insistent on May 9, threatening her with torture if she did not clarify certain points. She answered that even if they tortured her to death she would not reply differently, adding that in any case she would afterward maintain that any statement she might make had been extorted from her by force. In face of this commonsense fortitude her interrogators, by a majority of 10 to three, decided on May 12 that torture would be useless.

Joan was informed on May 23 of the decision of the University of Paris that if she persisted in her errors she would be turned over to the secular authorities. Only they, and not the church, could carry out the death sentence of a condemned heretic.

Abjuration, Relapse, and Execution

Apparently nothing further could be done. Joan was taken out of prison for the first time in four months on May 24 and conducted to the cemetery of the church of Saint-Ouen, where her sentence was to be read out. First she was made to listen to a sermon by one of the theologians in which he violently attacked Charles VII, provoking Joan to interrupt him because she thought he had no right to attack the king, a "good Christian," and should confine his strictures to her. After the sermon was ended, she asked that all the evidence on her words and deeds be sent to Rome. But her judges ignored her appeal to the Pope, to whom, under God, she would be answerable, and began to read out the sentence abandoning her to the secular power. Hearing this dreadful pronouncement, Joan quailed and declared she would do all that the church required of her. She was presented with a form of abjuration, which must already have been prepared. She hesitated in signing it, eventually doing so on condition that it was "pleasing to our Lord." She was then condemned to perpetual imprisonment or, as some maintain, to incarceration in a place habitually used as a prison. In any case, the judges required her to return to her former prison.

The vice-inquisitor had ordered Joan to put on women's clothes, and she obeyed. But two or three days later, when the judges and others visited her and found her again in male attire, she said she had made the change of her own free will, preferring men's clothes. They then pressed other questions, to which she answered that the voices of St. Catherine and St. Margaret had censured her "treason" in making an abjuration. These admissions were taken to signify relapse, and on May 29 the judges and 39 assessors agreed unanimously that she must be handed over to the secular officials.

The next morning, Joan received permission, unprecedented for a relapsed heretic, to make her confession and receive Communion. Accompanied by two Dominicans, she was then led to the Place du Vieux-Marché. There she endured one more sermon, and the sentence abandoning her to the secular arm—that is, to the English and their French collaborators—was read out in the presence of her judges and a great crowd. The executioner seized her, led her to the stake, and lit the pyre. A Dominican consoled Joan, who asked him to hold high a crucifix for her to see and to shout out the assurances of salvation so loudly that she should hear him above the roar of the flames. To the last she maintained that her voices were sent of God and had not deceived her. According to the rehabilitation proceedings of 1456, few witnesses of her death seem to have doubted her salvation, and they agreed that she died a faithful Christian. A few days later the English king and the University of Paris formally published the news of Joan's execution.

Almost 20 years afterward, on his entry into Rouen in 1450, Charles VII ordered an inquiry into the trial. Two years later the cardinal legate Guillaume d'Estouteville made a much more thorough investigation. Finally, on the order of Pope Calixtus III following a petition from the d'Arc family, proceedings were instituted in 1455–56 that revoked and annulled the sentence of 1431. Joan was canonized by Pope Benedict XV on May 16, 1920.

MIRA BAI

(b. 1450?, Kudaki, India—d. 1547?, Dwarka, Gujarat)

The Hindu mystic and poet Mira Bai wrote lyrical songs of devotion to the god Krishna that are still widely popular in northern India in the 21st century.

Mira Bai was a Rajput princess, the only child of Ratan Singh, younger brother of the ruler of Merta. Her royal education included music and religion as well as instruction in politics and government. An image of Krishna given to her during childhood by a holy man began a lifetime of devotion to Krishna, whom she worshipped as her Divine Lover.

Mira Bai was married in 1516 to Bhoj Raj, crown prince of Mewar. Her husband died in 1521, probably of battle wounds, and thereafter she was the victim of much persecution and intrigue at the hands of her brother-in-law when he ascended the throne, and by his successor, Vikram Singh. Mira Bai was something of a rebel, and her religious pursuits did not fit the established pattern for a Rajput princess and widow. She spent most of her days in her private temple dedicated to Krishna, receiving sadhus (holy men) and pilgrims from throughout India and composing songs of devotion. At least two attempts made on her life are alluded to in her poems. Once a poisonous snake was sent to her in a basket of flowers, but when she opened it, she found an image of Krishna; on another occasion she was given a cup of poison but drank it without any harm.

Finally, Mira Bai left Mewar and returned to Merta, but finding that her unconventional behaviour was not acceptable there either, she set out on a series of pilgrimages, eventually settling in Dwarka. In 1546 Udai Singh, who had succeeded Vikram Singh as *rana*, sent a delegation of Brahmans to bring her back to Mewar. Reluctant, she asked permission to spend the night at the temple of Ranchorji (Krishna) and the next morning was found to have disappeared. According to popular belief, she miraculously merged with the image of Ranchorji, but whether she actually died that night or slipped away to spend the rest of her years wandering in disguise is not known.

Mira Bai belonged to a strong tradition of *bhakti* (devotional) poets in medieval India who expressed their love of God through the analogy of human relations—a mother's love for her child, a friend for a friend, or a woman for her beloved. The immense popularity and charm of her lyrics lies in their use of everyday images and in the sweetness of emotions easily understood by the people of India.

ISABELLA I

(b. April 22, 1451, Madrigal de las Altas Torres, Castile—d. Nov. 26, 1504, Medina del Campo, Spain)

Together with her husband, Ferdinand II of Aragon (Ferdinand V of Castile), Queen Isabella I ruled Castile (1474–1504) and Aragon (1479–1504). Their rule effected the permanent union of Spain and the beginning of an overseas empire in the "New World," led by Christopher Columbus under Isabella's sponsorship.

Early Life

Isabella was the daughter of John II of Castile and his second wife, Isabella of Portugal. Three years after her birth, her half brother became king as Henry IV. Despite the fact that she had a younger brother, Alfonso, and that her early years were spent quietly with her mother at Arévalo, Isabella was soon drawn into Castilian politics. She was brought to court when she was 13 in order to be under the king's eye. At first the opposition to Henry IV gathered around Alfonso, but when the latter died in July 1468, the rebellious magnates naturally turned to Isabella. She did not, however, play the role thus designed for her, and the fruit of her wisdom was recognition as his heiress by Henry IV at the agreement known as the Accord of Toros de Guisando (Sept. 19, 1468).

As heiress of Castile, Isabella and her future marriage became a matter of increasing diplomatic activity at home and abroad. Portugal, Aragon, and France each put forward a marriage candidate. Henry seems to have wanted his half sister to marry Afonso V, king of Portugal. Between the Portuguese and Aragonese candidates, she herself, no doubt assisted in her decision by her small group of councillors, came down in favour of Ferdinand of Aragon. A third suitor, the French duc de Guiènne, was sidestepped, and without Henry's approval she married Ferdinand in October 1469 in the palace of Juan de Vivero, at Valladolid. The prospect of an Aragonese consort led to the development of an anti-Aragonese party that put forward the claims of a rival heiress, Henry's daughter Joan, known as la Beltraneja by those who believed that her true father was Beltrán de la Cueva, duque de Albuquerque. The king encouraged this group by going back on the accord of 1468 on the grounds that Isabella had shown disobedience to the crown in marrying Ferdinand without the royal consent.

He now rejected Isabella's claim to the throne and preferred that of Joan, for whom he sought the hand of the duc de Guiènne. Although Isabella and Henry were to some extent reconciled, the long-threatened war of succession broke out at once when the king died in 1474.

REIGN

When Henry died Isabella was in Segovia, which was secured for her claim. She was supported by an important group of Castilian nobles, including Cardinal Pedro González de Mendoza, the constable of Castile (a Velasco), and the admiral (an Enríquez), who was related to Ferdinand's mother. The opposing faction, which put forward the counterclaims of Joan, included the archbishop of Toledo; a former supporter, the master of Calatrava (an influential military order); and the powerful young Marqués de Villena. They were supported by Afonso V of Portugal, who hastened to invade Castile and there betrothed himself to Joan. The first four years of Isabella's reign were thus occupied by a civil war, which ended in defeat for her Castilian opponents and for the Portuguese king (Feb. 24, 1479). Upon the death of John II of Aragon in the same year, the kingdoms of Castile and Aragon came together in the persons of their rulers.

Spain emerged as a united country, but it was long before this personal union would lead to effective political unification. Indeed, in his first will (1475), Ferdinand made Isabella his heir in Aragon and openly declared the advantages his subjects would derive from the union with Castile. But each kingdom continued to be governed according to its own institutions.

The two sovereigns were certainly united in aiming to end the long process of Reconquista by taking over the kingdom of Granada—the last Muslim stronghold in Spain.

In the end, however, the conquest (which began in 1482) proved difficult and drawn out, and it strained the finances of Castile. Although some of the features of the campaign were medieval (such as the order of battle), others were novel. Isabella took a close interest in the conduct of the war and seems to have been responsible for improved methods of supply and for the establishment of a military hospital. In 1491 she and Ferdinand set up a forward head-quarters at Santa Fe, close to their ultimate objective, and there they stayed until Granada fell on Jan. 2, 1492.

While she was at Santa Fe, another event with which the queen was to become personally associated was in the making. Columbus visited her there to enlist support for the voyage that was to result in the European settlement of America. Although the story of her offering to pledge her jewels to help finance the expedition cannot be accepted, and Columbus secured only limited financial support from her, Isabella and her councillors must receive credit for making the decision to approve the momentous voyage. The terms on which the expedition was to set out to discover a new route to the Indies were drawn up on April 17, 1492. The New World that was explored as a result of that decision was, with papal confirmation, annexed to the crown of Castile, in accordance with existing practice in regard to such previous Atlantic discoveries as the Canary Islands.

The queen and her advisers hardly needed Columbus to remind them of the opportunity now offered for the spreading of Christianity. Yet the unexpected discoveries quickly brought fresh problems to Isabella, not the least of which was the relationship between the newly discovered "Indians" and the crown of Castile. The queen and her councillors were more ready to recognize the rights of the Indians than was Columbus; she ordered some of those he had brought back as slaves to be released. The queen was still concerned with these problems when she died in 1504.

Meanwhile, in 1480, the Inquisition had been set up in Andalusia. There is little doubt that this represented the culmination of a long and popular movement against non-Christians and doubtful converts, which had manifested itself frequently in the late Middle Ages in Castile. The expulsion in 1492 of those Jews who refused conversion was the logical result of the establishment of the Inquisition. Yet, however meritorious the expulsion may have seemed at the time in order to achieve greater religious and political unity, judged by its economic consequences alone, the loss of this valuable element in Spanish society was a serious mistake.

HALLMARKS OF HER REIGN

It is difficult to disentangle Isabella's personal responsibility for the achievements of her reign from those of Ferdinand. But, undoubtedly, she played a large part in establishing the court as a centre of influence. With her blue eyes, her fair or chestnut hair, and her jewels and magnificent dresses, she must have made a striking figure. At the same time display was matched with religious feeling. Her choice of spiritual advisers brought to the fore such different and remarkable men as Hernando de Talavera and Cardinal Cisneros. A policy of reforming the Spanish churches had begun early in the 15th century, but the movement gathered momentum only under Isabella and Talavera.

When, in 1492, Talavera became archbishop of Granada, his place at the queen's side was taken by Cisneros, for whom the monarchs secured the crucial position of archbishop of Toledo in 1495. The monarchs were interested in the reform of the secular clergy and still more in the orders of monks, friars, and nuns; Isabella took a particular interest in the reform of the Poor Clares, an order of Franciscan nuns. Although when she died there was still much to be done, the rulers and Cisneros together had gone far toward achieving their goals.

Although Isabella (who was known by the epithet "the Catholic," Spanish: "la Católica") was intensely pious and orthodox in her beliefs, she could be both imperious and pertinacious in her dealings with the papacy. This was particularly true when she thought the pope was making bad appointments to Spanish benefices or in any way encroaching on the customary rights of the crown over the Spanish churches. For example, for the vacant see of Cuenca in 1478 she rejected the Italian cardinal appointed by the pope, who four years later accepted her alternative Spanish candidate. Subsequently, she successfully rejected the suggestion that the pope's nephew should become archbishop of Sevilla. In seeking to control appointments to Castilian sees, Isabella was not simply inspired by national sentiments. She also sought candidates of high standards; judged by her choices of men such as Talavera and Cisneros, Isabella was remarkably effective in achieving her objective.

Isabella was almost as interested in education as she was in religion. After she reached the age of 30, she acquired proficiency in Latin. At court she encouraged such notable scholars as Pietro Martire d'Anghiera, whom she set up as the head of a new palace school for the sons of the nobility. Naturally, many of the outstanding literary works of her reign, such as Antonio de Nebrija's *Gramática Castellana* (1492; "Castilian Grammar"), were dedicated to her. She was also the patron of Spanish and Flemish artists, and part of her extensive collection of pictures survives.

LATER YEARS

The last decade of her reign took place against a background of family sorrows brought about by the deaths of her only son and heir, Juan (1497); of her daughter Isabella, queen of Portugal, in childbirth (1498); and of her grandchild Miguel (1500), who might have brought about a personal union between Spain and Portugal. Instead, her daughter Joan, wife of Philip I and mother of the Holy Roman emperor Charles V, became the heiress of Castile. However, this offered little comfort to the queen because by 1501 Joan had already shown signs of the mental imbalance that would later earn her the title of "the Mad."

One of the achievements of Isabella's last decade was undoubtedly the success with which she and Ferdinand, acting on her initiative, extended their authority over the military orders of Alcántara, Calatrava, and Santiago, thus giving the crown control over their vast property and patronage. These orders had been exploited for too long by the nobility and were the subject of intense rivalry among those who sought to be elected master of one or other of them. In 1487 Ferdinand became grand master of Calatrava, and by 1499 he had acquired the grand masterships of Alcántara and Santiago. With the capture of Granada, the main work of the orders had been done, and a process that envisaged their ultimate absorption into the lands of the crown was logical and sensible. Throughout her long reign, Isabella also strove to strengthen royal authority at the expense of the Cortes (Spanish parliament) and the towns.

Good sense and statesmanship were equally reflected in Isabella's will and codicil. Because she left no memoirs, her will is in many ways the most reliable picture of her. In it she sums up her aspirations and her awareness of how much she and Ferdinand had been unable to do. With prudence she comments on the basis of her political program—the unity of the states of the Iberian Peninsula, the maintenance of control over the Strait of Gibraltar, and a policy of expansion into Muslim North Africa, of just rule for the Indians of the New World, and of reform in the church at home. If the overall impression is inevitably piecemeal, it is also clear that Isabella gave to her successors an exceptional document. It assures scholars that in allotting to Isabella the foremost place among their rulers, Spaniards do not misjudge this remarkable woman.

TERESA OF ÁVILA

(b. March 28, 1515, Ávila, Spain—d. Oct. 4, 1582, Alba de Tormes; canonized 1622; feast day October 15)

The Spanish nun called Teresa of Ávila or Teresa of Jesus was one of the great mystics and religious women of the Roman Catholic church, and author of spiritual classics. She was the originator of the Carmelite Reform, which restored and emphasized the austerity and contemplative character of primitive Carmelite life. Teresa was canonized in 1622 and elevated to doctor of the church in 1970 by Pope Paul VI, the first woman to be so honoured.

Born Teresa de Cepeda y Ahumadaentered, she lost her mother in 1529. Despite her father's opposition, she joined the Carmelite Convent of the Incarnation at Ávila, probably in 1535. Within two years her health collapsed, and she was an invalid for three years, during which time she developed a love for prayer. After her recovery, however, she stopped praying. She continued for 15 years in a state divided between a worldly and a divine spirit, until, in 1555, she underwent a religious awakening.

In 1558 Teresa began to consider the restoration of Carmelite life to its original observance of austerity, which had relaxed in the 14th and 15th centuries. Her reform required utter withdrawal so that the nuns could meditate on divine law and, through a prayerful life of penance, exercise what she termed "our vocation of reparation" for the sins of mankind. In 1562, with Pope Pius IV's authorization, she opened the first convent (St. Joseph's) of the Carmelite Reform. A storm of hostility came from municipal and religious personages, especially because the convent existed without endowment, but she staunchly insisted on poverty and subsistence only through public alms.

John Baptist Rossi, the Carmelite prior general from Rome, went to Ávila in 1567 and approved the reform, directing Teresa to found more convents and to establish monasteries. In the same year, while at Medina del Campo, Spain, she met a young Carmelite priest, Juan de Yepes (later St. John of the Cross, the poet and mystic), who she realized could initiate the Carmelite Reform for men. A year later Juan opened the first monastery of the Primitive Rule at Duruelo, Spain.

Despite frail health and great difficulties, Teresa spent the rest of her life establishing and nurturing 16 more convents throughout Spain. In 1575, while she was at the Sevilla (Seville) convent, a jurisdictional dispute erupted between the friars of the restored Primitive Rule, known as the Discalced (or "Unshod") Carmelites, and the observants of the Mitigated Rule, the Calced (or "Shod") Carmelites. Although she had foreseen the trouble and endeavoured to prevent it, her attempts failed. The Carmelite general, to whom she had been misrepresented, ordered her to retire to a convent in Castile and to cease founding additional convents; Juan was subsequently imprisoned at Toledo in 1577.

In 1579, largely through the efforts of King Philip II of Spain, who knew and admired Teresa, a solution was effected whereby the Carmelites of the Primitive Rule were given independent jurisdiction, confirmed in 1580 by a rescript of Pope Gregory XIII. Teresa, broken in health, was then directed to resume the reform. In journeys that covered hundreds of miles, she made exhausting missions and was fatally stricken en route to Ávila from Burgos.

Teresa's ascetic doctrine has been accepted as the classical exposition of the contemplative life, and her spiritual writings are among the most widely read. Her *Life of the Mother Teresa of Jesus* (1611) is autobiographical, while the *Book of the Foundations* (1610) describes the establishment of her convents. Her writings on the progress of the Christian soul toward God are recognized masterpieces: *The Way of Perfection* (1583), *The Interior Castle* (1588), *Spiritual Relations, Exclamations of the Soul to God* (1588), and *Conceptions on the Love of God*. Of her poems, 31 are extant; of her letters, 458.

MARY I

(b. Feb. 18, 1516, Greenwich, near London, Eng.—d. Nov. 17, 1558, London)

Mary I, also called Mary Tudor, was the first queen to rule England (1553–58) in her own right. She was known as Bloody Mary for her persecution of Protestants in a vain attempt to restore Roman Catholicism in England.

The daughter of King Henry VIII and the Spanish princess Catherine of Aragon, Mary as a child was a pawn in England's bitter rivalry with more powerful nations, being fruitlessly proposed in marriage to this or that potentate desired as an ally. A studious and bright girl, she was educated by her mother and a governess of ducal rank.

Betrothed at last to the Holy Roman emperor, her cousin Charles V (Charles I of Spain), Mary was commanded by him to come to Spain with a huge cash dowry. This demand ignored, he presently jilted her and concluded a more advantageous match. In 1525 she was named princess of Wales by her father, although the lack of official documents suggests she was never formally invested. She then held court at Ludlow Castle while new betrothal plans were made. Mary's life was radically disrupted, however, by her father's new marriage to Anne Boleyn.

As early as the 1520s Henry had planned to divorce Catherine in order to marry Anne Boleyn, claiming that since Catherine had been his deceased brother's wife, her union with Henry was incestuous. The pope, however, refused to recognize Henry's right to divorce Catherine, even after the divorce was legalized in England. In 1534 Henry broke with Rome and established the Church of England. The allegation of incest, in effect, made Mary a bastard. Anne Boleyn, the new queen, bore the king a daughter, Elizabeth (the future queen), forbade Mary access to her parents, stripped her of her title of princess, and forced her to act as lady-in-waiting to the infant Elizabeth. Mary never saw her mother again, though, despite great danger, they corresponded secretly.

Anne's hatred pursued Mary so relentlessly that she feared execution, but having her mother's courage and all her father's stubbornness, she would not admit to the illegitimacy of her birth. Nor would she enter a convent when ordered to do so.

After Anne fell under Henry's displeasure, he offered to pardon Mary if she would acknowledge him as head of the Church of England and admit the "incestuous illegality" of his marriage to her mother. She refused to do so until her cousin, the emperor Charles, persuaded her to give in, an action she was to regret deeply.

Henry was now reconciled to her and gave her a household befitting her position and again made plans for her betrothal. She became godmother to Prince Edward, his son by Jane Seymour, the third queen.

Mary was now the most important European princess. Although plain, she was a popular figure, with a fine contralto singing voice and great linguistic ability. She was, however, not able to free herself of the epithet of bastard, and her movements were severely restricted. Husband after husband proposed for her failed to reach the altar. When Henry married Catherine Howard, however, Mary was granted permission to return to court, and in 1544, although still considered illegitimate, she was granted succession to the throne after Edward and any other legitimate children who might be born to Henry.

Edward VI succeeded his father in 1547 and, swayed by religious fervour and overzealous advisers, made English rather than Latin compulsory for church services. Mary, however, continued to celebrate mass in the old form in her private chapel and was once again in danger of losing her head.

Upon the death of Edward in 1553, Mary fled to Norfolk, as Lady Jane Grey had seized the throne and was recognized as queen for a few days. The country, however, considered Mary the rightful ruler, and within some days she made a triumphal entry into London. A woman of 37 now, she was forceful, sincere, bluff, and hearty like her father but, in contrast to him, disliked cruel punishments and the signing of death warrants.

Insensible to the need of caution for a newly crowned queen, unable to adapt herself to novel circumstances, and lacking self-interest, Mary longed to bring her people back to the church of Rome. To achieve this end, she was determined to marry Philip II of Spain, the son of the emperor Charles V and 11 years her junior, though most of her advisers advocated her cousin Courtenay, earl of Devon, a man of royal blood.

Those English noblemen who had acquired wealth and lands when Henry VIII confiscated the Catholic monasteries had a vested interest in retaining them, and Mary's desire to restore Roman Catholicism as the state religion made them her enemies. Parliament, also at odds with her, was offended by her discourtesy to their delegates pleading against the Spanish marriage: "My marriage is my own affair," she retorted.

When in 1554 it became clear that she would marry Philip, a Protestant insurrection broke out under the leadership of Sir Thomas Wyatt. Alarmed by Wyatt's rapid advance toward London, Mary made a magnificent speech rousing citizens by the thousands to fight for her. Wyatt was defeated and executed, and Mary married Philip, restored the Catholic creed, and revived the laws against heresy.

For three years rebel bodies dangled from gibbets, and heretics were relentlessly executed, some 300 being burned at the stake. Thenceforward the queen, now known as Bloody Mary, was hated, her Spanish husband distrusted and slandered, and she herself blamed for the vicious slaughter. An unpopular, unsuccessful war with France, in which Spain was England's ally, lost Calais, England's last toehold in Europe. Still childless, sick, and grief stricken, she was further depressed by a series of false pregnancies. She died on Nov. 17, 1558, in London, and with her died all that she did.

CATHERINE DE MÉDICIS

(b. April 13, 1519, Florence [Italy] — d. Jan. 5, 1589, Blois, France)

One of the most influential personalities of the Catholic-Huguenot wars was Catherine de Médicis, queen consort of Henry II of France (reigned 1547–59) and subsequently regent of France (1560–74). Three of her sons were kings of France: Francis II, Charles IX, and Henry III.

Early Life

Catherine (Italian: Caterina) was the daughter of Lorenzo de' Medici, duke of Urbino, and Madeleine de La Tour d'Auvergne, a Bourbon princess related to many of the French nobility. Orphaned within days, Catherine was highly educated, trained, and disciplined by nuns in Florence and Rome and married in 1533 by her uncle, Pope Clement VII, to Henry, duc d'Orléans, who inherited the French crown from his father, Francis I, in April 1547. Artistic, energetic, and extraverted, as well as discreet, courageous, and gay, Catherine was greatly esteemed at the dazzling court of Francis I, from which she derived both her political attitudes and her passion for building. Of the chateaus she designed herself—including the Tuileries—Chenonceaux was her unfinished masterpiece.

In spite of Henry's abiding attachment to his mistress Diane de Poitiers, Catherine's marriage was not unsuccessful and, after 10 anxious years, she bore him 10 children, of whom 4 boys and 3 girls survived. She herself supervised their education. Thus occupied, Catherine lived privately though she was appointed regent in 1552 during Henry's absence at the siege of Metz. Her ability and eloquence were acclaimed after the Spanish victory of Saint-Quentin in Picardy in 1557, possibly the origin of her perpetual fear of Spain, which remained, through changing circumstances, the touchstone of her judgments. It is essential to understand this in order to discern the coherence of her career.

Political Crises

Catherine's first great political crisis came in July 1559 upon the accidental death of Henry II, a traumatic bereavement from which it is doubtful that she ever recovered. Under her son, Francis II, power was retained by the Guise brothers. Thus began her lifelong struggle — explicit in her correspondence—with these extremists who, supported by Spain and the papacy, sought to dominate the crown and extinguish its independence in the commingled interests of European Catholicism and personal aggrandizement. It is also necessary to understand this political struggle of the Catholic crown with its own ultramontane extremists and to perceive its fluctuations in changing circumstances, in order to realize the fundamental consistency of Catherine's career. Her essentially moderate influence was first perceptible during the Conspiracy of Amboise (March 1560), an instance of tumultuous petitioning by the Huguenot gentry, primarily against Guisard persecution in the name of the king. Her merciful Edict of Amboise (March 1560) was followed in May by that of Romorantin, which distinguished heresy from sedition, thereby detaching faith from allegiance.

Catherine's second great political crisis came with the premature death on Dec. 5, 1560, of Francis II, whose royal authority the Guises had monopolized. Catherine succeeded in obtaining the regency for Charles IX, with Antoine de Bourbon, king of Navarre and first prince of the blood, as lieutenant general, to whom the Protestants vainly looked for leadership.

CIVIL WARS

The 10 years from 1560 to 1570 were, politically, the most important of Catherine's life. They witnessed the first three civil wars and her desperate struggle against the Catholic extremists for the independence of the crown, the maintenance of peace, and the enforcement of limited toleration. In 1561, with the support of the distinguished chancellor Michel de L'Hospital, she began by trying to propitiate the leaders of both religious factions, to effect reforms and economies by unassailably traditional methods, and to settle the religious conflict. Religious reconciliation was the conveners' purpose of the Colloquy of Poissy (September–November 1561). Catherine appointed a mixed commission of moderates that devised two formulas of consummate ambiguity, by which they hoped to resolve the basic, Eucharist controversy. Possibly Catherine's most concrete achievement was the Edict of January 1562, which followed the failure of reconciliation. This afforded the Calvinists licensed coexistence with specific safeguards. Unlike the proposals of Poissy, the edict was law, which the Protestants accepted and the Catholics rejected. This rejection was one basic element in the outbreak of civil war in 1562, in which—as she had predicted—Catherine fell, politically, into the clutches of the extremists, because the Catholic crown might protect its Protestant subjects in law but could not defend them in arms. Thenceforth the problem of religion was one of power, public order, and administration.

Catherine ended the first civil war in March 1563 by the Edict of Amboise, an attenuated version of the Edict of January. In August 1563 she declared the king of age in the Parlement of Rouen and, from April 1564 to January 1566, conducted him on a marathon itinerary round France. Its principal purpose was to execute the edict and, through a meeting at Bayonne in June 1565, to seek to strengthen peaceful relations between the crown and Spain and to negotiate for Charles's marriage to Elizabeth of Austria. During the period 1564–68, Catherine was unable, for complex reasons, to withstand the cardinal Lorraine, statesman of the Guises, who largely provoked the second and third civil wars. She quickly terminated the second (September 1567–March 1568) with the Peace of Longjumeau, a renewal of Amboise. But she was unable to avert its revocation (August 1568), which heralded the third civil war. She was not primarily responsible for the more far-reaching Treaty of Saint-Germain (August 1570), but she succeeded in disgracing the Guises.

For the next two years Catherine's policy was one of peace and general reconciliation. This she envisaged in terms of the marriage of her daughter Marguerite to the young Protestant leader, Henry of Navarre (later Henry IV of France), and alliance with England through the marriage of her son Henry, duc d'Anjou, or, failing him, his younger brother François, duc d'Alençon, to Queen Elizabeth. The complexity of Catherine's position during these years cannot be briefly explained. To some extent she was eclipsed by Louis of Nassau and a group of Flemish exiles and youthful Protestants who surrounded the king and urged him to make war upon Spain in the Netherlands, which Catherine inevitably resisted.

THE MASSACRE OF ST. BARTHOLOMEW'S DAY

The issue of war or peace in the Netherlands was closely linked with the Massacre of St. Bartholomew's Day in Paris on Aug. 23–24, 1572. Upon this occasion, following an abortive attempt against the life of the admiral Gaspard de Coligny, he and a number of his principal lieutenants, together with several thousand Huguenots, were killed. Catherine traditionally has been blamed for these events, which have therefore fashioned the interpretation not only of her subsequent, but frequently also of her previous, career, resulting in the familiar myth of the wicked Italian queen. There are two principal reasons for this. First, after some hesitation and inconsistency, the king assumed the responsibility by a declaration of August 26 in the Parlement of Paris, and "the crown" has been taken to mean Catherine. The second reason for the traditional inculpation of Catherine is the work of the pamphleteers and the polemical nature of the historiography of the event. It is impossible to establish the origin of the assault upon Coligny, but, as a member of the court—the royal family and the council—Catherine was among those who appear to have authorized not the massacre itself but the death of the admiral and his principal followers. This and the subsequent royal declaration of August 26 are both explained by the danger of the situation—after the unsuccessful assault upon Coligny—in which the infuriated Huguenots allegedly threatened the court with extinction and the kingdom with war.

LAST YEARS

After the Massacre of St. Bartholomew's Day, Catherine was more concerned with the election of Anjou to the throne of Poland (May 1573) than the prosecution of the fourth civil war. Upon the death of Charles IX a year later, she assumed the regency with the support of the Parlement until the return from Poland of Henry III in August. Catherine placed high hopes in her favourite, Henry, for the regeneration of France, for which she longed, but not without simultaneous misgivings, knowing his weakness of character and his previous subjection to the Catholics. For these reasons Catherine neither sought to dominate Henry nor to rule in his place but rather suffered him to exploit her and strove with unremitting pains to supply his deficiencies.

Until the death of Alençon in 1584, much of her attention was devoted to restraining his dangerous ambitions, which again threatened to involve France in hostilities with Spain. After the Treaty of Joinville (December 1584) between the Guises and Spain, at Henry's bidding,

Catherine, though gravely ill, returned to this dual threat. But after three months of continuous effort, in order to avert a public breach between the crown and the Guises, she was obliged, by the Treaty of Nemours (July 1585), to commit the king to making war against the Huguenots. Having failed with the Guises, the crown turned to Navarre, the Protestant leader who, as heir presumptive, had an interest in the preservation of the throne. In July 1586 Catherine undertook the arduous journey to see him at Saint-Brice near Cognac. But there was nothing to which Navarre could safely commit himself. Thus, despite the heroic efforts of Catherine's old age, France was sinking into chaos when she died at Blois eight months before the murder of Henry III. Nevertheless, her ultimate achievement was to have saved the kingdom just long enough to ensure the succession of the Bourbon Henry IV, by whom the royal authority was restored.

ELIZABETH I

(b. Sept. 7, 1533, Greenwich, near London, Eng.—d. March 24, 1603, Richmond, Surrey)

Elizabeth I was queen of England (1558–1603) during a period, often called the Elizabethan Age, when England asserted itself vigorously as a major European power in politics, commerce, and the arts. Although her small kingdom was threatened by grave internal divisions, Elizabeth's blend of shrewdness, courage, and majestic self-display inspired ardent expressions of loyalty and helped unify the nation against foreign enemies. The adulation bestowed upon her both in her lifetime and in the ensuing centuries was not altogether a spontaneous effusion; it was the result of a carefully crafted, brilliantly executed campaign in which the queen fashioned herself as

This rare full-length portrait of Elizabeth I, by Flemish artist Steven van der Meulen, gives a distinct sense of the queen's strength and majesty. AFP/ Getty Images

the glittering symbol of the nation's destiny. This political symbolism, common to monarchies, had more substance than usual, for the queen was by no means a mere figurehead.

While she did not wield the absolute power of which Renaissance rulers dreamed, she tenaciously upheld her authority to make critical decisions and to set the central policies of both state and church. The latter half of the 16th century in England is justly called the Elizabethan Age. Rarely has the collective life of a whole era been given so distinctively personal a stamp.

CHILDHOOD

Elizabeth was the daughter of the Tudor king Henry VIII and his second wife, Anne Boleyn. Henry had defied the pope and broken England from the authority of the Roman Catholic church in order to dissolve his marriage with his first wife, Catherine of Aragon, who had borne him a daughter, Mary. Since the king ardently hoped that Anne Boleyn would give birth to the male heir regarded as the key to stable dynastic succession, the birth of a second daughter was a bitter disappointment that dangerously weakened the new queen's position. Before Elizabeth reached her third birthday, her father had her mother beheaded on charges of adultery and treason. Moreover, at Henry's instigation, an act of Parliament declared his marriage with Anne Boleyn invalid from the beginning, thus making their daughter Elizabeth illegitimate, as Roman Catholics had all along claimed her to be.

When in 1537 Henry's third wife, Jane Seymour, gave birth to a son, Edward, Elizabeth receded still further into relative obscurity, but she was not neglected. Despite his capacity for monstrous cruelty, Henry VIII treated all his children with what contemporaries regarded as affection; Elizabeth was present at ceremonial occasions and was declared third in line to the throne. She spent much of the time with her half brother Edward and, from her 10th year onward, profited from the loving attention of her stepmother, Catherine Parr, the king's sixth and last wife.

Under a series of distinguished tutors, of whom the best known is the Cambridge humanist Roger Ascham, Elizabeth received the rigorous education normally reserved for male heirs, consisting of a course of studies centring on classical languages, history, rhetoric, and moral philosophy. "Her mind has no womanly weakness," Ascham wrote with the unselfconscious sexism of the age, "her perseverance is equal to that of a man, and her memory long keeps what it quickly picks up." In addition to Greek and Latin, she became fluent in French and Italian, attainments of which she was proud and which were in later years to serve her well in the conduct of diplomacy. Thus steeped in the secular learning of the Renaissance, the quick-witted and intellectually serious princess also studied theology, imbibing the tenets of English Protestantism in its formative period. Her association with the Reformation is critically important, for it shaped the future course of the nation, but it does not appear to have been a personal passion.

POSITION UNDER EDWARD VI AND MARY

With her father's death in 1547 and the accession to the throne of her frail 10-year-old brother Edward, Elizabeth's life took a perilous turn. Her guardian, the dowager queen Catherine Parr, almost immediately married Thomas Seymour, the lord high admiral. Handsome, ambitious, and discontented, Seymour began to scheme against his powerful older brother, Edward Seymour, protector of the realm during Edward VI's minority. In January 1549, shortly after the death of Catherine Parr, Thomas Seymour was arrested for treason and accused of plotting to marry Elizabeth in order to rule the kingdom. Repeated interrogations of Elizabeth and her servants led to the charge that even when his wife was alive Seymour had on several occasions behaved in a flirtatious and overly familiar manner toward the young princess. Under humiliating close questioning and in some danger, Elizabeth was extraordinarily circumspect and poised. When she was told that Seymour had been beheaded, she betrayed no emotion.

The need for circumspection, self-control, and political acumen became even greater after the death of the Protestant Edward in 1553 and the accession of Elizabeth's older half sister Mary, a religious zealot set on returning England, by force if necessary, to the Roman Catholic faith. This attempt, along with her unpopular marriage to the ardently Catholic king Philip II of Spain, aroused bitter Protestant opposition. In a charged atmosphere of treasonous rebellion and inquisitorial repression, Elizabeth's life was in grave danger. For though, as her sister demanded, she conformed outwardly to official Catholic observance, she inevitably became the focus and the obvious beneficiary of plots to overthrow the government and restore Protestantism.

Arrested and sent to the Tower of London after Sir Thomas Wyatt's rebellion in January 1554, Elizabeth narrowly escaped her mother's fate. Two months later, after extensive interrogation and spying had revealed no conclusive evidence of treason on her part, she was released from the Tower and placed in close custody for a year at Woodstock. The difficulty of her situation eased somewhat, though she was never far from suspicious scrutiny. Throughout the unhappy years of Mary's childless reign, with its burning of Protestants and its military disasters, Elizabeth had continued to protest her innocence, affirm her unwavering loyalty, and proclaim her pious abhorrence of heresy. It was a sustained lesson in survival through self-discipline and the tactful manipulation of appearances.

ACCESSION

At the death of Mary on Nov. 17, 1558, Elizabeth came to the throne amid bells, bonfires, patriotic demonstrations, and other signs of public jubilation. Her entry into London and the great coronation procession that followed were masterpieces of political courtship. Elizabeth's smallest gestures were scrutinized for signs of the policies and tone of the new regime: When an old man in the crowd turned his back on the new queen and wept, Elizabeth exclaimed confidently that he did so out of gladness; when a girl in an allegorical pageant presented her with a Bible in English translation—banned under Mary's reign—Elizabeth kissed the book, held it up reverently, and then laid it on her breast. When the abbot and monks of Westminster Abbey came to greet her in broad daylight with candles in their hands, she briskly dismissed them with the words, "Away with those torches! We can see well enough." Spectators were thus assured that under Elizabeth England had returned, cautiously but decisively, to the Reformation.

The first weeks of her reign were not entirely given over to symbolic gestures and public ceremonial. The queen began at once to form her government and issue proclamations. She reduced the size of the Privy Council, in part to purge some of its Catholic members and in part to make it more efficient as an advisory body; she began a restructuring of the enormous royal household; she carefully balanced the need for substantial administrative and judicial continuity with the desire for change; and she assembled a core of experienced and trustworthy advisers, including William Cecil, Nicholas Bacon, Francis Walsingham, and Nicholas Throckmorton. Chief among these was Cecil (afterward Lord Burghley), whom Elizabeth appointed her principal secretary of state on the morning of her accession and who was to serve her (first in this capacity and after 1571 as lord treasurer) with remarkable sagacity and skill for 40 years.

THE WOMAN RULER IN A PATRIARCHAL WORLD

Custom and teaching had reinforced a widespread conviction, that while men were naturally endowed with authority, women were temperamentally, intellectually, and morally unfit to govern. Apologists for the queen countered that there had always been significant exceptions, such as the biblical Deborah, the prophetess who had judged Israel. Crown lawyers, moreover, elaborated a mystical legal theory known as "the king's two bodies." When she ascended the throne, according to this theory, the queen's whole being was profoundly altered: her mortal "body natural" was wedded to an immortal "body politic." Her physical body was subject to the imperfections of all human beings (including those specific to womankind), but the body politic was timeless and perfect. Hence in theory the queen's gender was no threat to the stability and glory of the nation.

Elizabeth made it immediately clear that she intended to rule in more than name only and that she would not subordinate her judgment to that of any one individual or faction. This she managed in large part through her cultivation of the role of the Virgin Queen wedded to her kingdom; the cult she established around this persona was a gradual creation that unfolded over many years, but its roots may be glimpsed at least as early as 1555. At that time, Queen Mary had proposed to marry her sister to the staunchly Catholic duke of Savoy; the usually cautious and impassive Elizabeth burst into tears, declaring that she had no wish for any husband. Other matches were proposed and summarily rejected. But in this vulnerable period of her life there were obvious reasons for Elizabeth to bide her time and keep her options open. When she herself became queen, speculation about a suitable match immediately intensified, for if she died childless, the Tudor line would come to an end. The nearest heir was the Catholic Mary, Queen of Scots, the granddaughter of Henry VIII's sister Margaret.

The queen's marriage was critical not only for the question of succession but also for the tangled web of international diplomacy. England, isolated and militarily weak, was sorely in need of the major alliances that an advantageous marriage could forge. Important suitors eagerly came forward: Philip II of Spain, who hoped to renew the link between Catholic Spain and England; Archduke Charles of Austria; Erik XIV, king of Sweden; Henry, duke d'Anjou and later king of France; François, duke d'Alençon; and others. Many scholars think it unlikely that Elizabeth ever seriously intended to marry any of these aspirants to her hand, for the dangers always outweighed the possible benefits, but she skillfully played one off against another and kept the marriage negotiations going for months, even years, at one moment seeming on the brink of acceptance, at the next veering away toward vows of perpetual virginity.

Elizabeth was courted by English suitors as well, most assiduously by her principal favourite, Robert Dudley, earl of Leicester. As master of the horse and a member of the Privy Council, Leicester was constantly in attendance on the queen, who displayed toward him all the signs of an ardent romantic attachment. When in September 1560

Leicester's wife, Amy Robsart, died in a suspicious fall, the favourite seemed poised to marry his royal mistress — so at least widespread rumours had it — but, though the queen's behaviour toward him continued to generate scandalous gossip, the decisive step was never taken. Elizabeth's resistance to a marriage she herself seemed to desire may have been politically motivated, for Leicester had many enemies at court and an unsavory reputation in the country at large. But in October 1562 the queen nearly died of smallpox, and, faced with the real possibility of a contested succession and a civil war, even rival factions were likely to have countenanced the marriage.

Probably at the core of Elizabeth's decision to remain single was an unwillingness to compromise her power. Though she patiently received petitions and listened to anxious advice, she zealously retained her power to make the final decision in all crucial affairs of state. Unsolicited advice could at times be dangerous: when in 1579 a pamphlet was published vehemently denouncing the queen's proposed marriage to the Catholic duke d'Alençon, its author John Stubbs and his publisher William Page were arrested and had their right hands chopped off.

Elizabeth's performances — her displays of infatuation, her apparent inclination to marry the suitor of the moment — often convinced even close advisers, so that the level of intrigue and anxiety, always high in royal courts, often rose to a feverish pitch. Far from trying to allay the anxiety, the queen seemed to augment and use it, for she was skilled at manipulating factions. This skill extended beyond marriage negotiations and became one of the hallmarks of her regime. A powerful nobleman would be led to believe that he possessed unique influence over the queen, only to discover that a hated rival had been led to a comparable belief. Royal favour — apparent intimacies, public honours, the bestowal of such valuable perquisites as land grants and monopolies—would give way to royal aloofness or, still worse, to royal anger.

A similar blend of charm and imperiousness character-ized the queen's relations with Parliament, on which she had to depend for revenue. Many sessions of Parliament, particularly in the early years of her rule, were more than cooperative with the queen; they had the rhetorical air of celebrations. But under the strain of the marriage-and-succession question, the celebratory tone, which masked serious policy differences, began over the years to wear thin, and the sessions involved complicated, often acrimonious negotiations between crown and commons. Elizabeth had a rare gift for combining calculated displays of intransigence with equally calculated displays of graciousness and, on rare occasions, a prudent willingness to concede. Whenever possible, she transformed the language of politics into the language of love, likening herself to the spouse or the mother of her kingdom.

RELIGIOUS QUESTIONS AND THE FATE OF MARY, QUEEN OF SCOTS

Elizabeth restored England to Protestantism. The Act of Supremacy, passed by Parliament and approved in 1559, revived the antipapal statutes of Henry VIII and declared the queen supreme governor of the church, while the Act of Uniformity established a slightly revised version of the second Edwardian prayer book as the official order of worship. Priests, temporal officers, and men proceeding to university degrees were required to swear an oath to the royal supremacy or lose their positions; absence from Sunday church service was punishable by a fine; royal commissioners sought to ensure doctrinal and liturgical conformity. Many of the nobles and gentry, along with a majority of the common people, remained loyal to the old faith, but all the key positions in the government and church were held by Protestants who employed patronage, pressure, and propaganda, as well as threats, to secure an outward observance of the religious settlement.

Yet she shunned the demands of militant Protestants, who pressed for a drastic reform of the church hierarchy and church courts, a purging of residual Catholic elements in the prayer book and ritual, and a vigorous searching out and persecution of recusants. Elizabeth had no interest in probing the inward convictions of her subjects; provided that she could obtain public uniformity and obedience, she was willing to let the private beliefs of the heart remain hidden. This policy was consistent with her own survival strategy, her deep conservatism, and her personal dislike of evangelical fervour.

If Elizabeth's religious settlement was threatened by Protestant dissidents, it was equally threatened by the recalcitrance and opposition of English Catholics. In 1569 a rebellion of feudal aristocrats and their followers in the staunchly Catholic north of England was put down by savage military force; while in 1571 the queen's informers and spies uncovered an international conspiracy against her life, known as the Ridolfi Plot. Both threats were linked at least indirectly to Mary, Queen of Scots, who had been driven from her own kingdom in 1568 and had taken refuge in England. The presence, more prisoner than guest, of the woman whom the Roman Catholic church regarded as the rightful queen of England posed a serious political and diplomatic problem for Elizabeth, a problem greatly exacerbated by Mary's restless ambition and penchant for conspiracy. Elizabeth judged that it was too dangerous to let Mary leave the country, but at the same time she firmly rejected the advice of Parliament and many of her councillors that Mary should be executed. So a captive, at once ominous, malevolent, and pathetic, Mary remained.

The alarming increase in religious tension, political intrigue, and violence was not only an internal, English concern. In 1570 Pope Pius V excommunicated Elizabeth and absolved her subjects from any oath of allegiance that they might have taken to her. The immediate effect was to make life more difficult for English Catholics, who were the objects of a suspicion that greatly intensified in 1572 after word reached England of the St. Bartholomew's Day massacre of Protestants (Huguenots) in France. Tension and official persecution of recusants increased in the wake of the daring clandestine missionary activities of English Jesuits, trained on the Continent and smuggled back to England. Elizabeth was under great pressure to become more involved in the continental struggle between Roman Catholics and Protestants, in particular to aid the rebels fighting the Spanish armies in the Netherlands. But she was very reluctant to become involved, in part because she detested rebellion, even rebellion undertaken in the name of Protestantism, and in part because she detested expenditures. Eventually, after vacillations that drove her councillors to despair, she agreed first to provide some limited funds and then, in 1585, to send a small expeditionary force to the Netherlands.

Fears of an assassination attempt against Elizabeth increased after Pope Gregory XIII proclaimed in 1580 that it would be no sin to rid the world of such a miserable heretic. In 1584 Europe's other major Protestant leader, William of Orange, was assassinated. Elizabeth herself showed few signs of concern—throughout her life she was a person of remarkable personal courage—but the anxiety of the ruling elite was intense. Government spies under the direction of Sir Francis Walsingham had by this time discovered Mary to be thoroughly implicated in plots against the queen's life. When Walsingham's men in 1586 uncovered the Babington Plot, another conspiracy to murder Elizabeth, the wretched queen of Scots, her secret correspondence intercepted and her involvement clearly proved, was doomed. Mary was tried and sentenced to death. Parliament petitioned that the sentence be carried out without delay. For three months the queen hesitated and then with every sign of extreme reluctance signed the death warrant. When the news was brought to her that on Feb. 8, 1587, Mary had been beheaded, Elizabeth responded with an impressive show of grief and rage. It is impossible to know how many people believed Elizabeth's professions of grief.

For years Elizabeth had cannily played a complex diplomatic game with the rival interests of France and Spain. State-sanctioned privateering raids, led by Sir Francis Drake and others, on Spanish shipping and ports alternated with conciliatory gestures and peace talks. But by the mid-1580s word reached London that the Spanish king, Philip II, had begun to assemble an enormous fleet that would sail to the Netherlands, join forces with a waiting Spanish army led by the duke of Parma, and then proceed to an invasion and conquest of Protestant England. Always reluctant to spend money, the queen had nonetheless authorized sufficient funds during her reign to maintain a fleet of maneuverable, well-armed fighting ships. When in July 1588 the Armada reached English waters, the queen's ships, in one of the most famous naval encounters of history, defeated the enemy fleet, which then was all but destroyed by terrible storms.

THE QUEEN'S IMAGE

Elizabeth possessed a vast repertory of fantastically elaborate dresses and rich jewels. Her passion for dress was bound up with political calculation and an acute self-consciousness about her image. She tried to control the royal portraits that circulated widely in England and abroad, and her appearances in public were dazzling displays of wealth and magnificence. Artists, including poets like Edmund Spenser and painters like Nicholas Hilliard, celebrated her in a variety of mythological guises—as Diana, the chaste goddess of the moon; Astraea, the goddess of justice; Gloriana, the queen of the fairies—and Elizabeth, in addition to adopting these fanciful roles, appropriated to herself some of the veneration that pious Englishmen had directed to the Virgin Mary.

Nevertheless the last decade of Elizabeth's reign began to reveal a severe strain in her ability to control not only her own image, but also her country's political, religious, and economic forces. Bad harvests, persistent inflation, and unemployment caused hardship and a loss of public morale. Charges of corruption and greed led to widespread popular hatred of many of the queen's favourites. A series of disastrous military attempts to subjugate the Irish culminated in a crisis of authority with her last great favourite, Robert Devereux, the proud earl of Essex, who had undertaken to defeat rebel forces led by Hugh O'Neill, earl of Tyrone. Essex returned from Ireland against the queen's orders, insulted her in her presence, and then made a desperate, foolhardy attempt to raise an insurrection. He was tried for treason and executed on Feb. 25, 1601.

Elizabeth continued to make brilliant speeches, to exercise her authority, and to receive the extravagant compliments of her admirers, but she was, as Sir Walter Raleigh remarked, "a lady surprised by time," and her long reign was drawing to a close. She suffered from bouts of melancholy and ill health and showed signs of increasing debility. Her more astute advisers—among them Lord Burghley's son, Sir Robert Cecil, who had succeeded his father as her principal counselor—secretly entered into correspondence with the likeliest claimant to the throne, James VI of Scotland.

Having reportedly indicated James as her successor, Elizabeth died quietly. The nation enthusiastically welcomed its new king. But in a very few years the English began to express nostalgia for the rule of "Good Queen Bess." Long before her death she had transformed herself into a powerful image of female authority, regal magnificence, and national pride, and that image has endured to the present.

ARTEMISIA GENTILESCHI

(b. July 8, 1593, Rome, Papal States [Italy]—d. 1652/53, Naples, Kingdom of Naples)

The Italian painter Artemisia Gentileschi was the daughter of Orazio Gentileschi, a follower of the revolutionary Baroque painter Caravaggio. She herself was an important second-generation proponent of Caravaggio's dramatic realism.

A pupil of her father and of his friend the landscape painter Agostino Tassi, Artemisia painted at first in a style indistinguishable from her father's somewhat lyrical interpretation of Caravaggio's example. Her first known work is *Susanna and the Elders* (1610), an accomplished work long attributed to her father. She also painted two versions of a scene already essayed by Caravaggio (but never attempted by her father), *Judith Beheading Holofernes* (c. 1612–13; c. 1620). She was raped by Tassi, and, when he did not fulfill his promise to marry her, Orazio Gentileschi in 1612 brought him to trial. During that event Artemisia was forced to give evidence under torture.

Shortly after the trial she married a Florentine, and in 1616 she joined Florence's Academy of Design, the first

Portrait of a Lady, Three-Quarter Length Seated, Dressed in a Gold Embroidered Elaborate Costume, *oil on canvas by Artemisia Gentileschi, 17th century.* In a private collection

woman to do so. While in Florence she began to develop her own distinct style. Unlike many other women artists of the 17th century, she specialized in history painting rather than still life and portraiture. In Florence she was associated with the Medici court and painted an *Allegory of Inclination* (c. 1616) for the series of frescoes honouring the life of Michelangelo in the Casa Buonarotti. Her colours are more brilliant than her father's, and she continued to employ the tenebrism made popular by Caravaggio long after her father had abandoned that style.

Artemisia Gentileschi was in Rome for a time and also in Venice. About 1630 she moved to Naples, and in 1638 she arrived in London, where she worked alongside her father for King Charles I. They collaborated on the ceiling paintings of the Great Hall in the Queen's House in Greenwich. After Orazio's death in 1639, she stayed on in London for at least several more years. According to her biographer Baldinucci (who appended her life to that of her father), she painted many portraits and quickly surpassed her father's fame. Later, probably in 1640 or 1641, she settled in Naples, where she painted several versions of the story of David and Bathsheba, but little is known of the final years of her life.

OKUNI

(fl. 17th century)

The Japanese dancer Okuni is credited with founding the popular Japanese art form known as Kabuki. Although many extant contemporary sources such as paintings, drawings, and diaries have shed light on Okuni's life, the accuracy of such primary sources has been difficult to establish. Very little is known about her life for certain.

Okuni was also called Izumo no Okuni (Okuni of Izumo) because she is said to have been an attendant at the Grand Shrine of Izumo, the oldest Shintō shrine in Japan. It is possible that she was a temple dancer or even a prostitute. She formed a troupe of female dancers who in 1603 gave a highly popular performance of dances and light sketches on a makeshift stage set up in the dry bed of the Kamo River in Kyōto. The performance was a strong departure from the older, traditional Noh drama style, in which the actors engaged in slow, deliberate movements. It was so popular that she arranged a variety of other similar events. According to some accounts, Okuni dressed as a young man while she performed certain dances. The company's lusty and unrestrained dance dramas soon became known throughout Japan—the style acquiring the name Okuni Kabuki—and other troupes of female dancers were formed.

Okuni's company and the newer groups normally had the patronage of the nobility, but their appeal was directed toward ordinary townspeople, and the themes of their dramas and dances were taken from everyday life. The popularity of *onna* ("women's") Kabuki remained high until women's participation was officially banned in 1629 by the shogun (military ruler) Tokugawa Iemitsu, who thought that the sensuality of the dances had a deleterious effect on public morality. Not only were the dances considered suggestive, but the dancers themselves earned extra money by means of prostitution. (The ban on women's performing Kabuki lasted until the Meiji Restoration in 1868.) For a time, as in Elizabethan theatre, boys and young men performed the female roles while dressed as women. In 1652 their involvement was also banned by the shogun for moral reasons. Older male dancers subsequently took over these roles.

Ariyoshi Sawako's work of fiction *Izumo no Okuni* (1969; *Kabuki Dancer*) is an imagined biography of Okuni that provides an enlightened look at 16th- and 17th-century Japanese culture.

CHRISTINA

(b. Dec. 8, 1626, Stockholm, Swed.—d. April 19, 1689, Rome [Italy]

Christina was the queen of Sweden (1644–54) who stunned all of Europe by abdicating her throne. She subsequently attempted, without success, to gain the crowns of Naples and of Poland. One of the wittiest and most learned women of her age, Christina is best remembered for her lavish sponsorship of the arts and her influence on European culture.

Christina (Swedish: Kristina) was the daughter of King Gustav II Adolf and Maria Eleonora of Brandenburg. After her father died in the Battle of Lützen, Christina, his only heir, became queen-elect before the age of six. By his orders she was educated as a prince, with the learned theologian Johannes Matthiae as her tutor. Five regents headed by the chancellor Axel Oxenstierna governed the country. Her brilliance and strong will were evident even in her childhood. Oxenstierna himself instructed her in politics and first admitted her to council meetings when she was 14.

An assiduous politician, Christina was able to keep the bitter class rivalries that broke out after the Thirty Years' War from lapsing into civil war but was unable to solve the desperate financial problems caused by the long years of fighting.

Highly cultured and passionately interested in learning, she rose at five in the morning to read and invited eminent foreign writers, musicians, and scholars to her court. The

French philosopher René Descartes himself taught her philosophy and died at her court. For her wit and learning, all Europe called her the Minerva of the North; she was, however, extravagant, too free in giving away crown lands, and intent on a luxurious court in a country that could not support it and did not want it. Her reign was, nevertheless, beneficent. It saw the first Swedish newspaper (1645) and the first countrywide school ordinance; science and literature were encouraged, and new privileges were given to the towns. Trade, manufactures, and mining also made great strides.

Christina's abdication after 10 years of rule shocked and confused the Christian world. She pleaded that she was ill and that the burden of ruling was too heavy for a woman. The real reasons, however, are unclear and still disputed. Among those that are often cited are her aversion to marriage, her secret conversion to Roman Catholicism, and her discomfort (after spending most of her life in the company of men) with her own femininity. She chose her cousin Charles X Gustav as her successor, and, when he was crowned on June 6, 1654, the day of her abdication, Christina left Sweden immediately.

In December 1655 Pope Alexander VII received Christina in splendour at Rome. He was, however, soon disillusioned with his famous convert, who opposed public displays of piety. Although she was far from beautiful (short and pockmarked, with a humped right shoulder), Christina, by her manners and personality, created a sensation in Rome. Missing the activity of ruling, she entered into negotiations with the French chief minister, Cardinal Mazarin, and with the duke di Modena to seize Naples (then under the Spanish crown), intending to become queen of Naples and to leave the throne to a French prince at her death. This scheme collapsed in 1657, during a visit by Christina to France. While staying at the palace of Fontainebleau, she ordered the summary execution of her equerry, Marchese Gian Rinaldo Monaldeschi, alleging that he had betrayed her plans to the Holy See. Her refusal to give reasons for this action, beyond insisting on her royal authority, shocked the French court, nor did the pope welcome her return to Rome.

In spite of this scandal, Christina lived to become one of the most influential figures of her time, the friend of four popes, and a munificent patroness of the arts. Always extravagant, she had financial difficulties most of her life: the revenues due from Sweden came slowly or not at all. She visited Sweden in 1660 and in 1667. On the second journey, while staying in Hamburg, she had Pope Clement IX's support in an attempt to gain another crown, that of her second cousin John II Casimir Vasa, who had abdicated the throne of Poland; but her failure seemed to please her since this meant that she could return to her beloved Rome. There she had formed a strong friendship with Cardinal Decio Azzolino, a clever, charming, prudent man, leader of a group of cardinals active in church politics. It was generally believed in Rome that he was her lover, a view sustained by her letters, which were decoded in the 19th century. With him, she, too, became active in church politics, insisting for years on the pursuance of the Christian war against the Turks. Pope Innocent XI, who pushed this war to its victorious conclusion, stopped her pension at her own urgent request in order to add it to the war treasury. In 1681, having secured a trustworthy administrator for her lands in Sweden, Christina at last became financially secure.

Christina's extraordinary taste in the arts has influenced European culture since her time. Her palace, the Riario (now the Corsini, on the Lungara in Rome), contained the greatest collection of paintings of the Venetian school ever assembled, as well as other notable paintings, sculpture, and medallions. It became the meeting place of men of letters and musicians. The Arcadia Academy (Accademia dell'Arcadia) for philosophy and literature, which she founded, still exists in Rome. It was at her instigation that the Tordinona, the first public opera house in Rome, was opened, and it was she who recognized the genius of and sponsored the composer Alessandro Scarlatti, who became her choirmaster, and Arcangelo Corelli, who directed her orchestra. The sculptor and architect Giovanni Bernini, her friend, considered her his saviour when she commissioned the art historian Filippo Baldinucci to write his biography while he was being discredited in 1680. Her enormous collection of books and manuscripts is now in the Vatican library. She was renowned, too, for her militant protection of personal freedoms, for her charities, and as protectress of the Jews in Rome.

Christina died in 1689. Her tomb is in St. Peter's Basilica in Rome.

MARIA THERESA

(b. May 13, 1717, Vienna, Austria—d. Nov. 29, 1780, Vienna)

A key figure in the power politics of 18th-century Europe, Maria Theresa, archduchess of Austria and queen of Hungary and Bohemia (1740–80), was the wife and empress of the Holy Roman emperor Francis I (reigned 1745–65) and mother of the Holy Roman emperor Joseph II (reigned 1765–90). Upon her accession, the War of the Austrian Succession (1740–48) erupted, challenging her inheritance of the Habsburg lands. This contest with Prussia was followed by two more, the Seven Years' War (1756–63) and the War of the Bavarian Succession (1778–79), which further checked Austrian power.

EARLY LIFE

Maria Theresa (German: Maria Theresia) was the eldest daughter of the Holy Roman emperor Charles VI and Elizabeth of Brunswick-Wolfenbüttel. The death of an only son prompted Charles, the only living prince of his line, to promulgate the so-called Pragmatic Sanction, a royal act, eventually recognized by most powers, whereby female issue was entitled to succeed to the domains of the Habsburgs. (Since nearly every major European nation coveted some part of the Habsburg domains, their consent to the Pragmatic Sanction must be taken as nothing more than an act of convenience.) Maria Theresa thus became a pawn on Europe's political chessboard. In 1736 she married Francis Stephen of Lorraine. Because of French objections to the union of Lorraine with the Habsburg lands, Francis Stephen had to exchange his ancestral duchy for the right of succession to the Grand Duchy of Tuscany. The marriage was a love match, and 16 children were born to the couple, of whom 10 survived to adulthood.

WAR OF THE AUSTRIAN SUCCESSION

On Oct. 20, 1740, Charles VI died, and the war of succession he had striven so hard to forestall broke out before the end of the year. Charles left the Habsburg state at the lowest point of its prestige, its coffers empty, its capital beset by unrest. The naive courage with which Maria Theresa assumed her heritage (and made her husband co-regent) astounded Europe's chancelleries. Her refusal to negotiate with Frederick II (later the Great) of Prussia, who had invaded Silesia, her most prosperous province, appalled the senescent councillors of her late father. Her successful appearance before the refractory Hungarian Estates, ending with an appeal for a mass levy of troops, gave her a European reputation for diplomatic skill. When the elector Charles Albert of Bavaria—one of the princes who had joined Frederick in assaulting Habsburg territories—was elected emperor, Maria Theresa was mortified; that dignity, little more than titular by then, had in practice been hereditary in her family for 300 years. Upon the death of Charles Albert (1745), she secured for her husband, Francis, the imperial crown, which the law denied to women.

DOMESTIC REFORMS

Realizing the need for a sizable standing army and in order to maintain one, Maria Theresa accepted the plans of Count Friedrich Wilhelm Haugwitz—the first in a succession of remarkable men of intellect she was to draw into her council. In the face of the opposition of many noblemen, she managed to reduce drastically (except in Hungary) the powers of the various dominions' estates, which had held the monarchy's purse strings since time immemorial. In the further process of abolishing tax exemptions held by the great landowners, who dominated those assemblies, she hit on the notion of a "God-pleasing equality." Yet she did not question the justice of the manorial lord's claim on the labour of his hereditary subjects. Only many years later did peasant riots in famine-stricken Bohemia, as well as the reported cruelty of Hungarian magnates, cause her to limit the use of forced labour. "The peasantry must be able to sustain itself as well as pay taxes . . . ," she wrote.

Practical, if not always fiscal, considerations, rather than doctrinaire humanitarianism, guided all of Maria Theresa's reforms. An enlarged central administration—from which the judiciary was separated in 1749—and a repeatedly reorganized treasury required knowledgeable civil servants and judges; and their training was, to her mind, the sole purpose of higher education. She approved drastic changes that her physician, the Dutchman Gerhard van Swieten, carried through at the universities (such as the introduction of textbooks, the linking of the medical school of the University of Vienna with the embryonic public health service, and the sovereign's right to veto the election of deans by the faculties) even as he took them out of the hands of the Jesuits, to whose Society she herself was devoted. (She was the last of the Catholic monarchs to close its establishments.) Deeply pious, strictly observant, and intolerant to the point of bigotry, she was moving, nonetheless, toward subordinating the church to the authority of the state.

FOREIGN RELATIONS

Neither the peace of 1745 (by which Austria ceded Silesia to Prussia) nor the peace of 1748 (which ended Maria Theresa's war with the rest of her enemies) ended her efforts to modernize the army. The dazzling ideas of her new chancellor, Wenzel Anton von Kaunitz, fired her determination to recover Silesia, indeed, to destroy Prussia. In a famous "reversal of alliances" (1756) she threw over England, the old ally and "banker" of the Habsburgs, and allied herself with France, their ancient foe. Moreover, she had entered into a treaty with Russia, a newcomer to European rivalries. She paid but scant attention to the global ramifications of the ensuing Seven Years' War. When its end sealed the loss of Silesia and left the monarchy with a mountain of debts, she became a champion of peace. As late as 1779 she single-handedly frustrated another full-scale war with Prussia, risked by her self-opinionated firstborn, Joseph II, who on his father's demise had become co-regent in the Habsburg dominions (and been elected emperor).

Though Francis had not been a faithful husband, Maria Theresa never wavered in her love, and his sudden death in 1765 plunged her into prolonged grief. She emerged from it, her zeal for activity nowise impaired. A new public-debt policy, the settlement of the empty spaces of Hungary, the drafting of a penal code to supplant the tangle of local systems, and a kind of poor law—these were but some of the innovations in which she herself took a hand, with her common sense doing service for the book learning she lacked. In step with the enforced retreat of the church from secular affairs, she came to feel that it was incumbent on the state to control the intellectual life of its subjects. It was she who institutionalized government censorship; on the other hand, it was she, too, who launched plans for compulsory primary education.

LATE YEARS

Although Maria Theresa pedantically supervised her children's upbringing and education, she was to experience many disappointments in connection with them. Of her sons, only Leopold of Tuscany (later Emperor Leopold II), though difficult as a child, lived up to her hopes. Her special affection belonged to Maria Christina, who was allowed to marry for love and on whom Maria Theresa showered vast gifts of money. Three of her daughters, married off to unprepossessing Bourbons—in Parma, Naples, and France—again and again irritated their mother with their strong will or their follies; to her dying day she bombarded one of these, Queen Marie-Antoinette of France, with practical advice, moral exhortations, and dire warnings of the future.

But it was the running conflict with her son Joseph that clouded the years of her widowhood most. His flirting with the "new philosophy" of the Enlightenment frightened her, his admiration of Frederick the Great offended her, and his foreign enterprises filled her with trepidation. There were threats of abdication on both his part and hers. When Joseph, supported by Kaunitz, pressured her into agreeing to share in the (first) partition of Poland in 1772, she loudly bewailed the immorality of the action. And while she had shrugged off ridicule on such occasions as her setting up a public morals squad (the "chastity commission" of popular parlance) or, prude though she was, her enlisting the help of Louis XV's mistress, Mme de Pompadour, in order to obtain the French alliance, the accusation of "lachrymose hypocrisy" raised in foreign courts during the Polish affair distressed her.

Grown enormously stout and in poor health, she spent more and more of her time in suburban Schönbrunn, whose palace owed its reconstruction to her initiative. She was still trying to hold off the approach of the new age. Ironically, her own pragmatic reforms had smoothed the road to the enlightened despotism that was to mark the reign of her son and successor, Joseph II. She died in November 1780.

To the Habsburg monarchy, a dynastic agglomeration of disparate lands, Maria Theresa gave a measure of unity. A princess of engaging naturalness, she was one of the most capable rulers of her house and, according to one historian, "the most human of the Habsburgs."

CATHERINE II

(b. April 21 [May 2, New Style], 1729, Stettin, Prussia [now Szczecin, Poland]—d. Nov. 6 [Nov. 17], 1796, Tsarskoye Selo [now Pushkin], near St. Petersburg, Russia)

C atherine II, better known as Catherine the Great (Russian: Yekaterina Velikaya), was a German-born empress of Russia (1762–96), who led her country into full participation in the political and cultural life of Europe, carrying on the work begun by Peter the Great. With her ministers she reorganized the administration and law of the Russian Empire and extended Russian territory, adding the Crimea and much of Poland.

EARLY LIFE AND EXPERIENCE

Sophie Friederike Auguste von Anhalt-Zerbst was the daughter of an obscure German prince, Christian August von Anhalt-Zerbst, but she was related through her mother to the dukes of Holstein. At age 14 she was chosen to be the wife of Karl Ulrich, duke of Holstein-Gottorp, grandson of Peter the Great and heir to the throne of Russia as the grand duke Peter. In 1744 Catherine arrived in Russia, assumed the title of Grand Duchess Catherine Alekseyevna, and married her young cousin the following year. The marriage was a complete failure; the following 18 years were filled with deception and humiliation for her.

Russia at the time was ruled by Peter the Great's daughter, the empress Elizabeth, whose 20-year reign greatly stabilized the monarchy. Devoted to much pleasure and luxury and greatly desirous of giving her court the brilliancy of a European court, Elizabeth prepared the way for Catherine, who would not have become empress if her husband had been at all normal. He was extremely neurotic, rebellious, obstinate, perhaps impotent, nearly alcoholic, and, most seriously, a fanatical worshipper of Frederick II of Prussia, the foe of the empress Elizabeth. Catherine, by contrast, was clearheaded and ambitious. Her intelligence, flexibility of character, and love of Russia gained her much support.

She was humiliated, bored, and regarded with suspicion while at court, but she found comfort in reading extensively and in preparing herself for her future role as sovereign. Although a woman of little beauty, Catherine possessed considerable charm, a lively intelligence, and extraordinary energy. During her husband's lifetime alone, she had at least three lovers; if her hints are to be believed, none of her three children, not even the heir apparent Paul, was fathered by her husband. Her true passion, however, was ambition; since Peter was incapable of ruling, she saw quite early the possibility of eliminating him and governing Russia herself.

The empress Elizabeth died on Dec. 25, 1761 (Jan. 5, 1762, New Style), while Russia, allied with Austria and France, was engaged in the Seven Years' War against Prussia. Shortly after Elizabeth's death, Peter, now emperor, ended Russia's participation in the war and concluded an alliance with Frederick II of Prussia. He made no attempt to hide his hatred of Russia and his love of his native Germany. Discrediting himself endlessly by his foolish actions, he also prepared to rid himself of his wife. Catherine had only to strike. She had the support of the army, especially the regiments at St. Petersburg, where Grigory Orlov, her lover, was stationed. The court and public opinion in both capitals (Moscow and St. Petersburg) were allied with her as well. She was also supported by the "enlightened" elements of aristocratic society, since she was known for her liberal opinions and admired as one of the most cultivated persons in Russia.

On June 28 (July 9, New Style), 1762, she led the regiments that had rallied to her cause into St. Petersburg and had herself proclaimed empress and autocrat in the Kazan Cathedral. Peter III abdicated and was assassinated eight days later. Although Catherine probably did not order the murder of Peter, it was committed by her supporters, and public opinion held her responsible. In September 1762, she was crowned with great ceremony in Moscow, the ancient capital of the tsars, and began a reign that was to span 34 years as empress of Russia under the title of Catherine II.

Early Years as Empress

Despite Catherine's personal weaknesses, she was above all a ruler. Truly dedicated to her adopted country, she intended to make Russia a prosperous and powerful state. Since her early days in Russia she had dreamed of establishing a reign of order and justice, of spreading education, creating a court to rival Versailles, and developing a national culture that would be more than an imitation of French models. Her projects obviously were too numerous to carry out, even if she could have given her full attention to them.

Her most pressing practical problem, however, was to replenish the state treasury, which was empty when Elizabeth died; this she did in 1762 by secularizing the property of the clergy, who owned one-third of the land and serfs in Russia. The Russian clergy was reduced to a group of state-paid functionaries, losing what little power had been left to it by the reforms of Peter the Great. Since her coup d'etat and Peter's suspicious death demanded both discretion and stability in her dealings with other nations, she continued to preserve friendly relations with Prussia, Russia's old enemy, as well as with the country's traditional allies, France and Austria. In 1764 she resolved the problem of Poland, a kingdom lacking definite boundaries and coveted by three neighbouring powers, by installing one of her old lovers, Stanisław Poniatowski, a weak man entirely devoted to her, as king of Poland.

Her attempts at reform, however, were less than satisfying. A disciple of the English and French liberal philosophers, she saw very quickly that the reforms advocated by Montesquieu or Jean-Jacques Rousseau, which were difficult enough to put into practice in Europe, did not at all correspond to the realities of an anarchic and backward Russia. In 1767 she convened a commission composed of delegates from all the provinces and from all social classes (except the serfs) for the purpose of ascertaining the true wishes of her people and framing a constitution. The debates went on for months and came to nothing. Catherine's Instruction to the Commission was a draft of a constitution and a code of laws. It was considered too liberal for publication in France and remained a dead letter in Russia.

Frustrated in her attempts at reform, Catherine seized the pretext of war with Turkey in 1768 to change her policy; henceforth, emphasis would be placed above all on national grandeur. Since the reign of Peter the Great, the Ottoman Empire had been the traditional enemy of Russia; inevitably, the war fired the patriotism and zeal of Catherine's subjects. Although the naval victory at Çeşme in 1770 brought military glory to the empress, Turkey had not yet been defeated and continued fighting. At that point, Russia encountered unforeseen difficulties.

First, a terrible plague broke out in Moscow; along with the hardships imposed by the war, it created a climate of disaffection and popular agitation. In 1773 Yemelyan Pugachov, a former officer of the Don Cossacks, pretending to be the dead emperor Peter III, incited the greatest uprising of Russian history prior to the revolution of 1917. Starting in the Ural region, the movement spread rapidly through the vast southeastern provinces, and in June 1774 Pugachov's Cossack troops prepared to march on Moscow.

At this point, the war with Turkey ended in a Russian victory, and Catherine sent her crack troops to crush the rebellion. Defeated and captured, Pugachov was beheaded in 1775, but the terror and chaos he inspired were not soon forgotten. Catherine now realized that for her the people were more to be feared than pitied, and that, rather than freeing them, she must tighten their bonds.

Before her accession to power, Catherine had planned to emancipate the serfs, on whom the economy of Russia, which was 95 percent agricultural, was based. The serf was the property of the master, and the fortune of a noble was evaluated not in lands but in the "souls" he owned. When confronted with the realities of power, however, Catherine saw very quickly that emancipation of the serfs would never be tolerated by the owners, whom she depended upon for support, and who would throw the country into disorder once they lost their own means of support. Reconciling herself to an unavoidable evil without much difficulty, Catherine turned her attention to organizing and strengthening a system that she herself had condemned as inhuman. She imposed serfdom on the Ukrainians who had until then been free. By distributing the so-called crown lands to her favourites and ministers, she worsened the lot of the peasants, who had enjoyed a certain autonomy. At the end of her reign, there was scarcely a free peasant left in Russia, and, because of more systematized control, the condition of the serf was worse than it had been before Catherine's rule.

Thus, 95 percent of the Russian people did not in any way benefit directly from the achievements of Catherine's reign. Rather, their forced labour financed the immense expenditures required for her ever-growing economic, military, and cultural projects. In these undertakings, at least, she proved herself to be a good administrator and could claim that the blood and sweat of the people had not been wasted.

INFLUENCE OF POTEMKIN

In 1774, the year of Russia's defeat of Turkey, Grigory Potemkin, who had distinguished himself in the war, became Catherine's lover, and a brilliant career began for this official of the minor nobility, whose intelligence and abilities were equalled only by his ambition. He was to be the only one of Catherine's favourites to play an extensive political role. Ordinarily, the empress did not mix business and pleasure; her ministers were almost always selected for their abilities. In Potemkin she found an extraordinary man whom she could love and respect and with whom she could share her power. As minister he had unlimited powers, even after the end of their liaison, which lasted only two years.

Potemkin must be given part of the credit for the somewhat extravagant splendour of Catherine's reign. He had a conception of grandeur that escaped the rather pedestrian German princess, and he understood the effect it produced on the people. A great dreamer, he was avid for territories to conquer and provinces to populate; an experienced diplomat with a knowledge of Russia that Catherine had not yet acquired and as audacious as Catherine was methodical, Potemkin was treated as an equal by the empress up to the time of his death in 1791. They complemented and understood each other, and the ambitious minister expressed his respect for his sovereign through complete devotion to her interests.

The annexation of the Crimea from the Turks in 1783 was Potemkin's work. Through that annexation and the acquisition of the territories of the Crimean Khanate, which extended from the Caucasus Mountains to the Bug River in southwestern Russia, Russia held the north shore of the Black Sea and was in a position to threaten the existence of the Ottoman Empire and to establish a foothold in the Mediterranean. Catherine also sought to renew the alliance with Austria, Turkey's neighbour and enemy, and renounced the alliance with Prussia and England, who were alarmed by Russian ambitions. Yet, during Catherine's reign, the country did not become involved in a European war, because the empress scrupulously adhered to the territorial agreements she had concluded with several western European nations.

Catherine's glorification reached its climax in a voyage to the Crimea arranged by Potemkin in 1787. In a festive Arabian Nights atmosphere, the empress crossed the country to take possession of her new provinces; the emperor of Austria, the king of Poland, and innumerable diplomats came to honour her and to enjoy the splendours of what became known as "Cleopatra's fleet," because Catherine and her court traveled partly by water. She dedicated new towns bearing her name and announced that she ultimately intended to proceed to Constantinople.

EFFECTS OF THE FRENCH REVOLUTION

Catherine, like all the crowned heads of Europe, felt seriously threatened by the French Revolution. The divine right of royalty and the aristocracy was being questioned, and Catherine, although a "friend of the Enlightenment," had no intention of relinquishing her own privileges: "I am an aristocrat, it is my profession." In 1790 the writer A. N. Radishchev, who attempted to publish a work openly critical of the abuses of serfdom, was tried, condemned to death, then pardoned and exiled. Ironically, the sentiments Radishchev expressed were very similar to

Catherine's Instruction of 1767. Next, Poland, encouraged by the example of France, began agitating for a liberal constitution. In 1792, under the pretext of forestalling the threat of revolution, Catherine sent in troops and the next year annexed most of the western Ukraine, while Prussia helped itself to large territories of western Poland. After the national uprising led by Tadeusz Kościuszko in 1794, Catherine wiped Poland off the map of Europe by dividing it between Russia, Prussia, and Austria in 1795.

Catherine's last years were darkened by the execution of Louis XVI, the advance of the revolutionary armies, and the spread of radical ideas. The empress realized, moreover, that she had no suitable successor. She considered her son Paul an incompetent and unbalanced man; her grandson Alexander was too young yet to rule.

ASSESSMENT

Russians, even Soviet Russians, continue to admire Catherine, the German, the usurper and profligate, and regard her as a source of national pride. Non-Russian opinion of Catherine is less favourable. Because Russia under her rule grew strong enough to threaten the other great powers, and because she was in fact a harsh and unscrupulous ruler, she figured in the Western imagination as the incarnation of the immense, backward, yet forbidding country she ruled. One of Catherine's principal glories is to have been a woman who, just as Elizabeth I of England and Queen Victoria gave their names to periods of history, became synonymous with a decisive epoch in the development of her country.

At the end of Catherine's reign, Russia had expanded westward and southward over an area of more than 200,000 square miles, and the Russian rulers' ancient dream of access to the Bosporus Strait (connecting the

Black Sea with the Aegean) had become an attainable goal. At the end of her reign Catherine claimed that she had reorganized 29 provinces under her administrative reform plan. An uninhibited spender, she invested funds in many projects. More than a hundred new towns were built; old ones were expanded and renovated. As commodities were plentiful, trade expanded and communications developed. These achievements, together with the glory of military victories and the fame of a brilliant court, to which the greatest minds of Europe were drawn, have won her a distinguished place in history.

Catherine's critics acknowledge her energy and administrative ability but point out that the achievements of her reign were as much due to her associates and to the unaided, historical development of Russian society as to the merits of the empress. And when they judge Catherine the woman, they treat her severely.

Her private life was admittedly not exemplary. She had young lovers up to the time of her unexpected death from a stroke at the age of 67. After the end of her liaison with Potemkin, who perhaps was her morganatic husband, the official favourite changed at least a dozen times; she chose handsome and insignificant young men, who were only, as one of them himself said, "kept girls." Although in reality devoted to power above all else, she dreamed endlessly of the joys of a shared love, but her position isolated her. She did not love her son Paul, the legitimate heir, whose throne she occupied. On the other hand, she adored her grandsons, particularly the eldest, Alexander, whom she wished to succeed her. In her friendships she was loyal and generous and usually showed mercy toward her enemies.

Yet it cannot be denied that she was also egotistical, pretentious, and extremely domineering, above all a woman of action, capable of being ruthless when her own interest or that of the state was at stake. As she grew older she also became extremely vain: there was some excuse, as the most distinguished minds of Europe heaped flatteries on her that even she ultimately found exaggerated.

A friend of Voltaire and Denis Diderot, she carried on an extensive correspondence with most of the important personages of her time. She was a patron of literature and a promoter of Russian culture; she herself wrote, established literary reviews, encouraged the sciences, and founded schools. Her interests and enthusiasms ranged from construction projects to lawmaking and the collection of art objects; she touched on everything, not always happily but always passionately. She was a woman of elemental energy and intellectual curiosity, desiring to create as well as to control.

ELISABETH VIGÉE-LEBRUN

(b. April 16, 1755, Paris, France—d. March 30, 1842, Paris)

The French painter Marie-Louise-Elisabeth Vigée-Lebrun (also spelled LeBrun or Le Brun) was one of the most successful women artists (unusually so for her time) and was particularly noted for her portraits of women.

Her father and first teacher, Louis Vigée, was a noted portraitist who worked chiefly in pastels. In 1776 she married an art dealer, J.B.P. Lebrun. Her great opportunity came in 1779 when she was summoned to Versailles to paint a portrait of Queen Marie-Antoinette. The two women became friends, and in subsequent years Vigée-Lebrun painted more than 20 portraits of Marie-Antoinette in a great variety of poses and costumes. She also painted a great number of self-portraits, in the style of various artists whose work she admired. In 1783, because of her friendship with the queen, Vigée-Lebrun was grudgingly accepted into the Royal Academy.

On the outbreak of the Revolution in 1789, she left France and for 12 years lived abroad, traveling to Rome, Naples, Vienna, Berlin, St. Petersburg, and Moscow, painting portraits and playing a leading role in society. In 1801 she returned to Paris but, disliking Parisian social life under Napoleon, soon left for London, where she painted portraits of the court and of Lord Byron. Later she went to Switzerland (and painted a portrait of Mme de Staël) and then again (c. 1810) to Paris, where she continued to paint until her death.

Vigée-Lebrun was a woman of much wit and charm, and her memoirs, *Souvenirs de ma vie* (1835–37; "Reminiscences of My Life"; Eng. trans. *Memoirs of Madame Vigée Lebrun*), provide a lively account of her life and times. She was one of the most technically fluent portraitists of her era, and her pictures are notable for freshness, charm, and sensitivity of presentation. During her career, according to her own account, she painted 900 pictures, including some 600 portraits and about 200 landscapes.

MARIE-ANTOINETTE

(b. Nov. 2, 1755, Vienna, Austria—d. Oct. 16, 1793, Paris, France)

Marie-Antoinette was the queen consort of King Louis XVI of France (1774–93). Imprudent and an enemy of reform, she helped provoke the popular unrest that led to the French Revolution and to the overthrow of the monarchy in August 1792.

The 11th daughter of the Holy Roman emperor Francis I and Maria Theresa, Marie-Antoinette-Josèphe-Jeanne d'Autriche-Lorraine (Austria-Lorraine), born Maria Antonia Josepha Joanna von Österreich-Lothringen, was married in 1770 to the dauphin Louis, grandson of France's King

Louis XV. The timid, uninspiring Louis proved to be an inattentive husband; by the time he ascended the throne in 1774, Marie-Antoinette had withdrawn into the companionship of a small circle of court favourites.

Her extravagant court expenditures contributed—though to a minor degree—to the huge debt incurred by the French state in the 1770s and '80s. Louis XVI's inability to consummate their marriage and the queen's resultant childlessness in the 1770s inspired rivals—including the king's own brothers, who stood to inherit the throne if she did not produce a legitimate heir—to circulate slanderous reports of her alleged extramarital affairs. These vilifications culminated in the Affair of the Diamond Necklace (1785–86), in which the queen was unjustly accused of having formed an immoral relationship with a cardinal. The scandal discredited the monarchy and encouraged the nobles to oppose vigorously (1787–88) all the financial reforms advocated by the king's ministers.

During these crises, as in those to come, Marie-Antoinette proved to be stronger and more decisive than her husband. After a crowd stormed the Bastille on July 14, 1789, the queen failed to convince Louis to take refuge with his army at Metz. In August–September, however, she successfully prodded him to resist the attempts of the Revolutionary National Assembly to abolish feudalism and restrict the royal prerogative. As a result, she became the main target of the popular agitators, who attributed to her the celebrated and callous remark on being told that the people had no bread: "Let them eat cake!" ("Qu'ils mangent de la brioche!"). In October 1789 popular pressure compelled the royal family to return from Versailles to Paris, where they became hostages of the Revolutionary movement.

Six months later Marie-Antoinette opened secret communications with the comte de Mirabeau, a prominent member of the National Assembly who hoped to restore the authority of the crown. Nevertheless, her mistrust of Mirabeau prevented the king from following his advice. After Mirabeau died in April 1791, she turned for assistance to a group of émigrés. They arranged for the king and queen to escape from Paris on the night of June 20, but Revolutionary forces apprehended the royal couple at Varennes (June 25) and escorted them back to Paris.

Marie-Antoinette then attempted to shore up the rapidly deteriorating position of the crown by opening secret negotiations with Antoine Barnave, leader of the constitutional monarchist faction in the Assembly. Barnave persuaded the king to accept publicly the new constitution (September 1791), but the queen undermined Barnave's position by privately urging her brother, the Holy Roman emperor Leopold II, to conduct a counter-revolutionary crusade against France. Leopold avoided acceding to her demands. After France declared war on Austria in April 1792, Marie-Antoinette's continuing intrigues with the Austrians further enraged the French. Popular hatred of the queen provided impetus to the insurrection that overthrew the monarchy on Aug. 10, 1792.

Marie-Antoinette spent the remainder of her life in Parisian prisons. Louis XVI was executed on orders from the National Convention in January 1793, and in August the queen was put in solitary confinement in the Conciergerie. She was brought before the Revolutionary tribunal on Oct. 14, 1793, and was guillotined two days later.

MARY WOLLSTONECRAFT

(b. April 27, 1759, London, Eng. — d. Sept. 10, 1797, London)

The English writer Mary Wollstonecraft was a passionate advocate of educational and social equality for women.

The daughter of a farmer, Wollstonecraft taught school and worked as a governess, experiences that inspired her views in *Thoughts on the Education of Daughters* (1787). In 1788 she began working as a translator for the London publisher James Johnson, who published several of her works, including the novel *Mary: A Fiction* (1788). Her mature work on a woman's place in society is *A Vindication of the Rights of Woman* (1792), which calls for women and men to be educated equally.

Mary Wollstonecraft's A Vindication of the Rights of Woman *created quite a stir in its day, fueling the fight for women's rights and inspiring feminists everywhere.* Hulton Archive/Getty Images

In 1792 Wollstonecraft left England to observe the French Revolution in Paris, where she lived with an American, Captain Gilbert Imlay. In the spring of 1794 she gave birth to a daughter, Fanny. The following year, distraught over the breakdown of her relationship with Imlay, she attempted suicide.

Wollstonecraft returned to London to work again for Johnson and joined the influential radical group that gathered at his home, which included William Godwin, Thomas Paine, Thomas Holcroft, William Blake, and, after 1793, William Wordsworth. In 1796 she began a liaison with Godwin, and on March 29, 1797, Mary being pregnant, they were married. The marriage was happy but brief; Mary Wollstonecraft Godwin died 11 days after the birth of her second daughter, Mary. (This daughter would later marry Percy Bysshe Shelley and write *Frankenstein; or, The Modern Prometheus*, one of the great Romantic novels.)

Wollstonecraft's *A Vindication of the Rights of Woman* is one of the trailblazing works of feminism. Published in 1792, it argued that the educational system of her time deliberately trained women to be frivolous and incapable. She posited that an educational system that allowed girls the same advantages as boys would result in women who would be not only exceptional wives and mothers but also capable workers in many professions. Other early feminists had made similar pleas for improved education for women, but Wollstonecraft's work was unique in suggesting that the betterment of women's status be effected through such political change as the radical reform of national educational systems. Such change, she concluded, would benefit all society.

The publication of *Vindication* caused considerable controversy but failed to bring about any immediate reforms. From the 1840s, however, members of the incipient American and European women's movements resurrected some of the book's principles. It was a particular influence on American women's rights pioneers such as Elizabeth Cady Stanton and Margaret Fuller.

The life of Mary Wollstonecraft has been the subject of several biographies, beginning with her husband's *Memoirs of the Author of A Vindication of the Rights of Woman* (1798, reissued 2001, in an edition edited by Pamela Clemit and Gina Luria Walker). Those written in the 19th century tended to emphasize the scandalous aspects of her life and not her work. With the renewed interest in women's rights in the later 20th century, she again became the subject of several books. *The Collected Letters of Mary Wollstonecraft*, assembled by Janet Todd, was published in 2003.

GERMAINE DE STAËL

(b. April 22, 1766, Paris, France—d. July 14, 1817, Paris)

Germaine de Staël, the French-Swiss woman of letters, political propagandist, and conversationalist, epitomized the European culture of her time, bridging the history of ideas from Neoclassicism to Romanticism. As Madame de Staël, she also gained fame by maintaining a salon for leading intellectuals. Her writings include novels, plays, moral and political essays, literary criticism, history, autobiographical memoirs, and even a number of poems. Her most important literary contribution was as a theorist of Romanticism.

EARLY LIFE AND FAMILY

She was born Anne-Louise-Germaine Necker, the daughter of Swiss parents, in Paris. Her father was Jacques Necker, the Genevan banker who became finance minister to King Louis XVI. Her mother, Suzanne Curchod, the daughter of a French-Swiss pastor, assisted her husband's career by establishing a brilliant literary and political salon in Paris.

The young Germaine Necker early gained a reputation for lively wit, if not for beauty. While still a child, she was to be seen in her mother's salon, listening to, and even taking part in, the conversation with that lively intellectual curiosity that was to remain her most attractive quality. When she was 16, her marriage began to be considered. William Pitt the Younger was regarded as a possible husband, but she disliked the idea of living in England. She was married in 1786 to the Swedish ambassador in Paris, Baron Erik de Staël-Holstein. It was a marriage of convenience and ended in 1797 in formal separation. There were, however, three children: Auguste (b. 1790), who edited his mother's complete works; Albert (b. 1792); and Albertine (b. 1796), who was allegedly fathered by Benjamin Constant.

POLITICAL VIEWS

Before she was 21, Germaine de Staël had written a romantic drama, *Sophie, ou les sentiments secrets* (1786), and a tragedy inspired by Nicholas Rowe, *Jane Gray* (1790). But it was her *Lettres sur les ouvrages et le caractère de J.-J. Rousseau* (1788; *Letters on the Works and the Character of J.-J. Rousseau*) that made her known. There is in her thought an unusual and irreconcilable mixture of Rousseau's enthusiasm and Montesquieu's rationalism. Under the influence of her father, an admirer of Montesquieu, she adopted political views based on the English parliamentary monarchy. Favouring the French Revolution, she acquired a reputation for Jacobinism. Under the Convention, the elected body that abolished the monarchy, the moderate Girondin faction corresponded best to her ideas.

Protected by her husband's diplomatic status, she was in no danger in Paris until 1793, when she retreated to

Coppet, Switz., the family residence near Geneva. It was here that she gained fame by establishing a meeting place for some of the leading intellectuals of western Europe. Since 1789 she had been the mistress of Louis de Narbonne, one of Louis XVI's last ministers. He took refuge in England in 1792, where she joined him in 1793. She stayed at Juniper Hall, near Mickleham in Surrey, a mansion that had been rented since 1792 by French émigrés. There she met Fanny Burney (later Mme d'Arblay), but their friendship was cut short because Mme de Staël's politics and morals were considered undesirable by good society in England.

She returned to France, via Coppet, at the end of the Terror in 1794. A brilliant period of her career then began. Her salon flourished, and she published several political and literary essays, notably *De l'influence des passions sur le bonheur des individus et des nations* (1796; *A Treatise on the Influence of the Passions upon the Happiness of Individuals and of Nations*), which became one of the important documents of European Romanticism. She began to study the new ideas that were being developed particularly in Germany. She read the elderly Swiss critic Karl Viktor von Bonstetten; the German philologist Wilhelm von Humboldt; and, above all, the brothers August Wilhelm and Friedrich von Schlegel, who were among the most influential German Romanticists.

But it was her new lover, Benjamin Constant, the author and politician, who influenced her most directly in favour of German culture. Her fluctuating liaison with Constant started in 1794 and lasted 14 years, although after 1806 her affections found little response.

LITERARY THEORIES

At about the beginning of 1800 the literary and political character of Mme de Staël's thought became defined. Her literary importance emerged in *De la littérature considérée dans ses rapports avec les institutions sociales* (1800; *A Treatise of Ancient and Modern Literature* and *The Influence of Literature upon Society*). This complex work, though not perfect, is rich in new ideas and new perspectives — new, at least to France. The fundamental theory, which was to be restated and developed in the positivism of Hippolyte Taine, is that a work must express the moral and historical reality, the zeitgeist, of the nation in which it is conceived. She also maintained that the Nordic and classical ideals were basically opposed and supported the Nordic, although her personal taste remained strongly classical. Her two novels, *Delphine* (1802) and *Corinne* (1807), to some extent illustrate her literary theories, the former being strongly sociological in outlook, while the latter shows the clash between Nordic and southern mentalities.

BANISHMENT FROM PARIS

She was also an important political figure and was regarded by contemporary Europe as the personal enemy of Napoleon. With Constant and his friends she formed the nucleus of a liberal resistance that so embarrassed Napoleon that in 1803 he had her banished to a distance of 40 miles (64 km) from Paris. Thenceforward Coppet was her headquarters, and in 1804 she began what she called, in a work published posthumously in 1821, her *Dix Années d'exil* (*Ten Years' Exile*). From December 1803 to April 1804 she made a journey through Germany, culminating in a visit to Weimar, already established as the shrine of J. W. von Goethe and Friedrich von Schiller. In Berlin she met August Wilhelm von Schlegel, who was to become, after 1804, her frequent companion and counselor. Her guide in Germany, however, was a young Englishman, Henry Crabb Robinson, who was studying at Jena. The journey was interrupted in 1804 by news of the death of her father, whom she had always greatly admired. His death affected her deeply, but in 1805 she set out for Italy, accompanied by Schlegel and Simonde de Sismondi, the Genevan economist who was her guide on the journey. Returning in June 1805, she spent the next seven years of her exile from Paris for the most part at Coppet.

While *Corinne* can be considered the result of her Italian journey, the fruits of her visit to Germany are contained in her most important work, *De l'Allemagne* (1810; *Germany*). This is a serious study of German manners, literature and art, philosophy and morals, and religion in which she made known to her contemporaries the Germany of the Sturm und Drang movement (1770–1780). Its only fault is the distorted picture it gives, ignoring, for example, the violently nationalistic aspect of German Romanticism. Napoleon took it for an anti-French work, and the French edition of 1810 (10,000 copies) was seized and destroyed. It was finally published in England in 1813.

Meanwhile Mme de Staël, persecuted by the police, fled from Napoleon's Europe. Having married, in 1811, a young Swiss officer, "John" Rocca, in May 1812 she went to Austria and, after visiting Russia, Finland, and Sweden, arrived, in June 1813, in England. She was received with enthusiasm, although reproached by such liberals as Lord Byron for being more anti-Napoleonic than liberal and by the Tories for being too liberal. Her guide in England was Sir James Mackintosh, the Scottish publicist. She collected documents for, but never wrote, a *De l'Angleterre*: (the material for it can be found in the *Considérations sur la Révolution française* [1818; *Considerations on the Principal Events of the French Revolution*], which represents a return to Necker's ideas and holds up the English political system as a model for France).

On the Bourbon Restoration in 1814, Mme de Staël returned to Paris but was deeply disillusioned: the fall of

Napoleon had been followed by foreign occupation and had in no way reestablished liberty in France. During the Hundred Days she escaped to Coppet and in September 1815 set out again for Italy. In 1816 she returned to spend the summer at Coppet, where she was joined by Byron, in flight from England after his unhappy matrimonial experience. A strong friendship developed between the two writers.

Mme de Staël's health was declining. After Byron's departure she went to Paris for the winter. Though poorly received by the returned émigrés and suspected by the government, she held her salon throughout the winter and part of the spring, but after April 1817 she was an invalid. She died in Paris in July of that year.

ASSESSMENT

Germaine de Staël's purely literary importance is far exceeded by her importance in the history of ideas. Her novels and plays are now largely forgotten, but the value of her critical and historical work is undeniable. Though careless of detail, she had a clear vision of wider issues and of the achievements of civilization. Her involvement in, and understanding of, the events and tendencies of her time gave her an unusual position: it may be said that she helped the dawning 19th century to take stock of itself.

JANE AUSTEN

(b. Dec. 16, 1775, Steventon, Hampshire, Eng.—d. July 18, 1817, Winchester, Hampshire)

The English writer Jane Austen was the first writer to give the novel its distinctly modern character through her treatment of ordinary people in everyday life. Austen created the comedy of manners of middle-class life in the

England of her time in her novels, *Sense and Sensibility* (1811), *Pride and Prejudice* (1813), *Mansfield Park* (1814), *Emma* (1815), and *Northanger Abbey* and *Persuasion* (published posthumously, 1817).

LIFE

Jane Austen was born in the Hampshire village of Steventon, where her father, the Reverend George Austen, was rector. She was the second daughter and seventh child in a family of eight: six boys and two girls. Her closest companion throughout her life was her elder sister, Cassandra, who also remained unmarried. Their father was a scholar who encouraged the love of learning in his children. His wife, Cassandra (née Leigh), was a woman of ready wit, famed for her impromptu verses and stories. The great family amusement was acting.

Jane Austen's lively and affectionate family circle provided a stimulating context for her writing. Moreover, her experience was carried far beyond Steventon rectory by an extensive network of relationships by blood and friendship. It was this world—of the minor landed gentry and the country clergy, in the village, the neighbourhood, and the country town, with occasional visits to Bath and to London—that she was to use in the settings, characters, and subject matter of her novels.

Her earliest-known writings date from about 1787, and between then and 1793 she wrote a large body of material that has survived in three manuscript notebooks: *Volume the First*, *Volume the Second*, and *Volume the Third*. These contain plays, verses, short novels, and other prose that show Austen engaged in the parody of existing literary forms, notably sentimental fiction. Her passage to a more serious view of life from the exuberant high spirits and extravagances of her earliest writings is evident in *Lady*

Susan, a short novel-in-letters written about 1793–94 (and not published until 1871). This portrait of a woman bent on the exercise of her own powerful mind and personality to the point of social self-destruction is, in effect, a study of frustration and of woman's fate in a society that has no use for a woman's stronger, more "masculine," talents.

In 1802 it seems likely that Jane agreed to marry Harris Bigg-Wither, the 21-year-old heir of a Hampshire family, but the next morning changed her mind. There are also a number of mutually contradictory stories connecting her with someone with whom she fell in love but who died very soon after. Since Austen's novels are so deeply concerned with love and marriage, there is some point in attempting to establish the facts of these relationships. Unfortunately, the evidence is unsatisfactory and incomplete. Cassandra was a jealous guardian of her sister's private life, and after Jane's death she censored the surviving letters, destroying many and cutting up others. But Jane Austen's own novels provide indisputable evidence that their author understood the experience of love and of love disappointed.

The earliest of her novels, *Sense and Sensibility*, was begun about 1795 as a novel-in-letters called "Elinor and Marianne," after its heroines. Between October 1796 and August 1797 Austen completed the first version of *Pride and Prejudice*, then called "First Impressions." In 1797 her father wrote to offer it to a London publisher for publication, but the offer was declined. *Northanger Abbey*, the last of the early novels, was written about 1798 or 1799, probably under the title "Susan." In 1803 the manuscript of "Susan" was sold to the publisher Richard Crosby for £10. He took it for immediate publication, but, although it was advertised, unaccountably it never appeared.

Up to this time the tenor of life at Steventon rectory had been propitious for Jane Austen's growth as a novelist.

This stable environment ended in 1801, however, when George Austen, then aged 70, retired to Bath with his wife and daughters. For eight years Jane had to put up with a succession of temporary lodgings or visits to relatives, in Bath, London, Clifton, Warwickshire, and, finally, Southampton, where the three women lived from 1805 to 1809. In 1804 Jane began *The Watsons* but soon abandoned it. Also in 1804 her dearest friend, Mrs. Anne Lefroy, died suddenly, and in January 1805 her father died in Bath.

Eventually, in 1809, Jane's brother Edward was able to provide his mother and sisters with a large cottage in the village of Chawton, within his Hampshire estate, not far from Steventon. The prospect of settling at Chawton had already given Jane Austen a renewed sense of purpose, and she began to prepare *Sense and Sensibility* and *Pride and Prejudice* for publication. She was encouraged by her brother Henry, who acted as go-between with her publishers. She was probably also prompted by her need for money. Two years later Thomas Egerton agreed to publish *Sense and Sensibility*, which came out, anonymously, in November 1811. Both of the leading reviews, the *Critical Review* and the *Quarterly Review*, welcomed its blend of instruction and amusement. Meanwhile, in 1811 Austen had begun *Mansfield Park*, which was finished in 1813 and published in 1814. By then she was an established (though anonymous) author; Egerton had published *Pride and Prejudice* in January 1813, and later that year there were second editions of *Pride and Prejudice* and *Sense and Sensibility*. *Pride and Prejudice* seems to have been the fashionable novel of its season. Between January 1814 and March 1815, she wrote *Emma*, which appeared in December 1815. In 1816 there was a second edition of *Mansfield Park*, published, like *Emma*, by Lord Byron's publisher, John Murray. *Persuasion* (written August 1815–August 1816) was published posthumously, with *Northanger Abbey*, in December 1817.

The years after 1811 seem to have been the most rewarding of her life. She had the satisfaction of seeing her work in print and well reviewed and of knowing that the novels were widely read. They were so much enjoyed by the Prince Regent (later George IV) that he had a set in each of his residences; *Emma*, at a discreet royal command, was "respectfully dedicated" to him. The reviewers praised the novels for their morality and entertainment, admired the character drawing, and welcomed the homely realism as a refreshing change from the romantic melodrama then in vogue.

For the last 18 months of her life, she was busy writing. Early in 1816, at the onset of her fatal illness, she set down the burlesque *Plan of a Novel, According to Hints from Various Quarters* (first published in 1871). Until August 1816 she was occupied with *Persuasion*, and she looked again at the manuscript of "Susan" (*Northanger Abbey*).

In January 1817 she began *Sanditon*, a robust and self-mocking satire on health resorts and invalidism. This novel remained unfinished owing to Austen's declining health. She supposed that she was suffering from bile, but the symptoms make possible a modern clinical assessment that she was suffering from Addison's disease. Her condition fluctuated, but in April she made her will, and in May she was taken to Winchester to be under the care of an expert surgeon. She died on July 18, and six days later she was buried in Winchester Cathedral.

Her authorship was announced to the world at large by her brother Henry, who supervised the publication of *Northanger Abbey* and *Persuasion*. There was no recognition at the time that regency England had lost its keenest observer and sharpest analyst; no understanding that a miniaturist (as she maintained that she was and as she was then seen), a "merely domestic" novelist, could be seriously concerned with the nature of society and the quality of its culture; no grasp of Jane Austen as a historian of the emergence of regency society into the modern world. During her lifetime there had been a solitary response in any way adequate to the nature of her achievement: Sir Walter Scott's review of *Emma* in the *Quarterly Review* for March 1816, where he hailed this "nameless author" as a masterful exponent of "the modern novel" in the new realist tradition. After her death, there was for long only one significant essay, the review of *Northanger Abbey* and *Persuasion* in the *Quarterly* for January 1821 by the theologian Richard Whately. Together, Scott's and Whately's essays provided the foundation for serious criticism of Jane Austen: their insights were appropriated by critics throughout the 19th century.

NOVELS

Jane Austen's three early novels form a distinct group in which a strong element of literary satire accompanies the comic depiction of character and society.

Sense and Sensibility tells the story of the impoverished Dashwood sisters. Marianne is the heroine of "sensibility" — i.e., of openness and enthusiasm. She becomes infatuated with the attractive John Willoughby, who seems to be a romantic lover but is in reality an unscrupulous fortune hunter. He deserts her for an heiress, leaving her to learn a dose of "sense" in a wholly unromantic marriage with a staid and settled bachelor, Colonel Brandon, who is 20 years her senior. By contrast, Marianne's older sister, Elinor, is the guiding light of "sense," or prudence and discretion, whose constancy toward her lover, Edward Ferrars, is rewarded by her marriage to him after some distressing vicissitudes.

Pride and Prejudice describes the clash between Elizabeth Bennet, the daughter of a country gentleman, and Fitzwilliam Darcy, a rich and aristocratic landowner. Although Austen shows them intrigued by each other, she reverses the convention of "first impressions." "Pride" of rank and fortune and "prejudice" against Elizabeth's inferiority of family hold Darcy aloof, while Elizabeth is equally fired both by the "pride" of self-respect and by "prejudice" against Darcy's snobbery. Ultimately, they come together in love and self-understanding. The intelligent and high-spirited Elizabeth was Jane Austen's own favourite among all her heroines and is one of the most engaging in English literature.

Northanger Abbey combines a satire on conventional novels of polite society with one on Gothic tales of terror. Catherine Morland, the unspoiled daughter of a country parson, is the innocent abroad who gains worldly wisdom: first in the fashionable society of Bath and then at Northanger Abbey itself, where she learns not to interpret the world through her reading of Gothic thrillers. Her mentor and guide is the self-assured and gently ironic Henry Tilney, her husband-to-be.

In the three novels of Jane Austen's maturity, the literary satire, though still present, is more subdued and is subordinated to the comedy of character and society.

In its tone and discussion of religion and religious duty, *Mansfield Park* is the most serious of Austen's novels. The heroine, Fanny Price, is a self-effacing and unregarded cousin cared for by the Bertram family in their country house. Fanny emerges as a true heroine whose moral strength eventually wins her complete acceptance in the Bertram family and marriage to Edmund Bertram himself, after that family's disastrous involvement with the meretricious and loose-living Crawfords.

Of all Austen's novels, *Emma* is the most consistently comic in tone. It centres on Emma Woodhouse, a wealthy, pretty, self-satisfied young woman who indulges herself with meddlesome and unsuccessful attempts at match-making among her friends and neighbours. After a series of humiliating errors, a chastened Emma finds her destiny in marriage to the mature and protective George Knightley, a neighbouring squire who had been her mentor and friend.

Persuasion tells the story of a second chance, the reawakening of love between Anne Elliot and Captain Frederick Wentworth, whom seven years earlier she had been persuaded not to marry. Now Wentworth returns from the Napoleonic Wars with prize money and the social acceptability of naval rank; he is an eligible suitor acceptable to Anne's snobbish father and his circle. Anne discovers the continuing strength of her love for him.

Assessment

Although the birth of the English novel is to be seen in the first half of the 18th century in the work of Daniel Defoe, Samuel Richardson, and Henry Fielding, it is with Jane Austen that the novel takes on its distinctively modern character in the realistic treatment of unremarkable people in the unremarkable situations of everyday life. In her six novels—*Sense and Sensibility*, *Pride and Prejudice*, *Mansfield Park*, *Emma*, *Northanger Abbey*, and *Persuasion*—Austen created the comedy of manners of middle-class life in the England of her time, revealing the possibilities of "domestic" literature. Her repeated fable of a young woman's voyage to self-discovery on the passage through love to marriage focuses upon easily recognizable aspects of life. It is this concentration upon character and personality and upon the tensions between her heroines and their society that relates her novels more closely to the modern world than to the traditions of the 18th century. This modernity, together with the wit, realism, and timelessness of her prose style; her shrewd, amused sympathy; and the satisfaction to be found in stories so skillfully told, in novels so beautifully constructed, that helps to explain her continuing appeal for readers of all kinds. Modern critics remain fascinated by the commanding structure and organization of the novels, by the triumphs of technique that enable the writer to lay bare the tragicomedy of existence in stories of which the events and settings are apparently so ordinary and so circumscribed.

SACAGAWEA

(b. *c.* 1788, near the Continental Divide at the present-day Idaho-Montana border [U.S.]—d. Dec. 20, 1812?, Fort Manuel, on the Missouri River, Dakota Territory)

Acting as an interpreter for the Lewis and Clark Expedition (1804–06), the Shoshone Indian woman Sacagawea traveled thousands of wilderness miles, from the Mandan-Hidatsa villages in the Dakotas to the Pacific Northwest.

Separating fact from legend in Sacagawea's life is difficult; historians disagree on the dates of her birth and death and even on her name. In Hidatsa, Sacagawea (pronounced with a hard *g*) translates into "Bird Woman." Alternatively, Sacajawea means "Boat Launcher" in Shoshone. Others favor Sakakawea. The Lewis and Clark journals generally support the Hidatsa derivation.

A Lemhi Shoshone woman, Sacagawea was about 12 years old when a Hidatsa raiding party captured her near the Missouri River's headwaters about 1800. Enslaved and taken to their Knife River earth-lodge villages near present-day Bismarck, N.D., she was purchased by French Canadian fur trader Toussaint Charbonneau and became one of his plural wives about 1804. They resided in one of the Hidatsa villages, Metaharta.

When explorers Meriwether Lewis and William Clark arrived at the Mandan-Hidatsa villages and built Fort Mandan to spend the winter of 1804–05, they hired Charbonneau as an interpreter to accompany them to the Pacific Ocean. Because he did not speak Sacagawea's language and because the expedition party needed to communicate with the Shoshones to acquire horses to cross the mountains, the explorers agreed that the pregnant Sacagawea should also accompany them. On Feb. 11, 1805, she gave birth to a son, Jean Baptiste.

Departing on April 7, the expedition ascended the Missouri. On May 14, Charbonneau nearly capsized the white pirogue (boat) in which Sacagawea was riding. Remaining calm, she retrieved important papers, instruments, books, medicine, and other indispensable valuables that otherwise would have been lost. During the next week Lewis and Clark named a tributary of Montana's Mussellshell River "Sah-ca-gah-weah," or "Bird Woman's River," after her. She proved to be a significant asset in numerous ways: searching for edible plants, making moccasins and clothing, as

This drawing by E.S. Paxson shows Shoshone guide Sacagawea as she might have appeared while traveling with the explorers Lewis and Clark on their westward expedition. MPI/ Hulton Archive/Getty Images

well as allaying suspicions of approaching Native American tribes through her presence; a woman and child accompanying a party of men indicated peaceful intentions.

By mid-August the expedition encountered a band of Shoshones led by Sacagawea's brother Cameahwait. The reunion of sister and brother had a positive effect on Lewis and Clark's negotiations for the horses and guide that enabled them to cross the Rocky Mountains. Upon arriving at the Pacific coast, she was able to voice her opinion about where the expedition should spend the winter and was granted her request to visit the ocean to see a beached whale. She and Clark were fond of each other and performed numerous acts of kindness for one another, but romance between them occurred only in latter-day fiction.

Sacagawea was not the guide for the expedition, as some have erroneously portrayed her; nonetheless, she recognized landmarks in southwestern Montana and informed Clark that Bozeman Pass was the best route between the Missouri and Yellowstone rivers on their return journey. On July 25, 1806, Clark named Pompey's Tower (now Pompey's Pillar) on the Yellowstone after her son, whom Clark fondly called his "little dancing boy, Pomp."

The Charbonneau family disengaged from the expedition party upon their return to the Mandan-Hidatsa villages; Charbonneau eventually received $409.16 and 320 acres (130 hectares) for his services. Clark wanted to do more for their family, so he offered to assist them, eventually securing Charbonneau a position as an interpreter. The family traveled to St. Louis in 1809 to baptize their son and left him in the care of Clark, who had earlier offered to provide him with an education. Shortly after the birth of a daughter named Lisette, a woman identified only as Charbonneau's wife (but believed to be Sacagawea) died at the end of 1812 at Fort Manuel, near present-day Mobridge, S.D. Clark became the legal guardian of Lisette and Jean

Baptiste and listed Sacagawea as deceased in a list he compiled in the 1820s. Some biographers and oral traditions contend that it was another of Charbonneau's wives who died in 1812 and that Sacagawea went to live among the Comanches, started another family, rejoined the Shoshones, and died on Wyoming's Wind River Reservation on April 9, 1884. These accounts can likely be attributed to other Shoshone women who shared similar experiences as Sacagawea.

Sacagawea's son, Jean Baptiste, traveled throughout Europe before returning to enter the fur trade. He scouted for explorers and helped guide the Mormon Battalion to California before becoming an alcalde, a hotel clerk, and a gold miner. Lured to the Montana goldfields following the Civil War, he died en route near Danner, Ore., on May 16, 1866. Little is known of Lisette's whereabouts prior to her death on June 16, 1832; she was buried in the Old Catholic Cathedral Cemetery in St. Louis. Charbonneau died on Aug. 12, 1843.

Sacagawea has been memorialized with statues, monuments, stamps, and place names. In 2000 her likeness appeared on a gold-tinted dollar coin struck by the U.S. Mint. In 2001 U.S. President Bill Clinton granted her a posthumous decoration as an honorary sergeant in the regular army.

SOJOURNER TRUTH

(b. *c.* 1797, Ulster county, N.Y., U.S.—d. Nov. 26, 1883, Battle Creek, Mich.)

The eloquent African American evangelist and reformer Sojourner Truth applied her religious fervour to the abolitionist and women's rights movements.

Isabella was the daughter of slaves and spent her childhood as an abused chattel of several masters. Her first language was Dutch. Between 1810 and 1827 she bore at least five children to a fellow slave named Thomas. Just before New York state abolished slavery in 1827, she found refuge with Isaac Van Wagener, who set her free. (Her legal name was Isabella Van Wagener.) With the help of Quaker friends, she waged a court battle in which she recovered her small son, who had been sold illegally into slavery in the South. About 1829 she went to New York City with her two youngest children, supporting herself through domestic employment.

Since childhood Isabella had had visions and heard voices, which she attributed to God. In New York City she became associated with Elijah Pierson, a zealous missionary. Working and preaching in the streets, she joined his Retrenchment Society and eventually his household.

In 1843 she left New York City and took the name Sojourner Truth, which she used from then on. Obeying a supernatural call to "travel up and down the land," she sang, preached, and debated at camp meetings, in churches, and on village streets, exhorting her listeners to accept the biblical message of God's goodness and the brotherhood of man. In the same year, she was introduced to abolitionism at a utopian community in Northampton, Mass., and thereafter spoke in behalf of the movement throughout the state. In 1850 she traveled throughout the Midwest, where her reputation for personal magnetism preceded her and drew heavy crowds. She supported herself by selling copies of her book, *The Narrative of Sojourner Truth*, which she had dictated to Olive Gilbert.

Encountering the women's rights movement in the early 1850s, and encouraged by other women leaders, notably Lucretia Mott, she continued to appear before suffrage gatherings for the rest of her life. Sometime in the 1850s

Sojourner Truth settled in Battle Creek, Mich. At the beginning of the American Civil War, she gathered supplies for black volunteer regiments and in 1864 went to Washington, D.C., where she helped integrate streetcars and was received at the White House by President Abraham Lincoln. The same year, she accepted an appointment with the National Freedmen's Relief Association counseling former slaves, particularly in matters of resettlement. As late as the 1870s she encouraged the migration of freedmen to Kansas and Missouri. In 1875 she retired to her home in Battle Creek, where she remained until her death.

DOROTHEA DIX

(b. April 4, 1802, Hampden, District of Maine, Mass. [now in Maine], U.S.—d. July 17, 1887, Trenton, N.J.)

The American educator, social reformer, and humanitarian Dorothea Dix led the fight for the welfare of the mentally ill, and her efforts led to widespread reforms in the United States and abroad.

Dorothea Lynde Dix left her unhappy home at age 12 to live and study in Boston with her grandmother. By age 14 she was teaching in a school for young girls in Worcester, Mass., employing a curriculum of her own devising that stressed the natural sciences and the responsibilities of ethical living. In 1821 she opened a school for girls in Boston, where until the mid-1830s periods of intensive teaching were interrupted by periods of ill health. She eventually abandoned teaching and left Boston.

After nearly two years in England Dix returned to Boston, still a semi-invalid, and found to her amazement that she had inherited a sum of money sufficient to support her comfortably for life. But her Calvinist beliefs enjoined her from inactivity. Thus in 1841, when a young clergyman asked her to begin a Sunday school class in the East Cambridge House of Correction in Massachusetts, she accepted the challenge. In the prison she first observed the inhumane treatment of insane and mentally disturbed persons, who were incarcerated with criminals, irrespective of age or sex. They were left unclothed, in darkness, without heat or sanitary facilities; some were chained to the walls and flogged. Profoundly shocked, Dix traveled for nearly two years throughout the state, observing similar conditions in each institution she examined. In January 1843 she submitted to the Massachusetts legislature a detailed report of her thoroughly documented findings. Her dignity, compassion, and determination were effective in helping to pass a bill for the enlargement of the Worcester Insane Asylum. Dix then moved on to Rhode Island and later New York.

In the next 40 years Dix inspired legislators in 15 U.S. states and in Canada to establish state hospitals for the mentally ill. Her unflagging efforts directly effected the building of 32 institutions in the United States. She carried on her work even while on a convalescent tour of Europe in 1854–56, notably in Italy, where she prevailed upon Pope Pius IX to inspect personally the atrocious conditions she had discovered. Where new institutions were not required, she fostered the reorganization, enlargement, and restaffing—with well-trained, intelligent personnel— of already existing hospitals.

In 1845 Dix published *Remarks on Prisons and Prison Discipline in the United States* to advocate reforms in the treatment of ordinary prisoners. In 1861 she was appointed superintendent of army nurses for Civil War service. She was ill-suited to administration, however, and had great difficulty with the post. After the war she returned to her work with hospitals. When she died, it was in a hospital that she had founded.

CHARLOTTE AND EMILY BRONTË

(Respectively, b. April 21, 1816, Thornton, Yorkshire, Eng.—
d. March 31, 1855, Haworth, Yorkshire; b. July 30, 1818, Thornton,
Yorkshire, Eng.—d. Dec. 19, 1848, Haworth, Yorkshire)

Charlotte Brontë and Emily Brontë, were English writers whose works—notably *Jane Eyre* (1847; by Charlotte) and *Wuthering Heights* (1847; by Emily)—are considered classics of English literature. Their youngest sister, Anne, was also a writer, the author of *Agnes Grey* (1847) and *The Tenant of Wildfell Hall* (1848), but her works are little known.

The Brontë sisters' father was Patrick Brontë (1777–1861), an Anglican clergyman. Irish-born, he had changed his name from the more commonplace Brunty. After serving in several parishes, he moved with his wife, Maria Branwell Brontë, and their six small children to Haworth amid the Yorkshire moors in 1820, having been awarded a rectorship there. Soon after, Mrs. Brontë and the two eldest children (Maria and Elizabeth) died, leaving the father to care for the remaining three girls—Charlotte, Emily, and Anne—and a boy, Patrick Branwell. Their upbringing was aided by an aunt, Elizabeth Branwell, who left her native Cornwall and took up residence with the family at Haworth.

In 1824 Charlotte and Emily, together with their elder sisters before their deaths, attended Clergy Daughters' School at Cowan Bridge, near Kirkby Lonsdale, Lancashire. The fees were low, the food unattractive, and the discipline harsh. Charlotte condemned the school (perhaps exaggeratedly) long years afterward in *Jane Eyre*, under the thin disguise of Lowood; and the principal, the Rev. William Carus Wilson, has been accepted as the counterpart of Mr. Naomi Brocklehurst in the novel.

Charlotte and Emily returned home in June 1825, and for more than five years the Brontë children learned and played there, writing and telling romantic tales for one another and inventing imaginative games played out at home or on the desolate moors.

It is at this point that their paths diverged somewhat.

Charlotte Brontë's Life

In 1831 Charlotte was sent to Miss Wooler's school at Roe Head, near Huddersfield, where she stayed a year and made some lasting friendships; her correspondence with one of her friends, Ellen Nussey, continued until her death, and has provided much of the current knowledge of her life. In 1832 she came home to teach her sisters but in 1835 returned to Roe Head as a teacher. She wished to improve her family's position, and this was the only outlet that was offered to her unsatisfied energies. Branwell, moreover, was to start on his career as an artist, and it became necessary to supplement the family resources. The work, with its inevitable restrictions, was uncongenial to Charlotte. She fell into ill health and melancholia and in the summer of 1838 terminated her engagement.

In 1839 Charlotte declined a proposal from the Rev. Henry Nussey, her friend's brother, and some months later one from another young clergyman. At the same time Charlotte's ambition to make the practical best of her talents and the need to pay Branwell's debts urged her to spend some months as governess with the Whites at Upperwood House, Rawdon. Branwell's talents for writing and painting, his good classical scholarship, and his social charm had engendered high hopes for him; but he was fundamentally unstable, weak willed, and intemperate. He went from job to job and took refuge in alcohol and opium.

Meanwhile his sisters had planned to open a school together, which their aunt had agreed to finance, and in February 1842 Charlotte and Emily went to Brussels as pupils to improve their qualifications in French and acquire some German. The talent displayed by both brought them to the notice of Constantin Héger, a fine teacher and a man of unusual perception. After a brief trip home upon the death of her aunt, Charlotte returned to Brussels as a pupil-teacher. She stayed there during 1843 but was lonely and depressed. Her friends had left Brussels, and Madame Héger appears to have become jealous of her. The nature

Proving that (left to right) *Anne, Emily, and Charlotte Brontë were not the only talented ones in the family, Branwell, their brother, painted the women's portrait in 1834.* Rischgitz/Hulton Archive/Getty Images

of Charlotte's attachment to Héger and the degree to which she understood herself have been much discussed. His was the most interesting mind she had yet met, and he had perceived and evoked her latent talents. His strong and eccentric personality appealed both to her sense of humour and to her affections. She offered him an innocent but ardent devotion, but he tried to repress her emotions. The letters she wrote to him after her return may well be called love letters. When, however, he suggested that they were open to misapprehension, she stopped writing and applied herself, in silence, to disciplining her feelings. However they are interpreted, Charlotte's experiences at Brussels were crucial for her development. She received a strict literary training, became aware of the resources of her own nature, and gathered material that served her, in various shapes, for all her novels.

In 1844 Charlotte attempted to start a school that she had long envisaged in the parsonage itself, as her father's failing sight precluded his being left alone. Prospectuses were issued, but no pupils were attracted to distant Haworth.

In the autumn of 1845 Charlotte came across some poems by Emily, and this led to the publication of a joint volume of *Poems by Currer, Ellis and Acton Bell* (1846), or Charlotte, Emily, and Anne; the pseudonyms were assumed to preserve secrecy and avoid the special treatment that they believed reviewers accorded to women. The book was issued at their own expense. It received few reviews and only two copies were sold. Nevertheless, a way had opened to them, and they were already trying to place the three novels they had written. Charlotte failed to place *The Professor: A Tale* but had, however, nearly finished *Jane Eyre: An Autobiography*, begun in August 1846 in Manchester, where she was staying with her father, who had gone there for an eye operation. When Smith, Elder and Company, declining *The Professor*, declared themselves willing to consider a three-volume novel with more action and excitement in it, she completed and submitted it at once. *Jane Eyre* was accepted, published less than eight weeks later (on Oct. 16, 1847), and had an immediate success, far greater than that of the books that her sisters published the same year.

The months that followed were tragic ones. Branwell died in September 1848, Emily in December, and Anne in May 1849. Charlotte completed *Shirley: A Tale* in the empty parsonage, and it appeared in October. In the following years Charlotte went three times to London as the guest of her publisher; there she met the novelist William Makepeace Thackeray and sat for her portrait by George Richmond. She stayed in 1851 with the writer Harriet Martineau and also visited her future biographer, Mrs. Elizabeth Gaskell, in Manchester and entertained her at Haworth. *Villette* came out in January 1853. Meanwhile, in 1851, she had declined a third offer of marriage, this time from James Taylor, a member of Smith, Elder and Company. Her father's curate, Arthur Bell Nicholls (1817–1906), an Irishman, was her fourth suitor. It took some months to win her father's consent, but they were married on June 29, 1854, in Haworth church. They spent their honeymoon in Ireland and then returned to Haworth, where her husband had pledged himself to continue as curate to her father. He did not share his wife's intellectual life, but she was happy to be loved for herself and to take up her duties as his wife. She began another book, *Emma*, of which some pages remain. Her pregnancy, however, was accompanied by exhausting sickness, and she died in 1855.

CHARLOTTE'S WORKS

Charlotte's first novel, *The Professor* (published posthumously, 1857), shows her sober reaction from the indulgences of her girlhood. Told in the first person by an English tutor in Brussels, it is based on Charlotte's experiences there, with a reversal of sexes and roles.

Though there is plenty of satire and dry, direct phrasing in *Jane Eyre*, its success was the fiery conviction with which it presented a thinking, feeling woman, craving for love but able to renounce it at the call of impassioned self-respect and moral conviction. The book's narrator and main character, Jane Eyre, is an orphan and is governess to the ward of Mr. Rochester, the Byronic and enigmatic employer with whom she falls in love. Her love is reciprocated, but on the wedding morning it comes out that Rochester is already married and keeps his mad and depraved wife in the attics of his mansion. Jane leaves him, suffers hardship, and finds work as a village schoolmistress. When Jane learns, however, that Rochester has been maimed and blinded while trying vainly to rescue his wife from the burning house that she herself had set afire, Jane seeks him out and marries him.

There are melodramatic naïvetés in the story, and Charlotte's elevated rhetorical passages do not much appeal to modern taste, but she maintains her hold on the reader. The novel is subtitled *An Autobiography* and is written in the first person; but, except in Jane Eyre's impressions of Lowood, the autobiography is not Charlotte's. Personal experience is fused with suggestions from widely different sources, and the Cinderella theme may well come from Samuel Richardson's *Pamela*. The action is carefully motivated, and apparently episodic sections, like the return to Gateshead Hall, are seen to be necessary to the full expression of Jane's character and the working out of the threefold moral theme of love, independence, and forgiveness.

In her novel *Shirley*, Charlotte avoided melodrama and coincidences and widened her scope. Setting aside Maria Edgworth and Sir Walter Scott as national novelists, *Shirley* is the first regional novel in English, full of shrewdly depicted local material—Yorkshire characters, church and chapel, the cloth workers and machine breakers of her father's early manhood, and a sturdy but rather embittered feminism.

In *Villette* she recurred to the Brussels setting and the first-person narrative, disused in *Shirley*; the characters and incidents are largely variants of the people and life at the Pension Héger. Against this background she set the ardent heart, deprived of its object, contrasted with the woman happily fulfilled in love.

The influence of Charlotte's novels was much more immediate than that of *Wuthering Heights*. Her combination of romance and satiric realism had been the mode of nearly all the women novelists for a century. Her fruitful innovations were the presentation of a tale through the sensibility of a child or young woman, her lyricism, and the picture of love from a woman's standpoint.

EMILY BRONTË'S LIFE

In 1835, when Charlotte secured a teaching position at Miss Wooler's school at Roe Head, Emily accompanied her as a pupil but suffered from homesickness and remained only three months. In 1838 Emily spent six exhausting months as a teacher in Miss Patchett's school at Law Hill, near Halifax, and then resigned.

To keep the family together at home, Charlotte planned to keep a school for girls at Haworth. In February 1842 she and Emily went to Brussels to learn foreign languages and school management at the Pension Héger. Although Emily pined for home and for the wild moorlands, it seems that in Brussels she was better appreciated than Charlotte. In October, however, when her aunt died, Emily returned permanently to Haworth.

As recounted above, Charlotte's discovery that all three sisters — Charlotte, Emily, and Anne — had written verse led them to publish jointly a pseudonymous volume of verse, *Poems by Currer, Ellis and Acton Bell*; it contained 21 of Emily's poems, and a consensus of later criticism has accepted the fact that Emily's verse alone reveals true poetic genius.

By midsummer of 1847 Emily's *Wuthering Heights* and Anne's *Agnes Grey* had been accepted for joint publication by J. Cautley Newby of London, but publication was delayed until the appearance of their sister Charlotte's *Jane Eyre*, which was immediately and hugely successful. *Wuthering Heights*, when published in December 1847, did not fare well; critics were hostile, calling it too savage, too animal-like, and clumsy in construction. Only later did it come to be considered one of the finest novels in the English language.

Soon after the publication of her novel, Emily's health began to fail rapidly. She had been ill for some time, but now her breathing became difficult, and she suffered great pain. She died of tuberculosis in December 1848.

WUTHERING HEIGHTS

Emily Brontë's work on *Wuthering Heights* cannot be dated; she may well have spent a long time on this intense, solidly imagined novel. It is distinguished from other novels of the period by its dramatic and poetic presentation, its abstention from all comment by the author, and its unusual structure. It recounts in the retrospective narrative of an onlooker, which in turn includes shorter narratives, the impact of the waif Heathcliff on the two families of Earnshaw and Linton in a remote Yorkshire district at the end of the 18th century. Embittered by abuse and by the marriage of Cathy Earnshaw — who shares his stormy nature and whom he loves—to the gentle and prosperous Edgar Linton, Heathcliff plans a revenge on both families, extending into the second generation. Cathy's death in child-birth fails to set him free from his love-hate relationship with her, and the obsessive haunting persists until his death; the marriage of the surviving heirs of Earnshaw and Linton restores peace.

Sharing the family's dry humour and Charlotte's violent imagination, Emily diverges from her in making no use of the events of her own life and showing no preoccupation with her unmarried state or a governess's position. Work-ing, like her, within a confined scene and with a small group of characters, she constructs an action, based on profound and primitive energies of love and hate, which proceeds logically and economically, making no use of such coinci-dences as Charlotte relies on, requiring no rich romantic similes or rhetorical patterns, and confining the superb dialogue to what is immediately relevant to the subject. The book's sombre power and the elements of brutality in its characters puzzled and affronted some 19th-century opinion.

VICTORIA

(b. May 24, 1819, Kensington Palace, London, Eng.—d. Jan. 22, 1901, Osborne, near Cowes, Isle of Wight)

Victoria was queen of the United Kingdom of Great Britain and Ireland (1837–1901) and empress of India (1876–1901). She was the last monarch of the House of Hanover and gave her name to an era, the Victorian Age. During her reign the English monarchy took on its modern ceremonial character. She and her husband, Prince Consort Albert of Saxe-Coburg-Gotha, had nine children, through whose marriages were descended many of the royal families of Europe. By the end of her reign, the longest in English history, she had restored both dignity and popularity to a tarnished crown: an achievement of character, as well as of longevity. She will forever be noted for her high sense of duty, her transparent honesty, and the simplicity of her royal character.

Victoria first learned of her future role as a young princess during a history lesson when she was 10 years old. Almost four decades later Victoria's governess recalled that the future queen reacted to the discovery by declaring, "I will be good." This combination of earnestness and egotism marked Victoria as a child of the age that bears her name. The queen, however, rejected important Victorian values and developments. Although she hated pregnancy and childbirth, detested babies, and was uncomfortable in the presence of children, Victoria reigned in a society that idealized both motherhood and the family. She had no interest in social issues, yet the 19th century in Britain was an age of reform. She resisted technological change even while mechanical and technological innovations reshaped the face of European civilization. Most significantly, Victoria was a queen determined to retain political power; yet unwillingly and unwittingly she presided over the transformation of the sovereign's political role into a ceremonial one and thus preserved the English monarchy.

LINEAGE AND EARLY LIFE

On the death in 1817 of Princess Charlotte, daughter of the prince regent (later George IV), there was no surviving legitimate offspring of George III's 15 children. In 1818, therefore, three of his sons, the dukes of Clarence, Kent, and Cambridge, married to provide for the succession. The winner in the race to father the next ruler of Britain was Edward, duke of Kent, fourth son of King George III. His only child was christened Alexandrina Victoria. After his death and George IV's accession in 1820, Victoria became third in the line of succession to the throne after the duke of York (died 1827) and the duke of Clarence (subsequently William IV), whose own children died in infancy.

Victoria, by her own account, "was brought up very simply," principally at Kensington Palace. An important father figure to the orphaned princess was her uncle Leopold, her mother's brother, who lived at Claremont, near Esher, Surrey, until he became king of the Belgians in 1831. Victoria's childhood was made increasingly unhappy by the machinations of Sir John Conroy, an adviser to her German-born mother, the duchess of Kent. Persuaded by Conroy that the royal dukes posed a threat to her daughter, the duchess systematically isolated Victoria from her contemporaries and her father's family. Despite this treatment the strong-willed girl carried on, and when she ascended the throne in 1837, she did so alone.

ACCESSION TO THE THRONE

On June 20, 1837, Victoria learned of the death of William IV, third son of George III, and she became queen. As such, she who had never before had a room to herself, exiled her mother to a distant set of apartments when they moved into Buckingham Palace. Conroy was pensioned off. Even her beloved uncle Leopold was politely warned off discussions of English politics. "Alone" at last, she enjoyed her new-found freedom.

She later came to feel that it was "the least sensible and satisfactory time in her whole life"; but at the time it was exciting and enjoyable, the more so because of her romantic friendship with Lord Melbourne, the prime minister.

Melbourne was a crucial influence on Victoria, in many ways an unfortunate one. The urbane and sophisticated prime minister fostered the new queen's self-confidence and enthusiasm for her role; he also encouraged her to ignore or minimize social problems and to attribute all discontent and unrest to the activities of a small group of agitators. Moreover, because of Melbourne, Victoria became an ardent Whig.

Her constitutionally dangerous political partisanship contributed to the first two crises of her reign, both of which broke in 1839. The Hastings affair began when Lady Flora Hastings, a maid of honour who was allied and connected to the Tories, was forced by Victoria to undergo a medical examination for suspected pregnancy. The gossip, when it was discovered that the queen had been mistaken, became the more damaging when later in the year Lady Flora died of a disease that had not been diagnosed by the examining physician. The enthusiasm of the populace over the coronation (June 28, 1838) swiftly dissipated.

Between the two phases of the Hastings case "the bed-chamber crisis" intervened. When Melbourne resigned in May 1839, Sir Robert Peel, the Conservative leader and Melbourne's apparent successor, stipulated that the Whig ladies of the bedchamber (household "ladies in waiting" to the queen) should be removed. The queen imperiously refused, not without Melbourne's encouragement, and Peel therefore declined to take office, which Melbourne rather weakly resumed. "I was very young then," wrote the queen long afterward, "and perhaps I should act differently if it was all to be done again."

MARRIAGE TO ALBERT

Attracted by Albert's good looks and encouraged by her uncle Leopold, Victoria proposed to her cousin on Oct. 15, 1839, just five days after he had arrived at Windsor on a visit to the English court. She described her impressions of him in the journal she kept throughout her life: "Albert really is quite charming, and so extremely handsome . . . a beautiful figure, broad in the shoulders and a fine waist; my heart is quite *going*." They were married on Feb. 10, 1840, the queen dressed entirely in articles of British manufacture.

Children quickly followed. Victoria, the princess royal (the "Vicky" of the *Letters*), was born in 1840; in 1858 she married the crown prince of Prussia and later became the mother of the emperor William II. The Prince of Wales (later Edward VII) was born in 1841. Then followed Princess Alice, afterward grand duchess of Hesse, 1843; Prince Alfred, afterward duke of Edinburgh and duke of Saxe-Coburg-Gotha, 1844; Princess Helena (Princess Christian of Schleswig-Holstein), 1846; Princess Louise (duchess of Argyll), 1848; Prince Arthur (duke of Connaught), 1850; Prince Leopold (duke of Albany), 1853; and Princess Beatrice (Princess Henry of Battenberg), 1857. The queen's first grandchild was born in 1859, and her first great-grandchild in 1879. There were 37 great-grandchildren alive at her death.

Victoria never lost her early passion for Albert: "Without him everything loses its interest." Despite conflicts produced by the queen's uncontrollable temper and recurrent fits of depression, which usually occurred during and after pregnancy, the couple had a happy marriage. Victoria, however, was never reconciled to the childbearing that accompanied her marital bliss—the "shadow-side of marriage," as she called it.

At the beginning of their marriage the queen was insistent that her husband should have no share in the government of the country. Within six months, on Melbourne's repeated suggestion, the prince was allowed to start seeing the dispatches, then to be present when the queen saw her ministers. The concession became a routine, and during her first pregnancy the prince received a "key to the secret boxes." As one unwanted pregnancy followed another and as Victoria became increasingly dependent on her husband, Albert assumed an ever-larger political role. Victoria, once so enthusiastic about her role, came to conclude that "we women are not *made* for governing."

THE ALBERTINE MONARCHY

The prince came into his own to negotiate with Peel a compromise on the bedchamber question after the Melbourne government had been defeated in the general election of 1841. The following year Albert became effectively the queen's private secretary—according to himself, "her permanent minister."

A visible sign of the prince's power and influence was the building of the royal residences of Osborne, on the Isle of Wight, and Balmoral Castle in Scotland between 1845 and 1855. Victoria described Osborne as "our island home" and retreated there frequently; it was, however, at Balmoral that she was happiest. She liked the simpler life of the Highlands, and she took delight in the plain speech of John Brown, the Highland servant who stalked with Albert and became her personal attendant.

The royal couple's withdrawal to Scotland and the Isle of Wight bore witness to a new sort of British monarchy. In their quest for privacy and intimacy Albert and Victoria adopted a way of life that mirrored that of their middle-class subjects, admittedly on a grander scale. Although Albert was interested in intellectual and scientific matters, Victoria's tastes were closer to those of most of her people. She enjoyed the novels of Charles Dickens and patronized the circus and waxwork exhibitions. Both Victoria and Albert, however, differed from many in the middle class in their shared preference for nudes in painting and sculpture. Victoria was not the prude that many claimed her to be.

Victoria's delight in mingling with the Scottish poor at Balmoral did little to raise the level of her social awareness. Although in 1846 she and Albert supported the repeal of the Corn Laws (protectionist legislation that kept the price of British grain artificially high) in order to relieve distress in famine-devastated Ireland, they remained much more interested in and involved with the building of Osborne and foreign policy than in the tragedy of Ireland. Victoria, moreover, gave her full support to the government's policy of repression of the Chartists (advocates of far-reaching political and social reform) and believed the workers in her realm to be contented and loyal.

For both the queen and the prince consort the highlight of their reign came in 1851, with the opening of the Great Exhibition. Albert poured himself into the task of organizing the international trade show that became a symbol of the Victorian Age. Housed in the architectural marvel of the Crystal Palace, a splendid, greenhouse-inspired glass building erected in Hyde Park, the Great Exhibition displayed Britain's wealth and technological achievements to a wondering world.

FOREIGN AFFAIRS

By tradition the sovereign had a special part to play in foreign affairs and could conduct them alone with a secretary of state. Victoria and Albert had relatives throughout Europe and were to have more. Moreover, they visited and were visited by other monarchs. Albert was determined that this personal intelligence should not be disregarded and that the queen should never become a mere figurehead who represented the will of the foreign minister. The result was a clash with Lord Palmerston, the foreign secretary, who could look back on a career of high office beginning before the royal couple was born.

Even after Victoria insisted to Palmerston in 1850, "having once given her sanction to a measure, that it be not arbitrarily altered or modified by the minister," the foreign secretary continued to follow policies disapproved of by both Albert and Victoria, such as his encouragement of nationalist movements that threatened to dismember the Austrian Empire. Finally, after Palmerston expressed his approval of the coup d'état of Louis Napoleon (later Napoleon III) in 1851 without consulting the queen, the prime minister, Lord John Russell, dismissed him. Within a few months the immensely popular Palmerston was back in office, however, as home secretary. He would serve twice as prime minister.

On the eve of the Crimean War (1854–56) the royal pair encountered a wave of unpopularity, but there was a marked revival of royalist sentiment as the war wore on. The queen personally superintended the committees of ladies who organized relief for the wounded and eagerly seconded the efforts of Florence Nightingale: she visited crippled soldiers in the hospitals and instituted the Victoria Cross for gallantry.

With the death of Prince Albert on Dec. 14, 1861, the Albertine monarchy came to an end. Albert's influence on the queen was lasting. He had changed her personal habits and her political sympathies. From him she had received training in orderly ways of business, in hard work, in the expectation of royal intervention in ministry making at home, and in the establishment of a private (because royal) intelligence service abroad. The English monarchy too had changed.

DISRAELI'S INFLUENCE

After Albert's death Victoria descended into deep depression. Even after she conquered her depression, she remained in mourning and in partial retirement. She balked at performing the ceremonial functions expected of the monarch and withdrew to Balmoral and Osborne four months out of every year. After an initial period of respect and sympathy for the queen's grief, the public grew increasingly impatient with its absent sovereign.

Although Victoria resisted carrying out her ceremonial duties, she remained determined to retain an effective political role and to behave as Albert would have ordained. It was despite, yet because of, Albert that Victoria succumbed to Benjamin Disraeli. Albert had not liked him, but he was able to enter into the queen's grief, flatter her, restore her self-confidence, and make the lonely crown an easier burden. Behind all his calculated attacks on her affections there was a bond of mutual loneliness, a note of mystery and romanticism, and, besides, the return to good gossip. Disraeli, moreover, told the queen in 1868 that it would be "his delight and duty, to render the transaction of affairs as easy to your Majesty, as possible." Since the queen was only too ready to consider herself overworked, this approach was especially successful. On the other hand, the queen's former prime minister, William Gladstone, would never acknowledge that she was, as she put it, "dead beat," perhaps because he never was himself; Disraeli, however, tired easily. The contrast between Disraeli's lively, often malicious, gossipy letters and Gladstone's 40 sides of foolscap is obvious. And there was no Albert to give her a neat précis. The queen had no patience with Gladstone's moralistic (and, she believed, hypocritical) approach to politics and foreign affairs. His persistent and often tactless attempts to persuade her to resume her ceremonial duties especially enraged her.

Over the problem of Ireland their paths separated ever more widely. The queen (like the majority of her subjects) had little understanding of, or sympathy for, Irish grievances.

In all, she made but four visits to Ireland. The news of Gladstone's defeat in 1874 delighted the queen.

One of the bonds shared by Victoria and Disraeli was a romantic attachment to the East and the idea of empire. The queen was entranced by his imperialism and by his assertive foreign policy. She applauded his brilliant maneuvering, which led to the British purchase of slightly less than half of the shares in the Suez Canal in 1875 (a move that prevented the canal from falling entirely under French control), especially since he presented the canal as a personal gift to her: "It is just settled; you have it, Ma'am." The addition of "Empress of India" in 1876 to the royal title thrilled the queen even more. Victoria and Disraeli also agreed on their answer to the vexing "Eastern question"—what was to be done with the declining Turkish empire? Both held that Britain's best interests lay in supporting Turkey, the "Sick Man" of Europe. The fact that Gladstone took the opposing view, of course, strengthened their pro-Turkish sympathies. With the outbreak of a Russo-Turkish war in 1877, however, Disraeli had to restrain his bellicose sovereign, who demanded that Britain enter the war against Russia. At the Congress of Berlin in 1878 Disraeli emerged triumphant: Russian influence in the Balkans was reduced, and Britain gained control of the strategically located island of Cyprus. The queen was ecstatic.

Victoria's delight in Disraeli's premiership made further conflict with Gladstone inevitable. When the Conservative Party was defeated in 1880, she made no secret of her hostility toward Gladstone. She hoped he would retire, and she remained in correspondence with Lord Beaconsfield (as Disraeli had become). Despite her feelings about leading what she scornfully called a "Democratic Monarchy," Victoria did act as an important mediating influence between the two houses to bring about the compromise that resulted in the third parliamentary Reform Act in 1884.

Victoria never acclimatized herself to the effects of the new electorate on party organization. No longer was the monarchy normally necessary as cabinet maker. Yet the queen was reluctant to accept her more limited role. Thus, in 1886 she sought to avoid a third Gladstone ministry by attempting to form an anti-Radical coalition. Her attempt failed.

Last Years

In the Salisbury administration (1895–1902), with which her long reign ended, Victoria was eventually to find not only the sort of ministry with which she felt comfortable but one which lent a last ray of colour to her closing years by its alliance, through Joseph Chamberlain, with the mounting imperialism that she had so greatly enjoyed in Disraeli's day when he had made her empress of India.

The South African War (1899–1902) dominated her final years. The sufferings of her soldiers in South Africa aroused the queen to a level of activity and public visibility that she had avoided for decades. With a demanding schedule of troop inspections, medal ceremonies, and visits to military hospitals, Victoria finally became the exemplar of a modern monarch.

She remained, nevertheless, either aloof from or in opposition to many of the important political, social, and intellectual currents of the later Victorian period. She never reconciled herself to the advance of democracy, and she thought the idea of female suffrage anathema. The sufferings of an individual worker could engage her sympathy; the working class, however, remained outside her field of vision. Many of the movements of the day passed the aged queen by, many irritated her, but the stupendous hard work that Albert had taught her went on—the meticulous examination of the boxes, the regular signature of the papers. To the very end Victoria remained a passionate and strong-willed woman.

Those nearest to her came completely under her spell; all from the Prince of Wales down stood in considerable awe. Those who suffered her displeasure never forgot it, nor did she. Yielding to nobody else's comfort and keeping every anniversary, she lived surrounded by mementos, photographs, miniatures, busts, and souvenirs in chilly rooms at the end of drafty corridors, down which one tiptoed past Indian attendants to the presence. Nobody knocked; a gentle scratching on the door was all that she permitted. Every night at Windsor Albert's clothes were laid out on the bed, every morning fresh water was put in the basin in his room. She slept with a photograph—over her head—taken of his head and shoulders as he lay dead. When she died, after a short and painless illness, she was buried beside Prince Albert in the mausoleum at Frogmore near Windsor.

SUSAN B. ANTHONY AND ELIZABETH CADY STANTON

(Respectively, b. Feb. 15, 1820, Adams, Mass., U.S.—d. March 13, 1906, Rochester, N.Y.; b. Nov. 12, 1815, Johnstown, N.Y., U.S.—d. Oct. 26, 1902, New York, N.Y.)

Susan B. Anthony and Elizabeth Cady Stanton led the women's rights movement and were crusaders for woman suffrage in the United States. Their work helped pave the way for the Nineteenth Amendment (1920) to the Constitution, giving women the right to vote.

SUSAN B. ANTHONY

Susan Brownell Anthony was reared in the Quaker tradition in a home pervaded by a tone of independence and moral zeal. She was a precocious child and learned to read and write at age three. After the family moved from Massachusetts to Battensville, N.Y., in 1826, she attended a district school, then a school set up by her father, and finally a boarding school near Philadelphia. In 1839 she took a position in a Quaker seminary in New Rochelle, N.Y. After teaching at a female academy in upstate New York (1846–49), she settled in her family home, now near Rochester, N.Y. There she met many leading abolitionists, including Frederick Douglass, Parker Pillsbury, Wendell Phillips, William Henry Channing, and William Lloyd Garrison. Soon the temperance movement enlisted her sympathy; after meeting Amelia Bloomer and, through her, Elizabeth Cady Stanton, so did that of woman suffrage.

The rebuff of Anthony's attempt to speak at a temperance meeting in Albany in 1852 prompted her to organize the Woman's New York State Temperance Society, of which Stanton became president. The episode also pushed Anthony farther in the direction of women's rights advocacy. In a short time she became known as one of the cause's most zealous, serious advocates, a dogged and tireless worker whose personality contrasted sharply with that of her friend and coworker Stanton. She was also a prime target of public and newspaper abuse.

While campaigning for a liberalization of New York's laws regarding married women's property rights, an end attained in 1860, Anthony served from 1856 as chief New York agent of Garrison's American Anti-Slavery Society. During the early phase of the Civil War she helped

Susan B. Anthony (left) *and Elizabeth Cady Stanton.* Library of Congress, Washington, D.C. (neg. no. LC USZ 62 37938)

organize the Women's National Loyal League, which urged the case for emancipation. After the war she campaigned unsuccessfully to have the language of the Fourteenth Amendment altered to allow for woman as well as "Negro" suffrage, and in 1866 she became corresponding secretary of the newly formed American Equal Rights Association. Her exhausting speaking and organizing tour of Kansas in 1867 failed to win passage of a state enfranchisement law.

In 1868 Anthony became publisher, and Stanton editor, of a new periodical, *The Revolution*, originally financed by the eccentric George Francis Train. The same year, she represented the Working Women's Association of New York, which she had recently organized, at the National Labor Union convention. In January 1869 she organized a woman suffrage convention in Washington, D.C., and in May she and Stanton formed the National Woman Suffrage Association (NWSA). A portion of the organization deserted later in the year to join Lucy Stone's more conservative American Woman Suffrage Association, but the NWSA remained a large and powerful group and Anthony remained its principal leader and spokeswoman.

In 1870 she relinquished her position at *The Revolution* and embarked on a series of lecture tours to pay off the paper's accumulated debts. As a test of the legality of the suffrage provision of the Fourteenth Amendment, she cast a vote in the 1872 presidential election in Rochester, N.Y. She was arrested, convicted (the judge's directed verdict of guilty had been written before the trial began), and fined, and although she refused to pay the fine the case was carried no further. She traveled constantly, often with Stanton, in support of efforts in various states to win the franchise for women: California in 1871, Michigan in 1874, Colorado in 1877, and elsewhere. In 1890, after lengthy discussions, the rival suffrage associations were merged into the National American Woman Suffrage Association, and at Stanton's resignation in 1892 Anthony became president. Her principal lieutenant in later years was Carrie Chapman Catt.

By the 1890s Anthony had largely outlived the abuse and sarcasm that had attended her early efforts, and she emerged as a national heroine. Her visits to the World's Columbian Exposition in Chicago in 1893 and to the Lewis and Clark Exposition in Portland, Oregon, in 1905 were warmly received, as were her trips to London in 1899 and Berlin in 1904 as head of the U.S. delegation to the international Council of Women (which she helped found in 1888). In 1900, at the age of 80, she retired from the presidency of the National American Woman Suffrage Association, passing it on to Catt.

Principal among Anthony's written works are the first four volumes of the six-volume *History of Woman Suffrage*, written with Stanton and Matilda J. Gage. Various of her writings are collected in *The Elizabeth Cady Stanton-Susan B. Anthony Reader* (1992), edited by Ellen Carol DuBois, and *The Selected Papers of Elizabeth Cady Stanton and Susan B. Anthony* (1997), edited by Ann D. Gordon. With the issue of a new dollar coin in 1979, she became the first woman to be depicted on United States currency, although the honour was somewhat mitigated by popular rejection of the coin because its size was so similar to that of the 25-cent coin.

ELIZABETH CADY STANTON

Elizabeth Cady received a superior education at home, at the Johnstown Academy, and at Emma Willard's Troy Female Seminary, from which she graduated in 1832. While studying law in the office of her father, Daniel Cady, a U.S. congressman and later a New York Supreme Court judge, she learned of the discriminatory laws under which women lived and determined to win equal rights for her sex.

In 1840 she married Henry Brewster Stanton, a lawyer and abolitionist (she insisted that the word *obey* be dropped from the wedding ceremony). Later that year they attended the World's Anti-Slavery Convention in London, and she was outraged at the denial of official recognition to several women delegates, notably Lucretia C. Mott, because of their sex. She became a frequent speaker on the subject of women's rights and circulated petitions that helped secure passage by the New York legislature in 1848 of a bill granting married women's property rights.

In 1848 she and Mott issued a call for a women's rights convention to meet in Seneca Falls, N.Y. (where Stanton lived), on July 19–20 and in Rochester, N.Y., on subsequent days. At the meeting Stanton introduced her Declaration of Sentiments, modeled on the Declaration of Independence, that detailed the inferior status of women and that, in calling for extensive reforms, effectively launched the American women's rights movement. She also introduced a resolution calling for woman suffrage that was adopted after considerable debate.

From 1851 she worked closely with Susan B. Anthony. Together they remained active for 50 years after the first convention, planning campaigns, speaking before legislative bodies, and addressing gatherings in conventions, in lyceums, and in the streets. Stanton, the better orator and writer, was perfectly complemented by Anthony, the organizer and tactician. She wrote not only her own and many of Anthony's addresses but also countless letters and pamphlets, as well as articles and essays for numerous periodicals, including Amelia Bloomer's *Lily*, Paulina Wright Davis's *Una*, and Horace Greeley's *New York Tribune*. In 1854 Stanton received an unprecedented invitation to address the New York legislature. Her speech resulted in new legislation in 1860 granting married women the rights to their wages and to equal guardianship of their children.

During her presidency in 1852–53 of the short-lived Woman's State Temperance Society, which she and Anthony had founded, she scandalized many of her most ardent supporters by suggesting that drunkenness be made sufficient cause for divorce. Liberalized divorce laws continued to be one of her principal issues.

During the Civil War, Stanton again worked for abolitionism. In 1863 she and Anthony organized the Women's National Loyal League, which gathered more than 300,000 signatures on petitions calling for immediate emancipation. The movement to extend the franchise to African American men after the war, however, caused her bitterness and outrage, reemphasized the disenfranchisement of women, and led her and her colleagues to redouble their efforts for woman suffrage.

Stanton and Anthony made several exhausting speaking and organizing tours on behalf of woman suffrage. In 1868 Stanton became coeditor (with Parker Pillsbury) of the newly established weekly *The Revolution*, a newspaper devoted to women's rights. She continued to write fiery editorials until the paper's demise in 1870. She helped organize the National Woman Suffrage Association in 1869 and was named its president, a post she retained until 1890, when the organization merged with the rival American Woman Suffrage Association. She was then elected president of the new National American Woman Suffrage Association and held that position until 1892.

Stanton continued to write and lecture tirelessly. She was the principal author of the Declaration of Rights for Women presented at the Centennial Exposition in Philadelphia in 1876. In 1878 she drafted a federal suffrage amendment that was introduced in every Congress thereafter until women were granted the right to vote in 1920. With Susan B. Anthony and Matilda Joslyn Gage she compiled the first three volumes of the six-volume *History of Woman Suffrage*. She also published *The Woman's Bible*, 2 vol. (1895–98), and an autobiography, *Eighty Years and More* (1898).

FLORENCE NIGHTINGALE

(b. May 12, 1820, Florence [Italy]—d. Aug. 13, 1910, London, Eng.)

Florence Nightingale is best known as the foundational philosopher of modern nursing. She was also a statistician and social reformer.

Florence was a precocious child intellectually. Her father took particular interest in her education, guiding her through history, philosophy, and literature. She excelled in mathematics and languages and was able to read and write French, German, Italian, Greek, and Latin at an early age. Never satisfied with the traditional female skills of home management, she preferred to read the great philosophers and to engage in serious political and social discourse with her father.

As part of a liberal Unitarian family, Florence found great comfort in her religious beliefs. At the age of 16, she experienced one of several "calls from God." She viewed her particular calling as reducing human suffering. Nursing seemed the suitable route to serve both God and humankind. However, despite having cared for sick relatives and tenants on the family estates, her attempts to seek nurse's training were thwarted by her family as an inappropriate activity for a woman of her stature.

NURSING IN PEACE AND WAR

Despite family reservations, Nightingale was eventually able to enroll at the Institution of Protestant Deaconesses at Kaiserswerth in Germany for two weeks of training in July 1850 and again for three months in July 1851. There she learned basic nursing skills, the importance of patient observation, and the value of good hospital organization. In 1853 Nightingale sought to break free from her family environment. Through social connections, she became the superintendent of the Institution for Sick Gentle-women (governesses) in Distressed Circumstances, in London, where she successfully displayed her skills as an administrator by improving nursing care, working conditions, and efficiency of the hospital. After one year she began to realize that her services would be more valuable in an institution that would allow her to train nurses. She considered becoming the superintendent of nurses at King's College Hospital in London. However, politics, not nursing expertise, was to shape her next move.

In October 1853 the Turkish Ottoman Empire declared war on Russia, following a series of disputes over holy places in Jerusalem and Russian demands to exercise protection over the Orthodox subjects of the Ottoman sultan. The British and the French, allies of Turkey, sought to curb Russian expansion. The majority of the Crimean War was fought on the Crimean Peninsula in Russia. However, the British troop base and hospitals for the care of the sick and wounded soldiers were primarily established in Scutari (Üsküdar), across the Bosporus from Constantinople (Istanbul). The status of the care of the wounded was reported to the London *Times* by the first modern war correspondent, British journalist William Howard Russell. The newspaper reports stated that soldiers were treated by an incompetent and ineffective medical establishment and that the most basic supplies were not available for care. The British public raised an outcry over the treatment of the soldiers and demanded that the situation be drastically improved.

Sidney Herbert, secretary of state at war for the British government, wrote to Nightingale requesting that she lead a group of nurses to Scutari. At the same time, Nightingale wrote to her friend Liz Herbert, Sidney's wife, asking that she be allowed to lead a private expedition. Their letters crossed in the mail, but in the end their mutual requests were granted. Nightingale led an officially sanctioned party of 38 women, departing Oct. 21, 1854, and arriving in Scutari at the Barrack Hospital on November 5.

Not welcomed by the medical officers, Nightingale found conditions filthy, supplies inadequate, staff uncooperative, and overcrowding severe. Few nurses had access to the cholera wards, and Nightingale, who wanted to gain the confidence of army surgeons by waiting for official military orders for assistance, kept her party from the wards. Five days after Nightingale's arrival in Scutari, injured soldiers from the Battle of Balaklava and the Battle of Inkerman arrived and overwhelmed the facility. Nightingale said it was the "Kingdom of Hell."

In order to care for the soldiers properly, it was necessary that adequate supplies be obtained. Nightingale bought equipment with funds provided by the London *Times* and enlisted soldiers' wives to assist with the laundry.

Florence Nightingale began to revolutionize the practice of nursing while serving in a military hospital during the Crimean War. Hulton Archive/Getty Images

The wards were cleaned and basic care was provided by the nurses. Most important, Nightingale established standards of care, requiring such basic necessities as bathing, clean clothing and dressings, and adequate food. Attention was given to psychological needs through assistance in writing letters to relatives and through providing educational and recreational activities. Nightingale herself wandered the wards at night, providing support to the patients; this earned her the title of "Lady with the Lamp." She gained the respect of the soldiers and medical establishment alike. Her accomplishments in providing care and reducing the mortality rate to about 2 percent brought her fame in England through the press and the soldiers' letters.

In May 1855 Nightingale began the first of several excursions to the Crimea; however, shortly after arriving, she fell ill with "Crimean fever"—most likely brucellosis, which she probably contracted from drinking contaminated milk. Nightingale experienced a slow recovery, as no active treatment was available. The lingering effects of the disease were to last for 25 years, frequently confining her to bed because of severe, chronic pain.

On March 30, 1856, the Treaty of Paris ended the Crimean War. Nightingale remained in Scutari until the hospitals were ready to close, returning to her home in Derbyshire on Aug. 7, 1856, as a reluctant heroine.

HOMECOMING AND LEGACY

Although primarily remembered for her accomplishments during the Crimean War, Nightingale's greatest achievements centred on attempts to create social reform in health care and nursing. On her return to England, Nightingale was suffering the effects of both brucellosis and exhaustion. In September 1856 she met with Queen Victoria and Prince Albert to discuss the need for reform of the British military establishment. Nightingale kept meticulous records regarding the running of the Barrack Hospital, causes of illness and death, the efficiency of the nursing and medical staffs, and difficulties in purveyance. A Royal Commission was established, which based its findings on the statistical data and analysis provided by Nightingale. The result was marked reform in the military medical and purveyance systems.

In 1855, as a token of gratitude and respect for Nightingale, the Nightingale Fund was established. Through private donations, £45,000 was raised by 1859 and put at Nightingale's disposal. She used a substantial part of these monies to institute the Nightingale School of Nursing at St. Thomas' Hospital in London, which opened in 1860. The school formalized secular nursing education, making nursing a viable and respectable option for women who desired employment outside of the home. The model was taken worldwide by matrons (women supervisors of public health institutions). Nightingale's statistical models— such as the Coxcomb chart, which she developed to assess mortality—and her basic concepts regarding nursing remain applicable today. For these reasons she is considered the foundational philosopher of modern nursing.

Nightingale improved the health of households through her most famous publication, *Notes on Nursing: What It Is and What It Is Not*, which provided direction on how to manage the sick. This volume has been in continuous publication worldwide since 1859. Additional reforms were financed through the Nightingale Fund, and a school for the education of midwives was established at King's College Hospital in 1862. Believing that the most important location for the care of the sick was in the home, she established training for district nursing, which was aimed at improving the health of the poor and vulnerable. A second Royal Commission examined the health of India, resulting in major environmental reform, again based on Nightingale's statistical data.

Florence Nightingale was honoured in her lifetime by receiving the title of Lady of Grace of the Order of St. John of Jerusalem and by becoming the first woman to receive the Order of Merit. On her death in 1910, at Nightingale's prior request, her family declined the offer of a state funeral and burial in Westminster Abbey. Instead, she was honoured with a memorial service at St. Paul's Cathedral, London. Her burial is in the family plot in St. Margaret's Church, East Wellow, Hampshire.

HARRIET TUBMAN

(b. *c.* 1820, Dorchester county, Md., U.S.—d. March 10, 1913, Auburn, N.Y.)

Harriet Tubman was an American abolitionist who led hundreds of bondsmen to freedom in the North along the route of the Underground Railroad, an elaborate secret network of safe houses organized for that purpose.

Born into slavery, Araminta Ross later adopted her mother's first name, Harriet. From early childhood she worked variously as a maid, a nurse, a field hand, a cook, and a woodcutter. About 1844 she married John Tubman, a free black man.

In 1849, on the strength of rumours that she was about to be sold, Tubman fled to Philadelphia, leaving behind her husband, parents, and siblings. In December 1850 she made her way to Baltimore, Md., whence she led her sister and two children to freedom. That journey was the first of some 19 increasingly dangerous forays into Maryland in which, over the next decade, she conducted upward of 300 fugitive slaves along the Underground Railroad to Canada. By her extraordinary courage, ingenuity, persistence, and iron discipline, which she enforced upon her charges, Tubman became the railroad's most famous conductor and was known as the "Moses of her people." It has been said that she never lost a fugitive she was leading to freedom.

Rewards offered by slaveholders for Tubman's capture eventually totaled $40,000. Abolitionists, however, celebrated her courage. John Brown, who consulted her about his own plans to organize an antislavery raid of a federal armoury in Harpers Ferry, Va. (now in West Virginia), referred to her as "General" Tubman. About 1858 she bought a small farm near Auburn, New York, where she placed her aged parents (she had brought them out of Maryland in June 1857) and she lived thereafter. From 1862 to 1865, she served as a scout, as well as nurse and laundress, for Union forces in South Carolina. For the Second Carolina Volunteers, under the command of Colonel James Montgomery, Tubman spied on Confederate territory. When she returned with information about the locations of warehouses and ammunition, Montgomery's troops were able to make carefully planned attacks. For her wartime service Tubman was paid so little that she had to support herself by selling homemade baked goods.

After the Civil War Tubman settled in Auburn and began taking in orphans and the elderly, a practice that eventuated in the Harriet Tubman Home for Indigent Aged Negroes. The home later attracted the support of former abolitionist comrades and of the citizens of Auburn, and it continued in existence for some years after her death. In the late 1860s and again in the late 1890s she applied for a federal pension for her Civil War services. Some 30 years after her service, a private bill providing for $20 monthly was passed by Congress.

ELIZABETH BLACKWELL

(b. Feb. 3, 1821, Counterslip, Bristol, Gloucestershire, Eng.—d. May 31, 1910, Hastings, Sussex)

The Anglo-American physician Elizabeth Blackwell is considered to be the first woman medical doctor in modern times.

Born into a large, prosperous, and cultured family, Blackwell was well educated by private tutors. Financial reverses and the family's liberal social and religious views prompted them to immigrate to the United States in the summer of 1832. Soon after taking up residence in New York, her father, Samuel Blackwell, became active in abolitionist activities. The Blackwells moved to Jersey City, N.J., in 1835 and to Cincinnati, Ohio, in 1838. Soon after the move Blackwell's father died and left the family in poverty. To help support them, she and two sisters opened a private school. Later Elizabeth taught school in Henderson, Ky., and, in 1845–47, in North and South Carolina.

During the latter period, Blackwell undertook the study of medicine privately with sympathetic physicians, and in 1847 she began seeking admission to a medical school. All the leading schools rejected her application, but she was at length admitted, almost by fluke, to Geneva Medical College (a forerunner of Hobart College) in Geneva, New York. Her months there were extremely difficult. Townspeople and much of the male student body ostracized and harassed her, and she was at first even barred from classroom demonstration. She persevered, however, and in January 1849, ranked first in her class, she became the first woman in the United States to graduate from medical school and the first modern-day woman doctor of medicine.

In April of that year, having become a naturalized U.S. citizen, Blackwell traveled to England to seek further training. In May she went on to Paris, where, in June, she entered the midwives' course at La Maternité. While there she contracted an infectious eye disease that left her blind in one eye and forced her to abandon hope of becoming a surgeon. In October 1850 she returned to England and worked at St. Bartholomew's Hospital under Dr. (later Sir) James Paget. In the summer of 1851 she returned to New York, where she was refused posts in the city's hospitals and dispensaries and was even unable to rent private consulting quarters. Her private practice was very slow to develop, and in the meantime she wrote a series of lectures, published in 1852 as *The Laws of Life, with Special Reference to the Physical Education of Girls*.

In 1853 Blackwell opened a small dispensary in a slum district of New York City. Within a few years she was joined by her younger sister, Dr. Emily Blackwell, and by Dr. Marie E. Zakrzewska. In May 1857 the dispensary, greatly enlarged, was incorporated as the New York Infirmary for Women and Children. In January 1859, during a year-long lecture tour of Great Britain, she became the first woman to have her name placed on the British medical register. At the outbreak of the American Civil War in 1861, she helped organize the Woman's Central Association of Relief and the U.S. Sanitary Commission and worked mainly through the former to select and train nurses for war service.

In November 1868 a plan long in the perfecting, developed in large part in consultation with Florence Nightingale in England, bore fruit in the opening of the Woman's Medical College at the infirmary. Elizabeth Blackwell set very high standards for admission, academic and clinical training, and certification for the school, which continued in operation for 31 years; she herself occupied the chair of hygiene.

In 1869 Blackwell moved permanently to England. She established a successful private practice, helped organize the National Health Society in 1871, and in 1875 was appointed professor of gynecology at the London School of Medicine for Women. She retained the latter position until 1907, when an injury forced her to retire. Among her other writings are *The Religion of Health* (1871), *Counsel to Parents on the Moral Education of Their Children* (1878), *The Human Element in Sex* (1884), her autobiographical *Pioneer Work in Opening the Medical Profession to Women* (1895), and *Essays in Medical Sociology* (1902).

MARY BAKER EDDY

(b. July 16, 1821, Bow, near Concord, N.H., U.S.—d. Dec. 3, 1910, Chestnut Hill, Mass.)

The Christian religious reformer Mary Baker Eddy founded the religious denomination known as Christian Science.

Eddy was born to devout Congregationalists at a time when Puritan piety was a real, though residual, force in the religious life of New England. She struggled with serious illness from childhood, grieved over the death of a favourite brother when she was 20, became a widow at 22 after only a half year of marriage to George Glover, and, in 1849, lost both her mother and her fiancé within three weeks of each other. Her marriage in 1853 to Daniel Patterson eventually broke down, ending in divorce 20 years later after he deserted her. In 1856 she was plunged into virtual invalidism after Patterson and her father conspired to separate her from her only child, a 12-year-old son from her first marriage. She would not see her son again for nearly 25 years, and they met only a few times thereafter.

Eddy's understanding of her personal and physical misfortunes was greatly shaped by her Congregationalist upbringing. Her proclivity for religion was evident early on, and study of the Bible was the bedrock of her religious life. She was especially influenced by ministers in the "New Light" tradition of Jonathan Edwards, which emphasized the heart's outflowing response to God's majesty and love.

Yet as a teenager she also rebelled with others of her generation against the stark predestinarian Calvinism of what she called her father's "relentless theology." But whereas most Protestants who rejected Calvinism gravitated toward belief in a benign God, Eddy needed something more. Although she too believed in a benign God, she continued to ask how the reality of a God of love could possibly be reconciled with the existence of a world filled with so much misery and pain. She thus found herself confronting perhaps the most basic problem undermining Christian faith in her time.

THE PROCESS OF "DISCOVERY"

Eddy's spiritual quest took an unusual direction during the 1850s with the new medical system of homeopathy. Losing faith in medical systems based on materialistic premises, she hit on what some today would call the placebo effect. Her conviction that the cause of disease was rooted in the human mind and that it was in no sense God's will was confirmed by her contact from 1862 to 1865 with Phineas P. Quimby of Maine, a pioneer in what would today be called suggestive therapeutics. The degree of Quimby's influence on her has been controversial, but, as his own son affirmed, her intensely religious preoccupations remained distinct from the essentially secular cast of Quimby's thought. Though personally loyal to Quimby, she soon recognized that his healing method was based in mesmerism, or mental suggestion, rather than in the biblical Christianity to which she was so firmly bound.

Injured in a severe fall shortly after Quimby's death in early 1866, she turned, as she later recalled, to a Gospel account of healing and experienced a moment of spiritual illumination and discovery that brought not only immediate recovery but a new direction to her life. "That short experience," she later wrote, "included a glimpse of the great fact that I have since tried to make plain to others, namely, Life in and of Spirit; this Life being the sole reality of existence. I learned that mortal thought evolves a subjective state which it names matter, thereby shutting out the true sense of Spirit."

While the precise extent of her injuries is unclear, the transforming effect of the experience is beyond dispute. From 1866 on, she gained increasing conviction that she had made a spiritual discovery of overwhelming authority and power. The next nine years of scriptural study, healing work, and teaching climaxed in 1875 with the publication of her major work, *Science and Health*, which she regarded as spiritually inspired. It was in this major work that Eddy eventually included the basic tenets of the church:

1. As adherents of Truth, we take the inspired Word of the Bible as our sufficient guide to eternal Life.
2. We acknowledge and adore one supreme and infinite God. We acknowledge His Son, one Christ; the Holy Ghost or divine Comforter; and man in God's image and likeness.
3. We acknowledge God's forgiveness of sin in the destruction of sin and the spiritual understanding that casts out evil as unreal. But the belief in sin is punished so long as the belief lasts.
4. We acknowledge Jesus' atonement as the evidence of divine, efficacious Love, unfolding man's unity

with God through Christ Jesus, the Way-shower; and we acknowledge that man is saved through Christ, through Truth, Life, and Love as demonstrated by the Galilean Prophet in healing the sick and overcoming sin and death.

5. We acknowledge that the crucifixion of Jesus and his resurrection served to uplift faith to understand eternal Life, even the allness of Soul, Spirit, and the nothingness of matter.

6. And we solemnly promise to watch, and pray for that Mind to be in us which was also in Christ Jesus; to do unto others as we would have them do unto us; and to be merciful, just, and pure.

Although the first edition of *Science and Health* contained the essential structure of her teachings, Eddy continued to refine her statement of Christian Science in the years to come. For the rest of her life she continued to revise this "textbook" of Christian Science as the definitive statement of her teaching. In 1883 she added the words "with Key to the Scriptures" to the book's title to emphasize her contention that *Science and Health* did not stand alone but opened the way to the continuing power and truth of biblical revelation, especially the life and work of Jesus Christ.

To "reinstate primitive Christianity and its lost element of healing" was the stated purpose of the Church of Christ, Scientist, which she founded with 15 students in Lynn, Mass., in 1879.

WORK AS FOUNDER

A promising move to Boston in 1882 began with a jolting setback: the death of her third husband, Asa Gilbert Eddy, on whose support she had relied since their marriage in

1877. Nonetheless, during her years in Boston from 1882 to 1889, Christian Science began to make an impact on American religious life.

Boston was an intellectual centre where new ideas, especially in religion, traveled fast. Eddy contributed to the ferment in the religious life of New England, especially since she maintained that her teaching, while thoroughly Christian, offered a distinct alternative to both liberal and orthodox forms of Christianity.

The demands on her were enormous during this period. Eddy taught hundreds of students in the Massachusetts Metaphysical College, for which she obtained a charter in 1881. She continued to revise *Science and Health* and wrote a number of shorter works, including numerous articles for a monthly magazine she founded in 1883. And she also preached intermittently at Christian Science church services, which were attracting a growing number of disaffected mainstream Protestants.

Her successes in the 1880s, especially her conversions of mainstream Protestants, exposed her to growing criticism from concerned Boston ministers. The fledgling Christian Science movement was further threatened by internal schism and the rivalry of various "mind-cure" groups that appropriated her terminology but sought healing not through divine help but through the powers of the human mind, which she saw as engendering disease in the first place. In response to these challenges, Eddy's writings repeatedly underscored the biblical basis of her teachings and the Christian demands of practicing it. She also explicitly differentiated Christian Science from theosophy and spiritualism, both antecedents of 20th-century "New Age" movements.

Eddy moved to Concord, N.H., in 1889, eventually settling into a house, called Pleasant View, with a small staff. During the next decade she gained both authority within the movement and public recognition outside it. In 1892 she reorganized the church she had founded in 1879, establishing over the next decade its present structure as The Mother Church, The First Church of Christ, Scientist, and its worldwide branches. In 1895 she published the *Manual of The Mother Church*, a slim book of bylaws that she continued to revise until her death and that she intended would govern the church in perpetuity.

LAST YEARS AND ACHIEVEMENT

Eddy's growing public stature as a religious leader, together with the practical challenge her teachings posed to conventional religion and medicine, made her the subject of mounting controversy, as seen in a set of articles in 1902 and 1903 (published in book form in 1907 under the title *Christian Science*) by Mark Twain, who severely criticized Eddy while speaking at points warmly of her teaching. There was also a highly misleading series that ran in *McClure's Magazine* for two years and an unsuccessful lawsuit against her (the so-called "Next Friends Suit" of 1907) that Joseph Pulitzer's *New York World* newspaper orchestrated to question her mental competence.

Despite these personal attacks and occasional ill health (induced at least in part, she felt, by the hostility that fueled such attacks), Eddy accomplished much during the last decade of her long life. She put *Science and Health* through its last major revisions, completed the formal structuring of her church by entrusting greater responsibilities to its Board of Directors, and in 1908 founded *The Christian Science Monitor*, an international newspaper of recognized excellence.

Eddy's death in 1910 did not end the controversy over her character or her contribution to Christian thought and practice. Today's interest in women's studies, however, is prompting a fresh look at her life and influence, and feminists have often emphasized that her work had the effect of empowering women. Indeed, as she acknowledged, hers was a life of protest against conventional assumptions both in religion and in medicine. While she was not a feminist per se, she acted outside of conventional gender roles by founding and leading a significant American denomination, and she did support some feminist causes such as women's suffrage and the right of women to hold property.

Yet her aim was not to overturn traditional gender roles but to reinvigorate Christianity—to restore the role of spiritual healing in a living Christian faith. It is this tradition of spiritual healing that is perhaps the most controversial part of Eddy's legacy. Science is only beginning to grapple with some of the long-term questions raised by the church's practice of spiritual healing. These questions concern not only the medical evidence for spiritual healings, many of which have involved undiagnosed and psychosomatic disorders, but also the significance for religion of medically diagnosed conditions. While Eddy's character and the teachings of her church remain controversial, no single individual has focused more attention on this area of Christian experience.

CIXI

(b. Nov. 29, 1835, Beijing, China—d. Nov. 15, 1908, Beijing)

Cixi, who is also known as the Empress Dowager, was a consort of the Xianfeng emperor (reigned 1850–61), mother of the Tongzhi emperor (reigned 1861–75), adoptive mother of the Guangxu emperor (reigned 1875–1908), and a towering presence over the Chinese empire for almost half a century. Ruling through a clique of conservative, corrupt officials and maintaining authority over the

The Dowager Empress Cixi rose from being a lowly concubine to one of the most powerful women in Chinese history. Roger Viollet/Getty Images

Manchu imperial house (Qing dynasty, 1644–1911/12), she became one of the most powerful women in the history of China.

Cixi was one of the Xianfeng emperor's low-ranking concubines, but in 1856 she bore his only son. On Xianfeng's death, the six-year-old boy became the Tongzhi emperor, and state business was put in the hands of a regency council of eight elder officials. A few months later, after Gong Qinwang (Prince Gong), the former emperor's brother, was victorious in a palace coup, the regency was transferred to Cixi and Xianfeng's former senior consort, Ci'an. Gong became the prince counsellor.

Under this triumviral rule (but largely under Prince Gong's leadership), the government entered a temporary period of revitalization. The great Taiping Rebellion (1850–64), which had devastated South China, was quelled, as was the Nian Rebellion (1853–68) in the northern provinces. Schools were created for the study of foreign languages, a modern customs service was instituted, Western-style arsenals were constructed, and the first Chinese foreign service office was installed. Internally, an effort was made to end governmental corruption and to recruit men of talent.

Although the regency was terminated in 1873 after the Tongzhi emperor attained maturity, Cixi's involvement in state affairs continued. Following Tongzhi's death, Cixi's three-year-old nephew (whom she had adopted) was named the new heir. The two empress dowagers continued to act as regents, but after Ci'an's sudden death in 1881, Cixi became the sole holder of the office. Three years later, she dismissed Prince Gong.

In 1889 Cixi nominally relinquished control over the government to retire to the magnificent summer palace she had rebuilt northwest of Beijing. However, in 1898, a few years after the shocking defeat of the Chinese forces in the Sino-Japanese War (1894–95), the young Guangxu emperor, under the influence of a group of reformers, put through a number of radical proposals designed to renovate and modernize the Chinese government and to eliminate corruption. But conservative officials, who again used the military to institute a coup, collected around Cixi. The new reforms were reversed, and Cixi resumed the regency. Most historians believe that China's last chance for peaceful change thus ended.

The following year Cixi began to back those officials who were encouraging the anti-foreign Boxer rebels. In 1900 the Boxer Rebellion reached its peak; some 100 foreigners were killed, and the foreign legations in Beijing were surrounded. However, a coalition of foreign troops soon captured the capital, and Cixi was forced to flee the city and accept humiliating peace terms. Returning to Beijing in 1902, she finally began to implement many of the innovations that had been reversed in 1898, although the Guangxu emperor no longer participated in the government. The day before Cixi died, Guangxu's death was announced. Since then, it was generally believed that the emperor had been poisoned, but that fact was not substantiated until 2008 when a report was issued by Chinese researchers and police officials confirming that the emperor had been deliberately poisoned with arsenic. Although the report did not address who may have ordered his death—and there never has been any hard evidence of culpability—suspicion long has pointed toward the Empress Dowager.

MARY CASSATT

(b. May 22, 1844, Allegheny City [now part of Pittsburgh], Pa., U.S.—d. June 14, 1926, Château de Beaufresne, near Paris, France)

The American painter and printmaker Mary Cassatt, who was part of the group of Impressionists working in and around Paris, is noteworthy for her skillful and tender portraits of almost exclusively women and children.

Cassatt was the daughter of a banker and lived in Europe for five years as a young girl. She was tutored privately in art in Philadelphia and attended the Pennsylvania Academy of the Fine Arts in 1861–65, but she preferred a less academic approach and in 1866 traveled to Europe to study with such European painters as Jean-Léon Gérôme and Thomas Couture. Her first major showing was at the Paris Salon of 1872; four more annual Salon exhibitions followed.

In 1874 Cassatt chose Paris as her permanent residence and established her studio there. She shared with the Impressionists an interest in experiment and in using bright colours inspired by the out-of-doors. Edgar Degas became her friend; his style and that of Gustave Courbet inspired her own. Degas was known to admire her drawing especially, and at his request she exhibited with the Impressionists in 1879 and joined them in shows in 1880, 1881, and 1886. Like Degas, Cassatt showed great mastery of drawing, and both artists preferred unposed asymmetrical compositions. Cassatt also was innovative and inventive in exploiting the medium of pastels.

Initially, Cassatt painted mostly figures of friends or relatives and their children in the Impressionist style. After the great exhibition of Japanese prints held in Paris in 1890, she brought out her series of 10 coloured prints — e.g., *Woman Bathing* and *The Coiffure*—in which the influence of the Japanese masters Utamaro and Toyokuni is apparent. In these etchings, combining aquatint, drypoint, and soft ground, she brought her printmaking technique to perfection. Her emphasis shifted from form to line and pattern. The principal motif of her mature and perhaps most familiar period is mothers caring for small children—e.g., *The Bath* (c. 1892) and *Mother and Child* (1899).

In 1894 she purchased a château in Le Mesnil-Théribus and thereafter split her time between her country home and Paris. Soon after 1900 her eyesight began to fail, and by 1914 she had ceased working.

Cassatt urged her wealthy American friends and relatives to buy Impressionist paintings, and in this way, more than through her own works, she exerted a lasting influence on American taste. She was largely responsible for selecting the works that make up the H.O. Havemeyer Collection in the Metropolitan Museum of Art, New York City.

SARAH BERNHARDT

(b. Oct. 22/23, 1844, Paris, France—d. March 26, 1923, Paris)

The greatest French actress of the later 19th century, Sarah Bernhardt (also called The Divine Sarah, or in French, La Divine Sarah) was one of the best-known figures in the history of the stage.

EARLY LIFE AND TRAINING

Born Henriette-Rosine Bernard, Bernhardt was the illegitimate daughter of Julie Bernard, a Dutch courtesan who had established herself in Paris (the identity of her father is uncertain). As the presence of a baby interfered with her mother's life, Sarah was brought up at first in a *pension* and later in a convent. A difficult, willful child of delicate health, she wanted to become a nun, but one of her mother's lovers, the duke de Morny, Napoleon III's half brother, decided that she should be an actress and, when she was 16, arranged for her to enter the Paris Conservatoire, the government-sponsored school of acting. She was not considered a particularly promising student, and, although she revered some of her teachers, she regarded the Conservatoire's methods as antiquated.

Sarah Bernhardt left the Conservatoire in 1862 and, thanks to the duke's influence, was accepted by the national theatre company, the Comédie-Française, as a beginner on probation. During the obligatory three debuts required of probationers, she was scarcely noticed by the critics. Her contract with the Comédie-Française was canceled in 1863 after she slapped the face of a senior actress who had been rude to her younger sister. For a time she found employment at the Théâtre du Gymnase-Dramatique. After playing the role of a foolish Russian princess, she entered a period of soul-searching, questioning her talent for acting. During these critical months she became the mistress of Henri, prince de Ligne, and gave birth to her only child, Maurice. (Later Bernhardt was married to a Greek military-officer-turned-actor, Jacques Damala, but the marriage was short-lived, he dying of drug abuse. Throughout her life she had a series of affairs or liaisons with famous men, allegedly including the great French writer Victor Hugo, the actor Lou Tellegen, and the prince of Wales, the future Edward VII.)

In 1866 Bernhardt signed a contract with the Odéon Theatre and, during six years of intensive work with a congenial company there, gradually established her reputation. Her first resounding success was as Anna Damby in the 1868 revival of *Kean*, by the novelist and playwright Alexandre Dumas *père*. The same year, she played the role of Cordelia in *Le Roi Lear* there. Bernhardt's greatest triumph at the Odéon, however, came in 1869, when she played the minstrel Zanetto in the young dramatist François Coppée's one-act verse play *Le Passant* ("The Passerby")—a part that she played again in a command performance before Napoleon III.

During the Franco-German War in 1870, she organized a military hospital in the Odéon theatre. After the war, the reopened Odéon paid tribute to Hugo with a production of his verse-play *Ruy Blas*. As Queen Maria, Bernhardt charmed her audiences with the lyrical quality of her distinctive voice, which was memorably described as a "golden bell," though her critics usually called it "silvery," as resembling the tones of a flute.

In 1872 Bernhardt left the Odéon and returned to the Comédie-Française, where at first she received only minor parts. But she had a remarkable success there in the title role of Voltaire's *Zaïre* (1874), and she was soon given the chance to play the title role in Jean Racine's *Phèdre*, a part for which the critics supposed she lacked the resources needed to portray violent passion. Her performance, however, made them revise their estimate and write enthusiastic reviews. Another of her finest roles, her portrayal of Doña Sol in Hugo's *Hernani*, was said to have brought tears to the author's eyes.

She played Desdemona in Shakespeare's *Othello* in 1878, and, when the Comédie-Française appeared in London in 1879, Bernhardt played in the second act of *Phèdre* and achieved another triumph. She had now reached the head of her profession, and an international career lay before her. Bernhardt had become an expressive actress with a wide emotional range who was capable of great subtlety in her interpretations. Her grace, beauty, and charisma gave her a commanding stage presence, and the impact of her unique voice was reinforced by the purity of her diction. Her career was also helped by her relentless self-promotion and her unconventional behaviour both on and off the stage.

INTERNATIONAL SUCCESS

In 1880 Bernhardt formed her own traveling company and soon became an international idol. She spent her time acting with her own company, managing the theatres it used, and going on long international tours. She appeared fairly regularly in England and extended her itinerary to the European continent, the United States, and Canada. New York City saw her for the first time on Nov. 8, 1880, and eight visits to the United States followed. In 1891–93 she undertook a world tour that included Australia and South America. Aside from her appearances as Phèdre, there were two parts that audiences all over the world clamoured to see her act: Marguérite Gautier, the redeemed courtesan in *La Dame aux camélias* (*Camille*; "The Lady of the Camellias") of Alexandre Dumas *fils*, and the title role of the popular playwright Eugène Scribe's *Adrienne Lecouvreur*. She had first played these two roles in 1880.

In the 1880s a new element had entered her artistic life with the emergence of Victorien Sardou as chief playwright for melodrama. With Bernhardt in mind, Sardou wrote *Fédora* (1882), *Thédora* (1884), *La Tosca* (1887), and *Cléopâtre* (1890). Sardou, directing his own plays in which she starred, taught her a broad, flamboyant style of acting, relying for effect on lavish decors, exotic costumes, and pantomimic action.

Bernhardt played several male roles in the course of her career. She had made notable appearances as Hamlet in Paris and London in 1899. In one of her more famous parts, that of Napoleon's only son in Edmond Rostand's play *L'Aiglon* (1900), Bernhardt, then age 55, played a youth who died at age 21. She was also one of the first women known to have performed the title role in *Hamlet*.

In 1893 Bernhardt became the manager of the Théâtre de la Renaissance, and in 1899 she relocated to the former Théâtre des Nations, which she renamed the Théâtre Sarah Bernhardt and managed until her death in 1923. The theatre retained her name until the German occupation of World War II and is now known as the Théâtre de la Ville.

Bernhardt was made a member of the Legion of Honour in 1914. In 1905, during a South American tour, she had injured her right knee when jumping off the parapet in the last scene of *La Tosca*. By 1915 gangrene had set in, and her leg had to be amputated. Undaunted, the patriotic Bernhardt insisted on visiting the soldiers at the front during World War I while carried about in a litter chair. In 1916 she began her last tour of the United States, and her indomitable spirit sustained her during 18 grueling months on the road. In November 1918 she arrived back in France but soon set out on another European tour, playing parts she could act while seated. New roles were provided for her by the playwrights Louis Verneuil, Maurice Rostand, and Sacha Guitry. She collapsed during the dress rehearsal of the Guitry play *Un Sujet de roman* ("A Subject for a Novel") but recovered again sufficiently to take an interest in the Hollywood motion picture *La Voyante* ("The Clairvoyant"), which was being filmed in her own house in Paris at the time of her death.

In 1920 Bernhardt published a novel, *Petite Idole*, that is not without interest since the actress-heroine of the story constitutes an idealization of its author's own career and ambitions. Facts and fiction are difficult to disentangle in her autobiography, *Ma Double Vie: mémoires de Sarah Bernhardt* (1907; *My Double Life: Memoirs of Sarah Bernhardt*, also translated as *Memories of My Life*). Bernhardt's treatise on acting, *L'Art du théâtre* (1923; *The Art of the Theatre*), is revealing in its sections on voice training: the actress had always considered voice as the key to dramatic character.

SARAH WINNEMUCCA

(b. *c.* 1844, Humboldt Sink, Mex. [now in Nevada, U.S.]—d. Oct. 16, 1891, Monida, Mont., U.S.)

Sarah Winnemucca, whose Paiute name is variously given as Thoc-me-tony, Thocmectony, or Tocmectone ("Shell Flower"), was a Native American educator, lecturer, tribal leader, and writer best known for her book *Life Among the Piutes: Their Wrongs and Claims* (1883). Her writings, valuable for their description of Northern Paiute life and for their insights into the impact of white settlement, are among the few contemporary Native American works.

A granddaughter of Truckee and daughter of Winnemucca, both Northern Paiute chiefs, she lived during part of her childhood in the San Joaquin valley of California, where she learned both Spanish and English. After her return to Nevada she lived for a time with a white family and adopted the name Sarah (sometimes called Sally). In 1860 she briefly attended a convent school in San Jose, Calif., until objections from the parents of white students forced her to leave. During the Paiute War of 1860 and the subsequent increasingly frequent clashes between Native Americans and whites, she suffered the loss of several family members. She attempted the role of peacemaker on a few occasions and from 1868 to 1871 served as an interpreter at Camp McDermitt in northeastern Nevada. In 1872 she accompanied her tribe to a new reservation, the Malheur, in southeastern Oregon.

Winnemucca for a time was an interpreter for the reservation agent, but the appointment of a new and unsympathetic agent in 1876 ended her service as well as a period of relative quiet on the reservation. On the outbreak of the Bannock War in 1878, she learned that her father and others had been taken hostage and offered to help the army scout the Bannock territory. Covering more than a hundred miles of trail through Idaho and Oregon, Winnemucca located the Bannock camp, spirited her father and many of his companions away, and returned with valuable intelligence for General O.O. Howard. She was scout, aide, and interpreter to Howard during the resulting campaign against the Bannocks.

In 1879 she lectured in San Francisco on the plight of her tribe—many of whose members had been exiled along with belligerent Bannocks to a reservation in Washington Territory—and on the wrongs perpetrated by dishonest civilian Indian agents. Despite slanderous responses by agents and their friends, Winnemucca attracted the attention of President Rutherford B. Hayes. She was promised the return of her people to the Malheur reservation and a severalty allotment of land there, but the order issued to that effect was never executed.

After a year of teaching in a school for Native American children at Vancouver Barracks, Washington Territory, and her marriage late in 1881 to L. H. Hopkins, an army officer, Winnemucca, often known among whites as "the Princess," went on an eastern lecture tour to arouse public opinion. Aided by General Howard, Elizabeth Peabody, and others, the tour was a success, and sales of her *Life Among the Piutes: Their Wrongs and Claims* raised money for Winnemucca's expenses. She secured thousands of signatures on a petition calling for the promised allotment of reservation lands to individual Paiutes. Congress passed a bill to that end in 1884, but once again promises came to nothing. From 1883 to 1886 Winnemucca taught at a Paiute school near Lovelock, Nevada. In 1886 her husband died, and ill herself, Winnemucca moved to a sister's home in Monida, Mont., where she died in 1891.

EMMELINE AND CHRISTABEL PANKHURST

(Respectively, b. July 14, 1858, Manchester, Eng.—d. June 14, 1928, London; b. Sept. 22, 1880, Manchester, Eng.—d. Feb. 13, 1958, Los Angeles, Calif., U.S.)

Emmeline Pankhurst and Christabel Pankhurst were militant crusaders (mother and daughter) for woman suffrage in England. Emmeline's 40-year campaign achieved complete success in the year of her death, when British women obtained full equality in the voting franchise.

In 1879 Emmeline Goulden married Richard Marsden Pankhurst, a lawyer who was a friend of British philosopher and economist John Stuart Mill, as well as the author of the first woman suffrage bill in Great Britain (late 1860s) and of the Married Women's Property acts (1870, 1882). Ten years later she founded the Women's Franchise League, which secured (1894) for married women the right to vote in elections to local offices (not to the House of Commons). From 1895 Emmeline Pankhurst held a succession of municipal offices in Manchester, but her energies were increasingly in demand by the Women's Social and Political Union (WSPU), which she founded with her daughter, Christabel Harriette Pankhurst, in 1903, in Manchester.

Christabel Pankhurst (later Dame Christabel) advocated the use of militant tactics to win the vote for women in England. Reflecting the union's slogan, "Deeds not Words," Pankhurst, with Annie Kenney, unfurled a banner reading "Votes for Women" at a Liberal Party meeting in Manchester on Oct. 13, 1905. Her action received worldwide attention after she and Kenney were thrown out of the meeting for demanding a statement about votes for women. The two were arrested in the street for a technical assault on the police and, after having refused to pay fines, were sent to prison. Christabel subsequently directed a campaign that included direct physical action, hunger strikes, and huge open-air rallies.

Beginning in 1906, Emmeline Pankhurst directed WSPU activities from London. Regarding the Liberal government as the main obstacle to woman suffrage, she campaigned against the party's candidates at elections, and her followers interrupted meetings of Cabinet ministers. In 1908–09 Pankhurst was jailed three times, once for issuing a leaflet calling on the people to "rush the House of Commons." A truce that she declared in 1910 was broken when the government blocked a "conciliation" bill on woman suffrage. From July 1912 the WSPU turned to extreme militancy, mainly in the form of arson directed by Christabel from Paris, where she had gone to avoid arrest for conspiracy. Pankhurst herself was imprisoned, and, under the Prisoners Act of 1913 (the "Cat and Mouse Act"), by which hunger-striking prisoners could be freed for a time and then reincarcerated upon regaining their health to some extent, she was released and rearrested 12 times within a year, serving a total of about 30 days.

With the outbreak of World War I in 1914, Emmeline and Christabel called off the suffrage campaign, and the government released all suffragist prisoners. During the war, Christabel declared a suffrage truce and helped lead the war effort in England. Emmeline, meanwhile, continued to lecture on woman suffrage, visiting the United States, Canada, and Russia to encourage the industrial mobilization of women. She lived in the United States, Canada, and Bermuda for several years after the war. In 1926, upon returning to England, she was chosen Conservative candidate for an east London constituency, but her health failed before she could be elected. The Representation of the People Act of 1928, establishing voting equality for men and women, was passed a few weeks before her death.

Emmeline Pankhurst's autobiography, *My Own Story*, appeared in 1914. In later life, Christabel Pankhurst became a religious evangelist. In 1936 she was created a Dame Commander of the Order of the British Empire.

JANE ADDAMS

(b. Sept. 6, 1860, Cedarville, Ill., U.S.—d. May 21, 1935, Chicago, Ill.)

The American social reformer and pacifist Jane Addams is probably best known as the founder of Hull House in Chicago, one of the first social settlements in North America. She was cowinner (with Nicholas Murray Butler) of the Nobel Prize for Peace in 1931.

Addams graduated from Rockford Female Seminary in Illinois in 1881 and was granted a degree the following year when the institution became Rockford College. Following the death of her father in 1881, her own health problems, and an unhappy year at the Woman's Medical College, Philadelphia, she was an invalid for two years. During neither subsequent travel in Europe in 1883–85 nor her stay in Baltimore, Maryland, in 1885–87 did she find a vocation.

In 1887–88 Addams returned to Europe with a Rockford classmate, Ellen Gates Starr. On a visit to the Toynbee Hall settlement house (founded 1884) in the Whitechapel industrial district in London, Addams's vague leanings toward reform work crystallized. Upon returning to the United States, she and Starr determined to create something like Toynbee Hall. In a working-class immigrant district in Chicago, they acquired a large vacant residence built by Charles Hull in 1856, and, calling it Hull House, they moved into it on Sept. 18, 1889. Eventually the settlement included 13 buildings and a playground, as well as a camp near Lake Geneva, Wisconsin. Many prominent social workers and reformers—Julia Lathrop, Florence Kelley, and Grace and Edith Abbott—came to live at Hull House, as did others who continued to make their living in business or the arts while helping Addams in settlement activities.

Among the facilities at Hull House were a day nursery, a gymnasium, a community kitchen, and a boarding club for working girls. Hull House offered college-level courses in various subjects, furnished training in art, music, and crafts such as bookbinding, and sponsored one of the earliest little-theatre groups, the Hull House Players. In addition to making available services and cultural opportunities for the largely immigrant population of the neighbourhood, Hull House afforded an opportunity for young social workers to acquire training.

Addams worked with labour as well as other reform groups toward goals including the first juvenile-court law, tenement-house regulation, an eight-hour working day for women, factory inspection, and workers' compensation. She strove in addition for justice for immigrants and blacks, advocated research aimed at determining the causes of poverty and crime, and supported woman suffrage. In 1910 she became the first woman president of the National Conference of Social Work, and in 1912 she played an active part in the Progressive Party's presidential campaign for Theodore Roosevelt. At The Hague in 1915 she served as chairman

Her work on behalf of the down-trodden and underserved won activist Jane Addams a Nobel Prize for Peace in 1931. Hulton Archive/ Getty Images

of the International Congress of Women, following which was established the Women's International League for Peace and Freedom. She was also involved in the founding of the American Civil Liberties Union in 1920. In 1931 she was a cowinner of the Nobel Prize for Peace.

The establishment of the Chicago campus of the University of Illinois in 1963 forced the Hull House Association to relocate its headquarters. The majority of its original buildings were demolished, but the Hull residence itself was preserved as a monument to Jane Addams.

Among Addams's books are *Democracy and Social Ethics* (1902), *Newer Ideals of Peace* (1907), *Twenty Years at Hull-House* (1910), and *The Second Twenty Years at Hull-House* (1930).

ANNIE JUMP CANNON

(b. Dec. 11, 1863, Dover, Del., U.S.—d. April 13, 1941, Cambridge, Mass.)

Annie Jump Cannon was an American astronomer who specialized in the classification of stellar spectra.

Cannon was the oldest daughter of Wilson Cannon, a Delaware state senator, and Mary Jump. She studied physics and astronomy at Wellesley College, graduating in 1884. For several years thereafter she traveled and dabbled in photography and music. In 1894 she returned to Wellesley for a year of advanced study in astronomy, and in 1895 she enrolled at Radcliffe in order to continue her studies under Edward C. Pickering, who was director of the Harvard College Observatory.

In 1896 she was named an assistant at the Harvard Observatory, becoming one of a group known as "Pickering's Women." There, joining Williamina P.S. Fleming, Cannon devoted her energies to Pickering's ambitious project, begun in 1885, of recording, classifying, and cataloging the spectra of all stars down to those of the ninth magnitude. The scheme of spectral classification by surface temperature used for the project and later (1910) universally adopted was largely work that Cannon had developed from earlier systems, and she eventually obtained and classified spectra for more than 225,000 stars. Her work was published in nine volumes as the *Henry Draper Catalogue* (1918–24).

In 1911 Cannon succeeded Fleming as curator of astronomical photographs at the observatory, and in 1938 she was named William Cranch Bond Professor of Astronomy. After 1924 she extended her work, cataloging tens of thousands of additional stars down to the 11th magnitude for the two-volume *Henry Draper Extension* (1925, 1949). The work was an invaluable contribution to astronomy, bearing strongly on countless other problems and areas of research and exerting major influence on the evolution of the science of astronomy from one of mere observation to one of great theoretical and philosophical content. In the course of her work Cannon also discovered some 300 variable stars and five novae.

Among the numerous honours and awards accorded her were the first honorary doctorate from the University of Oxford to be awarded to a woman (1925) and the Henry Draper Medal of the National Academy of Sciences in 1931. She was also the first woman to become an officer in the American Astronomical Society. In 1933 she established that organization's Annie J. Cannon Award, which is given to a North American female astronomer (within five years of receiving a doctorate) for her distinguished contribution to astronomy. Cannon officially retired from the observatory in 1940 but carried on research until her death the next year.

MARIE CURIE

(b. Nov. 7, 1867, Warsaw, Poland, Russian Empire — d. July 4, 1934, near Sallanches, France)

The Polish-born French physicist Marie Curie (née Maria Skłodowska) is famous for her work on radioactivity.

She twice won the Nobel Prize: with Henri Becquerel and her husband, Pierre Curie, she was awarded the Nobel Prize for Physics in 1903; and she was the sole winner of the Nobel Prize for Chemistry in 1911. Marie Curie was the first woman to win a Nobel Prize, and she is the only woman to win the award in two different fields.

From childhood Maria Skłodowska was remarkable for her prodigious memory, and at age 16 she won a gold medal on completion of her secondary education at the Russian lycée. Because her father, a teacher of mathematics and physics, lost his savings through bad investment, she had to take work as a teacher and, at the same time, took part clandestinely in the nationalist "free university," reading in Polish to women workers. At 18 she took a post as governess, where she suffered an unhappy love affair. From her earnings she was able to finance her sister Bronisława's medical studies in Paris, on the understanding that Bronisława would in turn later help her to get an education.

In 1891 she went to Paris and, now using the name Marie, began to follow the lectures of Paul Appel, Gabriel Lippmann, and Edmond Bouty at the Sorbonne. There she met physicists who were already well known—Jean Perrin, Charles Maurain, and Aimé Cotton. Skłodowska worked far into the night in her student-quarters garret and virtually lived on bread and butter and tea. She came first in the *licence* of physical sciences in 1893. She began to work in Lippmann's research laboratory and in 1894 was placed second in the *licence* of mathematical sciences. It was in the spring of that year that she met Pierre Curie.

Their marriage (July 25, 1895) marked the start of a partnership that was soon to achieve results of world significance, in particular the discovery of polonium (so called by Marie in honour of her native land) in the summer of 1898 and that of radium a few months later. Following

Henri Becquerel's discovery (1896) of a new phenomenon (which she later called "radioactivity"), Marie Curie, looking for a subject for a thesis, decided to find out if the property discovered in uranium was to be found in other matter. She discovered that this was true for thorium at the same time as G. C. Schmidt did.

Turning her attention to minerals, she found her interest drawn to pitchblende, a mineral whose activity, superior to that of pure uranium, could be explained only by the presence in the ore of small quantities of an unknown substance of very high activity. Pierre Curie then joined her in the work that she had undertaken to resolve this problem and that led to the discovery of the new elements, polonium and radium. While Pierre Curie devoted himself chiefly to the physical study of the new radiations, Marie Curie struggled to obtain pure radium in the metallic state—achieved with the help of the chemist André-Louis Debierne, one of Pierre Curie's pupils. On the results of this research, Marie Curie received her doctorate of science in June 1903 and, with Pierre, was awarded the Davy Medal of the Royal Society. Also in 1903 they shared with Becquerel the Nobel Prize for Physics for the discovery of radioactivity.

The birth of her two daughters, Irène and Ève, in 1897 and 1904 did not interrupt Marie's intensive scientific work. She was appointed lecturer in physics at the École Normale Supérieure for girls in Sèvres (1900) and introduced there a method of teaching based on experimental demonstrations. In December 1904 she was appointed chief assistant in the laboratory directed by Pierre Curie.

The sudden death of Pierre Curie (April 19, 1906) was a bitter blow to Marie Curie, but it was also a decisive turning point in her career: henceforth she was to devote all her energy to completing alone the scientific work that they had undertaken. On May 13, 1906, she was appointed to the professorship that had been left vacant on her husband's death; she was the first woman to teach in the Sorbonne. In 1908 she became titular professor, and in 1910 her fundamental treatise on radioactivity was published. In 1911 she was awarded the Nobel Prize for Chemistry, for the isolation of pure radium. In 1914 she saw the completion of the building of the laboratories of the Radium Institute (Institut du Radium) at the University of Paris.

Throughout World War I, Marie Curie, with the help of her daughter Irène, devoted herself to the development of the use of X-radiography. In 1918 the Radium Institute, the staff of which Irène had joined, began to operate in earnest, and it was to become a universal centre for nuclear physics and chemistry. Marie Curie, now at the highest point of her fame and, from 1922, a member of the Academy of Medicine, devoted her researches to the study of the chemistry of radioactive substances and the medical applications of these substances.

In 1921, accompanied by her two daughters, Marie Curie made a triumphant journey to the United States, where President Warren G. Harding presented her with a gram of radium bought as the result of a collection among American women. She gave lectures, especially in Belgium, Brazil, Spain, and Czechoslovakia. She was made a member of the International Commission on Intellectual Co-operation by the Council of the League of Nations. In addition, she had the satisfaction of seeing the development of the Curie Foundation in Paris and the inauguration in 1932 in Warsaw of the Radium Institute, of which her sister Bronisława became director.

One of Marie Curie's outstanding achievements was to have understood the need to accumulate intense radioactive sources, not only to treat illness but also to maintain an abundant supply for research in nuclear physics; the resultant stockpile was an unrivaled instrument until the appearance after 1930 of particle accelerators. The existence in Paris at the Radium Institute of a stock of 1.5 grams of radium in which, over a period of several years, radium D and polonium had accumulated made a decisive contribution to the success of the experiments undertaken in the years around 1930 and in particular of those performed by Irène Curie in conjunction with Frédéric Joliot, whom she had married in 1926. This work prepared the way for the discovery of the neutron by Sir James Chadwick and, above all, for the discovery in 1934 by Irène and Frédéric Joliot-Curie of artificial radioactivity.

A few months after this discovery, Marie Curie died as a result of leukemia caused by the action of radiation. Her contribution to physics had been immense, not only in her own work, the importance of which had been demonstrated by the award to her of two Nobel Prizes, but because of her influence on subsequent generations of nuclear physicists and chemists.

In 1995 Marie Curie's ashes were enshrined in the Panthéon in Paris; she was the first woman to receive this honour for her own achievements.

GERTRUDE BELL

(b. July 14, 1868, Washington Hall, Durham, Eng.—d. July 12, 1926, Baghdad, Iraq)

The English traveler, administrator, and writer Gertrude Bell played a principal part in the establishment in Baghdad of the Hāshimite dynasty.

Gertrude Margaret Lowthian Bell's brilliant career at Oxford, where she took a first in history in 1887, was followed by some time spent in Tehrān, where her uncle

Sir Frank Lascelles was British minister. Returning to the political and intellectual salons in England and Europe for a decade, she did not until 1899 embark on the career of Arabian activities that made her famous. She visited Palestine and Syria in that year and was often back in the Middle East during the next decade, extending her travels to Asia Minor. But her heart was set on an Arabian journey, which she began in 1913, being the second woman (after Lady Anne Blunt) to visit Ha'il, where she was not favourably received, although she ever afterward favoured the Ibn Rashīd dynasty in its struggle against the Ibn Saʻūd dynasty. She never wrote a full account of this journey, though her literary output during the 20 years preceding World War I had been considerable, including *Safar Nameh* (1894), *Poems from the Divan of Hafiz* (1897), *The Desert and the Sown* (1907), *The Thousand and One Churches* (1909), and *Amurath to Amurath* (1911). Her vast correspondence was published in an edited form in two volumes by her stepmother in 1927.

Perhaps her greatest work was a masterly official report on the administration of Mesopotamia during the difficult period between the Armistice of 1918 and the Iraq rebellion of 1920. After a short period of war work in England and France, she plunged into the rough-and-tumble of Middle East politics, mainly in Mesopotamia, where she served in turn under Sir Percy Cox and Sir Arnold Wilson. She helped place the Hāshimite ruler Fayṣal I on the throne of Iraq in 1921. The last three years of her life were devoted to the creation of an archæological museum in Baghdad. She insisted, for the first time, that antiquities excavated should stay in the country of their origin, thereby ensuring that the National Museum of Iraq, which is her monument in the land she loved, would possess a splendid collection of Iraq's own antiquities. Facing ill health and profound loneliness, Bell took a fatal dose of sleeping pills.

MARIA MONTESSORI

(b. Aug. 31, 1870, Chiaravalle, near Ancona, Italy—d. May 6, 1952, Noordwijk aan Zee, Neth.)

The Italian educator Maria Montessori originated the educational system that bears her name. The Montessori system is based on belief in the creative potential of children, their drive to learn, and their right to be treated as individuals.

After graduating in medicine from the University of Rome in 1896—the first woman in Italy to do so—Montessori was appointed assistant doctor at the psychiatric clinic of the University of Rome, where she became interested in the educational problems of mentally retarded children. Between 1899 and 1901 she served as director of the State Orthophrenic School of Rome, where her methods proved extremely successful. From 1896 to 1906 she held a chair in hygiene at a women's college in Rome, and from 1900 to 1907 she lectured in pedagogy at the University of Rome, holding a chair in anthropology from 1904 to 1908. During these years she continued her studies of philosophy, psychology, and education.

In 1907 Montessori opened the first Casa dei Bambini ("Children's House"), a preschool for children ages three to six from the San Lorenzo slum district of Rome, applying her methods now to children of normal intelligence. Her successes led to the opening of other Montessori schools, and for the next 40 years she travelled throughout Europe, India, and the United States lecturing, writing, and establishing teacher-training programs. In 1922 she was appointed government inspector of schools in Italy, but left the country in 1934 because of the fascist rule. After periods in Spain and Ceylon (now Sri Lanka), she settled in The Netherlands.

Montessori scorned conventional classrooms, where "children, like butterflies mounted on pins, are fastened each to his place." She sought, instead, to teach children by supplying concrete materials and organizing situations conducive to learning with these materials.

She discovered that certain simple materials aroused in young children an interest and attention not previously thought possible. These materials included beads arranged in graduated-number units for premathematics instruction; small slabs of wood designed to train the eye in left-to-right reading movements; and graduated series of cylinders for small-muscle training. Children between three and six years old would work spontaneously with these materials, indifferent to distraction, for from a quarter of an hour to an hour. At the end of such a period, they would not seem tired, as after an enforced effort, but refreshed and calm. Undisciplined children became settled through such voluntary work. The materials used were designed specifically to encourage individual rather than cooperative effort. Group activity occurred in connection with shared housekeeping chores.

A large measure of individual initiative and self-direction characterized the Montessori philosophy, and self-education was the keynote of the plan. The teacher provided and demonstrated the special "didactic apparatus" but remained in the background, leaving the child to handle it for himself. In the Montessori system biological and mental growth are linked. "Periods of sensitivity," corresponding to certain ages, exist when a child's interest and mental capacity are best suited to the acquisition of certain specialized knowledge.

Montessori's methods are set forth in such books as *Il metodo della pedagogia scientifica* (1909; *The Montessori Method*), *The Advanced Montessori Method* (1917–18), *The Secret of Childhood* (1936), *Education for a New World* (1946),

To Educate the Human Potential (1948), and *La mente assorbente* (1949; *The Absorbent Mind*).

ROSA LUXEMBURG

(b. March 5, 1871, Zamość, Pol., Russian Empire [now in Poland]—d. Jan. 15, 1919, Berlin, Ger.)

The Polish-born German revolutionary and agitator Rosa Luxemburg, also called Bloody Rosa (German: Blutige Rosa) played a key role in the founding of the Polish Social Democratic Party and the Spartacus League, which grew into the Communist Party of Germany. As a political theoretician Luxemburg developed a humanitarian theory of Marxism, stressing democracy and revolutionary mass action to achieve international socialism.

Rosa Luxemburg was the youngest of five children of a lower middle-class Jewish family in Russian-ruled Poland. She became involved in underground activities while still in high school. Like many of her radical contemporaries from the Russian Empire who were faced with prison, she emigrated to Zürich (1889), where she studied law and political economy, receiving a doctorate in 1898.

In Zürich she became involved in the international socialist movement and met Georgy Valentinovich Plekhanov, Pavel Axelrod, and other leading representatives of the Russian social democratic movement, with whom, however, she soon began to disagree. Together with a fellow student, Leo Jogiches, who was to become a lifelong friend and sometime lover, she challenged both the Russians and the established Polish Socialist Party because of their support of Polish independence. Consequently, she and her colleagues founded the rival Polish Social Democratic Party, which was to become the nucleus of the future Polish Communist Party. The national issue became one of Luxemburg's main themes. To her, nationalism and national independence were regressive concessions to the class enemy, the bourgeoisie. She consistently underrated nationalist aspirations and stressed socialist international-ism. This became one of her major points of disagreement with Vladimir Lenin and his theory of national self-determination.

In 1898, after marrying Gustav Lübeck to obtain German citizenship, she settled in Berlin to work with the largest and most powerful constituent party of the Second International, the Social Democratic Party of Germany. Almost at once, she jumped into the revisionist controversy that divided the party. In 1898 the German revisionist Eduard Bernstein had argued that Marxist theory was essentially outdated and that socialism in highly industrialized nations could best be achieved through a gradualist approach, using trade-union activity and parliamentary politics. Luxemburg denied categorically this approach in *Sozialreform oder Revolution?* (1889; *Reform or Revolution?*), in which she defended Marxist orthodoxy and the necessity of revolution, arguing that parliament was nothing more than a bourgeois sham. Karl Kautsky, the leading theoretician of the Second International, agreed with her, and revisionism consequently became a socialist heresy both in Germany and abroad, though it continued to make headway, especially in the labour movement.

The Russian Revolution of 1905 proved to be the central experience in Rosa Luxemburg's life. Until then, she had believed that Germany was the country in which world revolution was most likely to originate. She now believed it would catch fire in Russia. She went to Warsaw, participated in the struggle, and was imprisoned. From these experiences emerged her theory of revolutionary mass action, which she propounded in *Massenstreik, Partei und Gewerkschaften* (1906; *The Mass Strike, the Political Party, and the Trade*

Unions). Luxemburg advocated the mass strike as the single most important tool of the proletariat, Western as well as Russian, in attaining a socialist victory. The mass strike, the spontaneous result of "objective conditions," would radicalize the workers and drive the revolution forward. In contrast to Lenin, she deemphasized the need for a tight party structure, believing that organization would emerge naturally from the struggle. For this, she has been repeatedly chastised by orthodox communist parties.

Released from her Warsaw prison, she taught at the Social Democratic Party school in Berlin (1907–14), where she wrote *Die Akkumulation des Kapitals* (1913; *The Accumulation of Capital*). In this analysis, she described imperialism as the result of a dynamic capitalism's expansion into underdeveloped areas of the world. It was during this time also that she began to agitate for mass actions and broke completely with the established Social Democratic party leadership of August Bebel and Kautsky, who disagreed with her incessant drive toward proletarian radicalization.

The Social Democratic Party backed the German government at the outbreak of World War I, but Rosa Luxemburg immediately went into opposition. In an alliance with Karl Liebknecht and other like-minded radicals, she formed the Spartakusbund, or Spartacus League, which was dedicated to ending the war through revolution and the establishment of a proletarian government. The organization's theoretical basis was Luxemburg's pamphlet *Die Krise der Sozialdemokratie* (1916; *The Crisis in the German Social Democracy*), written in prison under the pseudonym Junius. In this work she agreed with Lenin in advocating the overthrow of the existing regime and the formation of a new International strong enough to prevent a renewed outbreak of mass slaughter. The actual influence of the Spartacus group during the war, however, remained small.

Released from prison by the German revolution (November 1918), Luxemburg and Liebknecht immediately began agitation to force the new order to the left. They exercised considerable influence on the public and were a contributing factor in a number of armed clashes in Berlin. Like the Bolsheviks, Luxemburg and Liebknecht demanded political power for the workers' and soldiers' soviets but were frustrated by the conservative Socialist establishment and the army. In late December 1918, they became founders of the German Communist Party, but Luxemburg attempted to limit Bolshevik influence in this new organization. In fact, her *Die Russische Revolution* (1922; *The Russian Revolution*) chastised Lenin's party on its agrarian and national self-determination stands and its dictatorial and terrorist methods. Luxemburg always remained a believer in democracy as opposed to Lenin's democratic centralism. She was never able, however, to exercise a decisive influence on the new party, for she and Liebknecht were assassinated in 1919 by reactionary troops.

COLETTE

(b. Jan. 28, 1873, Saint-Sauveur-en-Puisaye, France—d. Aug. 3, 1954, Paris)

Colette is one of the outstanding French writers of the first half of the 20th century, whose best novels, largely concerned with the pains and pleasures of love, are remarkable for their command of sensual description. Her greatest strength as a writer is an exact sensory evocation of sounds, smells, tastes, textures, and colours of her world.

Sidonie-Gabrielle Colette was reared in a village in Burgundy, where her much-loved mother awakened her to the wonders of the natural world—everything that "germinates, blossoms, or flies." At age 20 and ill-prepared for both married life and the Paris scene, Colette married the writer and critic Henri Gauthier-Villars ("Willy"), 15 years her senior. He introduced her to the world of Parisian salons and the demimonde, and, not long after their marriage, he discovered her talent for writing.

Locking her in a room to encourage her to focus on the task at hand, Willy forced her to write — but published as his own work — the four "Claudine" novels, *Claudine à l'école* (1900; *Claudine at School*), *Claudine à Paris* (1901; *Claudine in Paris*), *Claudine en menage* (1902; republished as *Claudine amoureuse*, translated as *The Indulgent Husband*), and *Claudine s'en va: Journal d'Annie* (1903; *The Innocent Wife*). For these novels, Colette drew on her own experiences, both as a girl from the provinces and as a young married woman with a libertine husband, to produce scenes from the life of the young ingénue. Both Claudine and the passive, domestic Annie, who narrates the fourth Claudine book, reappear in Colette's *La Retraite sentimentale* (1907; *Retreat from Love*), which was published under the name Colette Willy.

Colette left Willy in 1906. Though her slightly salacious novels were wildly popular, as were the plays derived from them, she saw none of her earnings; Willy kept the royalties. Ever resourceful, she took a job as a music-hall performer, working long hours to keep poverty at bay. During these years (roughly 1906–10), she was involved with the Marquise de Balbeuf ("Missy"), an independently wealthy lesbian who affected male dress and mocked the masculine manner. This period of her life inspired *La Vagabonde* (1910; *The Vagabond*) and *L'Envers du music-hall* (1913; *Music-Hall Sidelights*). She was finally divorced from Willy in 1910, and in 1912 she married Henry de Jouvenel, editor in chief of the paper *Le Matin*, to which she contributed theatre chronicles and short stories. Their daughter (b. 1913) is the Bel-Gazou of the delightful animal story *La Paix chez les bêtes* (1916; some stories translated as *Dogs, Cats, & I*).

The writings she published up to this point belong to what Colette called her years of apprenticeship; she wrote of them in *Mes Apprentissages* (1936; *My Apprenticeships*). Her best work was produced after 1920 and followed two veins. The first vein followed the lives of the slightly depraved, postwar younger generation. Among these novels are *Chéri* (1920) and *La Fin de Chéri* (1926; *The Last of Chéri*), dealing with a liaison between a young man (Chéri) and an older woman, and *Le Blé en herbe* (1923; *The Ripening Seed*), which concerns a tender and acid initiation to love. The second vein looked back to the countryside of her enchanted childhood and away from the pleasures and disillusions of shallow love affairs. *La Maison de Claudine* (1922; *My Mother's House*) and *Sido* (1930) are her poetic meditations on these years.

After 1930 her life was both productive and serene. In 1935, having divorced de Jouvenel the previous year, she married the writer Maurice Goudeket. The marriage brought much happiness, as Goudeket recorded in his memoirs *Près de Colette* (1955; *Close to Colette*). During her last two decades, Colette wrote on a number of topics. In *Ces Plaisirs* (1932; "Those Pleasures," later published as *Le Pur et l'impur* [1941; *The Pure and the Impure*]), she examined aspects of female sexuality. *La Chatte* (1933; *The Cat*) and *Duo* (1934) are treatments of jealousy. *Gigi* (1944), the story of a girl reared by two elderly sisters to become a courtesan, was adapted for both stage and screen. A charming musical film version of 1958, starring Maurice Chevalier, Louis Jourdan, and a winsome Leslie Caron, enjoyed great popularity.

Colette was made a member of the Belgian Royal Academy (1935) and the French Académie Goncourt (1945) and a grand officer of the Legion of Honour—all honours rarely granted to women.

A delicate and humorous realist, Colette was the annalist of female existence. She wrote chiefly of women in traditional roles, such as husband hunters or discarded, aging, or déclassé mistresses. Her chosen format was the novella, her style a blend of the sophisticated and the natural, laced with all the subtle cadences of sensuous pleasures and intuitive acumen. From 1949 she was increasingly crippled by arthritis. She ended her days, a legendary figure surrounded by her beloved cats, confined to her beautiful Palais-Royal apartment overlooking Paris.

GERTRUDE STEIN

(b. Feb. 3, 1874, Allegheny City [now in Pittsburgh], Pa., U.S.— d. July 27, 1946, Neuilly-sur-Seine, France)

The eccentric Modernist writer and self-styled genius Gertrude Stein was known less for her writing than for the salon she held in her Paris home in the period between World Wars I and II.

Stein spent her infancy in Vienna and in Passy, France, and her girlhood in Oakland, California. She entered the Society for the Collegiate Instruction of Women (renamed Radcliffe College in 1894), where she studied psychology with the philosopher William James, and received her degree in 1898. She studied at Johns Hopkins Medical School from 1897 to 1902 and then, with her older brother Leo, moved first to London and then to Paris, where she was able to live by private means. She lived with Leo, who became an accomplished art critic, until 1909; thereafter she lived with her lifelong companion Alice B. Toklas (1877–1967).

Stein and her brother were among the first collectors of works by the Cubists and other experimental painters of the period, such as Pablo Picasso (who painted her portrait), Henri Matisse, and Georges Braque, several of whom became her friends. At her salon they mingled with expatriate American writers whom she dubbed the "Lost Generation," including Sherwood Anderson and Ernest Hemingway, and other visitors drawn by her literary reputation. Her literary and artistic judgments were revered, and her chance remarks could make or destroy reputations.

In her own work, she attempted to parallel the theories of Cubism, specifically in her concentration on the illumination of the present moment (for which she often relied on the present perfect tense) and her use of slightly varied repetitions and extreme simplification and fragmentation. The best explanation of her theory of writing is found in the essay *Composition and Explanation*, which is based on lectures that she gave at the Universities of Oxford and Cambridge and was issued as a book in 1926. Among her work that was most thoroughly influenced by Cubism is *Tender Buttons* (1914), which carries fragmentation and abstraction to an extreme.

Her first published book, *Three Lives* (1909), the stories of three working-class women, has been called a minor masterpiece. *The Making of Americans*, a long composition written in 1906–11 but not published until 1925, was too convoluted and obscure for general readers, for whom she remained essentially the author of such lines as "Rose is a rose is a rose is a rose." Her only book to reach a wide public was *The Autobiography of Alice B. Toklas* (1933), actually Stein's own autobiography. The performance in the United States of her *Four Saints in Three Acts* (1934), which the composer Virgil Thomson had made into an opera, led to a triumphal American lecture tour in 1934–35. Thomson also wrote the music for her second opera, *The Mother of Us All* (published 1947), based on the life of feminist Susan

B. Anthony. One of Stein's early short stories, "Q.E.D.," was first published in *Things as They Are* (1950).

The eccentric Stein was not modest in her self-estimation: "Einstein was the creative philosophic mind of the century, and I have been the creative literary mind of the century." She became a legend in Paris, especially after surviving the German occupation of France and befriending the many young American servicemen who visited her. She wrote about these soldiers in *Brewsie and Willie* (1946).

ISADORA DUNCAN

(b. May 26, 1877 or May 27, 1878, San Francisco, Calif., U.S.—d. Sept. 14, 1927, Nice, France)

The American dancer Isadora Duncan (born Angela Duncan) helped free ballet from its conservative restrictions through her teaching and performances and presaged the development of modern expressive dance. She was among the first to raise interpretive dance to the status of creative art.

Although Duncan's birth date is generally believed to have been May 27, 1878, her baptismal certificate, discovered in San Francisco in 1976, records the date of May 26, 1877. She was one of four children brought up in genteel poverty by their mother, a music teacher. As a child she rejected the rigidity of the classic ballet and based her dancing on more natural rhythms and movements, an approach she later used consciously in her interpretations of the works of such great composers as Brahms, Wagner, and Beethoven. Her earliest public appearances, in Chicago and New York City, met with little success, and at age 21 she left the United States to seek recognition abroad. With her meagre savings she sailed on a cattle boat for England.

At the British Museum her study of the sculptures of ancient Greece confirmed the classical use of those dance movements and gestures that hitherto instinct alone had caused her to practice and upon a revival of which her method was largely founded. Through the patronage of the celebrated actress Mrs. Patrick Campbell, she was invited to appear at the private receptions of London's leading hostesses, where her dancing, distinguished by a complete freedom of movement, enraptured those who were familiar only with the conventional forms of the ballet, which was then in a period of decay. It was not long before the phenomenon of a young woman dancing barefoot, as scantily clad as a woodland nymph, crowded theatres and concert halls throughout Europe. During her controversial first tour of Russia in 1905, Duncan made a deep impression on the choreographer Michel Fokine and on the art critic Serge Diaghilev, who as impresario was soon to lead a resurgence of ballet throughout western Europe. Duncan toured widely, and at one time or another she founded dance schools in Germany, Russia, and the United States, though none of these survived.

Her private life, quite as much as her art, kept her name in the headlines owing to her constant defiance of social taboos. The father of her first child, Deirdre, was the stage designer Gordon Craig, who shared her abhorrence of marriage; the father of her second child, Patrick, was Paris Singer, the heir to a sewing machine fortune and a prominent art patron. In 1913 a tragedy occurred from which Duncan never really recovered: The car in which her two children and their nurse were riding in Paris rolled into the Seine River and all three were drowned.

In an effort to sublimate her grief she was about to open another school when the advent of World War I put an end to her plans. Her subsequent tours in South America, Germany, and France were less successful than

Expressive movement, which stretched the boundaries of traditional dance in the late 19th century, was American dancer Isadora Duncan's stock in trade. Hulton Archive/Getty Images

before, but in 1920 she was invited to establish a school of her own in Moscow. To her revolutionary temperament, the Soviet Union seemed the land of promise. There she met Sergey Aleksandrovich Yesenin, a poet 17 years younger than she, whose work had won him a considerable reputation. She married him in 1922, sacrificing her scruples against marriage in order to take him with her on a tour of the United States. She could not have chosen a worse time for their arrival. Fear of the "Red Menace" was at its height, and she and her husband were unjustly labeled as Bolshevik agents. Leaving her native country once more, a bitter Duncan told reporters: "Good-bye America, I shall never see you again!" She never did. There followed an unhappy period with Yesenin in Europe, where his increasing mental instability turned him against her. He returned alone to the Soviet Union and, in 1925, committed suicide.

During the last years of her life Duncan was a somewhat pathetic figure, living precariously in Nice on the French Riviera, where she met with a fatal accident: her long scarf became entangled in the rear wheel of the car in which she was riding, and she was strangled. Her autobiography, *My Life*, was published in 1927 (reissued 1972).

Isadora Duncan was acclaimed by the foremost musicians, artists, and writers of her day, but she was often an object of attack by the less broad-minded. Her ideas were too much in advance of their time, and she flouted social conventions too flamboyantly to be regarded by the wider public as anything but an advocate of "free love." Certainly her place as a great innovator in dance is secure: her repudiation of artificial technical restrictions and reliance on the grace of natural movement helped to liberate the dance from its dependence on rigid formulas and on displays of brilliant but empty technical virtuosity, paving the way for the later acceptance of modern dance as it was developed by Mary Wigman, Martha Graham, and others.

MARGARET SANGER

(b. Sept. 14, 1879, Corning, N.Y., U.S.—d. Sept. 6, 1966, Tucson, Ariz.)

Margaret Sanger founded the birth-control movement in the United States and was an international leader in the field. In fact, she is credited with originating the term "birth control."

The sixth of 11 children, Margaret Louisa Higgins attended Claverack College and then took nurse's training in New York at the White Plains Hospital and the Manhattan Eye and Ear Clinic. She was married twice, to William Sanger in 1900 and, after a divorce, to J. Noah H. Slee in 1922. After a brief teaching career she practiced obstetrical nursing on the Lower East Side of New York City, where she witnessed the relationships among poverty, uncontrolled fertility, high rates of infant and maternal mortality, and deaths from botched illegal abortions. These observations made Sanger a feminist who believed in every woman's right to avoid unwanted pregnancies, and she devoted herself to removing the legal barriers to publicizing the facts about contraception.

In 1912 Sanger gave up nursing to devote herself to the cause of birth control. In 1914 she issued a short-lived magazine, *The Woman Rebel*, and distributed a pamphlet, *Family Limitation*, advocating her views. She was indicted for mailing materials advocating birth control, but the charges were dropped in 1916. Later that year she opened in Brooklyn the first birth-control clinic in the United States. She was arrested and charged with maintaining a "public nuisance," and in 1917 she served 30 days in the

Queens penitentiary. While she was serving time, the first issue of her periodical *The Birth Control Review* was published. Her sentencing and subsequent episodes of legal harrassment helped to crystallize public opinion in favour of the birth-control movement. Sanger's legal appeals prompted the federal courts first to grant physicians the right to give advice about birth-control methods and then, in 1936, to reinterpret the Comstock Act of 1873 (which had classified contraceptive literature and devices as obscene materials) in such a way as to permit physicians to import and prescribe contraceptives.

In 1921 Sanger founded the American Birth Control League, and she served as its president until 1928. The league was one of the parent organizations of the Birth Control Federation of America, which in 1942 became the Planned Parenthood Federation of America, with Sanger as honorary chairman. Sanger, who had traveled to Europe to study the issue of birth control there, also organized the first World Population Conference in Geneva in 1927, and she was the first president of the International Planned Parenthood Federation (founded 1953). Subsequently she took her campaign for birth control to Asian countries, especially India and Japan.

Among her numerous books are *What Every Mother Should Know* (1917), *My Fight for Birth Control* (1931), and *Margaret Sanger: An Autobiography* (1938).

HELEN KELLER

(b. June 27, 1880, Tuscumbia, Ala., U.S. — d. June 1, 1968, Westport, Conn.)

The American author and educator Helen Keller was blind and deaf. Her education and training represent an extraordinary accomplishment in the education of people with these disabilities.

Helen Keller (left) *with her teacher, Anne Sullivan.* Library of Congress, Washington, D.C.

Helen Adams Keller was afflicted at the age of 19 months with an illness (possibly scarlet fever) that left her blind, deaf, and mute. At age six she was examined by the Scottish-born American audiologist Alexander Graham Bell, who sent to her a 20-year-old teacher, Anne Sullivan (Macy) from the Perkins Institution for the Blind in Boston, which Bell's son-in-law directed. Sullivan, a remarkable teacher, remained with Keller from March 1887 until her own death in October 1936.

Within months Keller had learned to feel objects and associate them with words spelled out by finger signals on her palm, to read sentences by feeling raised words on cardboard, and to make her own sentences by arranging words in a frame. During 1888–90 she spent winters at the Perkins Institution learning braille. Then she began a slow process of learning to speak under Sarah Fuller of the Horace Mann School for the Deaf, also in Boston. She also learned to lip-read by placing her fingers on the lips and throat of the speaker while the words were simultaneously spelled out for her. At age 14 she enrolled in the Wright-Humason School for the Deaf in New York City, and at 16 she entered the Cambridge School for Young Ladies in Massachusetts. She won admission to Radcliffe College in 1900 and graduated cum laude in 1904.

Having developed skills never approached by any similarly disabled person, Keller began to write of blindness, a subject then taboo in women's magazines because of the relationship of many cases to venereal disease. Edward W. Bok accepted her articles for the *Ladies' Home Journal*, and other major magazines—*The Century*, *McClure's*, and *The Atlantic Monthly*—followed suit.

She wrote of her life in several books, including *The Story of My Life* (1903), *Optimism* (1903), *The World I Live In* (1908), *My Religion* (1927), *Helen Keller's Journal* (1938), and

The Open Door (1957). In 1913 she began lecturing (with the aid of an interpreter), primarily on behalf of the American Foundation for the Blind, for which she later established a $2 million endowment fund, and her lecture tours took her several times around the world. Her efforts to improve treatment of the deaf and the blind were influential in removing the disabled from asylums. She also prompted the organization of commissions for the blind in 30 states by 1937. Keller's childhood training with Anne Sullivan was depicted in William Gibson's play *The Miracle Worker* (New York opening, Oct. 19, 1959), which won the Pulitzer Prize in 1960 and was subsequently made into a motion picture (1962) that won two Academy Awards.

MARIE STOPES

(b. Oct. 15, 1880, Edinburgh, Scot.—d. Oct. 2, 1958, near Dorking, Surrey, Eng.)

Marie Stopes (in full Marie Charlotte Carmichael Stopes) was an advocate of birth control who, in 1921, founded the United Kingdom's first instructional clinic for contraception. Although her clinical work, writings, and speeches evoked violent opposition, especially from Roman Catholics, she greatly influenced the Church of England's gradual relaxation (from 1930) of its stand against birth control.

Stopes grew up in a wealthy, educated family; her father was an architect, her mother a scholar of Shakespeare and an advocate for the education of women. Stopes obtained a science degree (1902) from University College, London, which she completed in only two years. She went on to do postgraduate studies in paleobotany (fossil plants), earning a doctorate from the University of Munich in 1904. That same year she became an assistant lecturer of botany at the University of Manchester. She specialized in fossil plants and the problems of coal mining.

She married her first husband, a botanist named Reginald Ruggles Gates, in 1911. Stopes would later assert that her marriage was unconsummated and that she knew little about sex when she first married. Her failed marriage and its eventual annulment in 1916 played a large role in determining her future career, causing her to turn her attention to the issues of sex, marriage, and childbirth and their meaning in society. She initially saw birth control as an aid to marriage fulfillment and as a means to save women from the physical strain of excessive childbearing. In this regard for quality of life of the individual woman, she differed from most other early leaders of the birth-control movement, who were more concerned with social good, such as the elimination of overpopulation and poverty.

In 1918 Stopes married Humphrey Verdon Roe, cofounder of the A.V. Roe aircraft firm, who also had strong interests in the birth-control movement. He helped her in the crusade that she then began. Their original birth-control clinic—designed to educate women about the few methods of birth control available to them—was founded three years later, in the working-class Holloway district of London. That same year she became founder and president of the Society for Constructive Birth Control, a platform from which she spoke widely about the benefits of married women having healthy, desired babies. In the meantime she wrote *Married Love* and *Wise Parenthood* (both 1918), which were widely translated. Her *Contraception: Its Theory, History and Practice* (1923) was, when it first appeared, the most comprehensive treatment of the subject. After World War II she promoted birth control in East Asian countries.

ANNA PAVLOVA

(b. Jan. 31 [Feb. 12, New Style], 1881, St. Petersburg, Russia—d. Jan. 23, 1931, The Hague, Neth.)

The Russian ballerina Anna Pavlovna Pavlova was the most celebrated dancer of her time. Pavlova studied at the Imperial School of Ballet at the Mariinsky Theatre from 1891, joined the Imperial Ballet in 1899, and became a prima ballerina in 1906. In 1909 she went to Paris on the historic tour of the Ballets Russes. After 1913 she danced independently with her own company throughout the world.

The place and time of Pavlova's birth could hardly have been better for a child with an innate talent for dancing. Tsarist Russia maintained magnificent imperial schools for the performing arts. Entry was by examination, and, although Pavlova's mother was poor—Anna's father had died when she was two years old—the child was accepted for training at the Imperial School of Ballet at the Mariinsky Theatre in St. Petersburg in 1891.

Following ballet tradition, Pavlova learned her art from teachers who were themselves great dancers. She graduated to the Imperial Ballet in 1899 and rose steadily through the grades to become prima ballerina in 1906. By this time she had already danced *Giselle* with considerable success.

Almost immediately, in 1907, the pattern of her life began to emerge. That year, with a few other dancers, she went on a European tour to Riga, Stockholm, Copenhagen, Berlin, and Prague. She was acclaimed, and another tour took place in 1908. In 1909 the impresario Serge Diaghilev staged a historic season of Russian ballet in Paris, and Pavlova appeared briefly with the company there and later in London. But her experience of touring with a small group had given her a taste for independence, and she never became part of Diaghilev's closely knit Ballets Russes. Her destiny was not, as was theirs, to innovate but simply to show the beauties of classical ballet throughout the world. While she was still taking leave from the Mariinsky Theatre, she danced in New York City and London in 1910 with Mikhail Mordkin.

Once she left the Imperial Ballet in 1913, her frontiers were extended. For the rest of her life, with various partners (including Laurent Novikov and Pierre Vladimirov) and companies, she was a wandering missionary for her art, giving a vast number of people their introduction to ballet. Whatever the limitations of the rest of the company, which inevitably was largely a well-trained, dedicated band of young disciples, Pavlova's own performances left those who watched them with a lasting memory of disciplined grace, poetic movement, and incarnate magic. Her quality was, above all, the powerful and elusive one of true glamour.

Pavlova's independent tours, which began in 1914, took her to remote parts of the world. These tours were managed by her husband, Victor Dandré. The repertoire of Anna Pavlova's company was in large part conventional. They danced excerpts or adaptations of Mariinsky successes such as *Don Quixote, La Fille mal gardée* ("The Girl Poorly Managed"), *The Fairy Doll*, or *Giselle*, of which she was an outstanding interpreter. The most famous numbers, however, were the succession of ephemeral solos, which were endowed by her with an inimitable enchantment: *The Dragonfly, Californian Poppy, Gavotte*, and *Christmas* are names that lingered in the thoughts of her audiences, together with her single choreographic endeavour, *Autumn Leaves* (1918).

Pavlova's enthusiasm for ethnic dances was reflected in her programs. Polish, Russian, and Mexican dances were performed. Her visits to India and Japan led her to a serious study of their dance techniques. She compiled these studies into *Oriental Impressions*, collaborating on the Indian scenes with Uday Shankar, later to become one of the greatest performers of Indian dance, and in this way playing an important part in the renaissance of the dance in India.

Because she was the company's raison d'être, the source of its public appeal, and, therefore, its financial stability, Pavlova's burden was extreme. It was hardly surprising, therefore, that, by the end of her life, her technique was faltering, and she was relying increasingly on her unique qualities of personality.

Pavlova's personal life was undramatic apart from occasional professional headlines, as when, in 1911, she quarreled with Mordkin. For some time she kept secret her marriage to her manager, Victor Dandré, and there were no children; her maternal instincts spent themselves on her company and on a home for Russian refugee orphans, which she founded in Paris in 1920. She loved birds and animals. Her home in London, Ivy House, Hampstead, became famous for the ornamental lake with swans, beside which she was photographed and filmed, recalling her most famous solo, *The Dying Swan*, which the choreographer Michel Fokine had created for her in 1905. These film sequences are among the few extant of her and are included in a compilation called *The Immortal Swan*, together with some extracts from her solos filmed one afternoon in Hollywood, in 1924, by the actor Douglas Fairbanks, Sr.

VIRGINIA WOOLF

(b. Jan. 25, 1882, London, Eng.—d. March 28, 1941, near Rodmell, Sussex)

English writer Virginia Woolf is noted mainly for a group of novels that through their nonlinear approaches to narrative, exerted a major influence on the genre. While she is best known for her novels, especially *Mrs. Dalloway* (1925) and *To the Lighthouse* (1927), Woolf also wrote pioneering essays on artistic theory, literary history, women's writing, and the politics of power. A fine stylist, she experimented with several forms of biographical writing, composed painterly short fictions, and sent to her friends and family a lifetime of brilliant letters.

EARLY LIFE AND INFLUENCES

Born Adeline Virginia Stephen, she was the child of ideal Victorian parents. Her father, Leslie Stephen, was an eminent literary figure and the first editor (1882–91) of the *Dictionary of National Biography*. Her mother, Julia Jackson, possessed great beauty and a reputation for saintly self-sacrifice; she also had prominent social and artistic connections, which included Julia Margaret Cameron, her aunt and one of the greatest portrait photographers of the 19th century. Both Jackson's first husband, Herbert Duckworth, and Stephen's first wife, a daughter of the novelist William Makepeace Thackeray, had died unexpectedly, leaving her three children and him one.

Julia Jackson Duckworth and Leslie Stephen married in 1878, and four children followed: Vanessa (born 1879), Thoby (born 1880), Virginia (born 1882), and Adrian (born 1883). While these four children banded together against their older half siblings, loyalties shifted among them. Virginia was jealous of Adrian for being their mother's favourite. At age nine, she was the genius behind a family newspaper, the *Hyde Park Gate News*, that often teased Vanessa and Adrian. Vanessa mothered the others, especially Virginia, but the dynamic between need (Virginia's) and aloofness (Vanessa's) sometimes expressed itself as rivalry between Virginia's art of writing and Vanessa's of painting.

The Stephen family made summer migrations from their London town house near Kensington Gardens to the rather disheveled Talland House on the rugged Cornwall coast. That annual relocation structured Virginia's childhood world in terms of opposites: city and country, winter and summer, repression and freedom, fragmentation and wholeness. Her neatly divided, predictable world ended, however, when her mother died in 1895 at age 49. Virginia, at 13, ceased writing amusing accounts of family news. Almost a year passed before she wrote a cheerful letter to her brother Thoby. She was just emerging from depression when, in 1897, her half sister Stella Duckworth died at age 28, an event Virginia noted in her diary as "impossible to write of." Then in 1904, after her father died, Virginia had a nervous breakdown.

While Virginia was recovering, Vanessa supervised the Stephen children's move to the bohemian Bloomsbury section of London. There the siblings lived independent of their Duckworth half brothers, free to pursue studies, to paint or write, and to entertain. Leonard Woolf dined with them in November 1904, just before sailing to Ceylon (now Sri Lanka) to become a colonial administrator. Soon the Stephens hosted weekly gatherings of radical young people, including Clive Bell, Lytton Strachey, and John Maynard Keynes, all later to achieve fame as, respectively, an art critic, a biographer, and an economist.

Then, after a family excursion to Greece in 1906, Thoby died of typhoid fever. He was 26. Virginia grieved but did not slip into depression. She overcame the loss of Thoby and the "loss" of Vanessa, who became engaged to Bell just after Thoby's death, through writing. Vanessa's marriage (and perhaps Thoby's absence) helped transform conversation at the avant-garde gatherings of what came to be known as the Bloomsbury group into irreverent, sometimes bawdy repartee that inspired Virginia to exercise her wit publicly, even while privately she was writing her poignant *Reminiscences*—about her childhood and her lost mother—which was published in 1908. Viewing Italian art that summer, she committed herself to creating in language "some kind of whole made of shivering fragments," to capturing "the flight of the mind."

EARLY FICTION

Virginia Stephen determined in 1908 to "re-form" the novel by creating a holistic form embracing aspects of life that were "fugitive" from the Victorian novel. While writing anonymous reviews for the *Times Literary Supplement* and other journals, she experimented with such a novel, which she called *Melymbrosia*. In November 1910, Roger Fry, a new friend of the Bells, launched the exhibit "Manet and the Post-Impressionists," which introduced radical European art to the London bourgeoisie. Virginia was at once outraged over the attention that painting garnered and intrigued by the possibility of borrowing from the likes of artists Paul Cézanne and Pablo Picasso. As Clive Bell was unfaithful, Vanessa began an affair with Fry, and Fry began a lifelong debate with Virginia about the visual and verbal arts.

In the summer of 1911, Leonard Woolf returned from the East. After he resigned from the colonial service, Leonard and Virginia married in August 1912. She continued to work on her first novel; he wrote the anticolonialist novel *The Village in the Jungle* (1913) and *The Wise Virgins* (1914), a Bloomsbury exposé. Then he became a political writer and an advocate for peace and justice.

Between 1910 and 1915, Virginia's mental health was precarious. Nevertheless, she completely recast *Melymbrosia*

Dust jacket designed by Vanessa Bell for the first edition of Virginia Woolf's To the Lighthouse, *published by the Hogarth Press in 1927.* Between the Covers Rare Books, Merchantville, N.J.

as *The Voyage Out* in 1913. She based many of her novel's characters on real-life prototypes: Lytton Strachey, Leslie Stephen, her half brother George Duckworth, Clive and Vanessa Bell, and herself. Rachel Vinrace, the novel's central character, is a sheltered young woman who, on an excursion to South America, is introduced to freedom and sexuality (though from the novel's inception she was to die before marrying). Woolf first made Terence, Rachel's suitor, rather Clive-like; as she revised, Terence became a more sensitive, Leonard-like character. After an excursion up the Amazon, Rachel contracts a terrible illness that plunges her into delirium and then death. As possible causes for this disaster, Woolf's characters suggest everything from poorly washed vegetables to jungle disease to a malevolent universe, but the book endorses no explanation. That indeterminacy, at odds with the certainties of the Victorian era, is echoed in descriptions that distort perception: while the narrative often describes people, buildings, and natural objects as featureless forms, Rachel, in dreams and then delirium, journeys into surrealistic worlds. Rachel's voyage into the unknown began Woolf's voyage beyond the conventions of realism.

Woolf's manic-depressive worries (that she was a failure as a writer and a woman, that she was despised by Vanessa and unloved by Leonard) provoked a suicide attempt in September 1913. Publication of *The Voyage Out* was delayed until early 1915; then, that April, she sank into a distressed state in which she was often delirious. Later that year she overcame the "vile imaginations" that had threatened her sanity. She kept the demons of mania and depression mostly at bay for the rest of her life.

In 1917 the Woolfs bought a printing press and founded the Hogarth Press, named for Hogarth House, their home in the London suburbs. The Woolfs themselves (she was the compositor while he worked the press) published their own *Two Stories* in the summer of 1917. It consisted of Leonard's *Three Jews* and Virginia's *The Mark on the Wall*, the latter about contemplation itself.

Since 1910, Virginia had kept (sometimes with Vanessa) a country house in Sussex, and in 1916 Vanessa settled into a Sussex farmhouse called Charleston. She had ended her affair with Fry to take up with the painter Duncan Grant, who moved to Charleston with Vanessa and her children, Julian and Quentin Bell; a daughter, Angelica, would be born to Vanessa and Grant at the end of 1918. Charleston soon became an extravagantly decorated, unorthodox retreat for artists and writers, especially Clive Bell, who continued on friendly terms with Vanessa, and Fry, Vanessa's lifelong devotee.

Virginia had kept a diary, off and on, since 1897. In 1919 she envisioned "the shadow of some kind of form which a diary might attain to," organized not by a mechanical recording of events but by the interplay between the objective and the subjective. Her diary, as she wrote in 1924, would reveal people as "splinters & mosaics; not, as they used to hold, immaculate, monolithic, consistent wholes." Such terms later inspired critical distinctions, based on anatomy and culture, between the feminine and the masculine, the feminine being a varied but all-embracing way of experiencing the world and the masculine a mono-lithic or linear way. Critics using these distinctions have credited Woolf with evolving a distinctly feminine diary form, one that explores, with perception, honesty, and humour, her own ever-changing, mosaic self.

Proving that she could master the traditional form of the novel before breaking it, she plotted her next novel in two romantic triangles, with its protagonist Katharine in both. *Night and Day* (1919) answers Leonard's *The Wise Virgins*, in which he had his Leonard-like protagonist lose the Virginia-like beloved and end up in a conventional marriage. In *Night and Day*, the Leonard-like Ralph learns to value Katharine for herself, not as some superior being. And Katharine overcomes (as Virginia had) class and familial prejudices to marry the good and intelligent Ralph. This novel focuses on the very sort of details that Woolf had deleted from *The Voyage Out*: credible dialogue, realistic descriptions of early 20th-century settings, and investigations of issues such as class, politics, and suffrage.

Woolf was writing nearly a review a week for the *Times Literary Supplement* in 1918. Her essay *Modern Novels* (1919; revised in 1925 as *Modern Fiction*) attacked the "materialists" who wrote about superficial rather than spiritual or "luminous" experiences. The Woolfs also printed by hand, with Vanessa Bell's illustrations, Virginia's *Kew Gardens* (1919), a story organized, like a Post-Impressionistic painting, by pattern. With the Hogarth Press's emergence as a major publishing house, the Woolfs gradually ceased being their own printers.

In 1919 they bought a cottage in Rodmell village called Monk's House, which looked out over the Sussex Downs and the meadows where the River Ouse wound down to the English Channel. Virginia could walk or bicycle to visit Vanessa, her children, and a changing cast of guests at the bohemian Charleston and then retreat to Monk's House to write. She envisioned a new book that would apply the theories of *Modern Novels* and the achievements of her short stories to the novel form. In early 1920 a group of friends, evolved from the early Bloomsbury group, began a "Memoir Club," which met to read irreverent passages from their autobiographies. Her second presentation was an exposé of Victorian hypocrisy, especially that of George Duckworth, who masked inappropriate, unwanted caresses as affection honouring their mother's memory.

In 1921 Woolf's minimally plotted short fictions were gathered in *Monday or Tuesday*. Meanwhile, typesetting having heightened her sense of visual layout, she began a new novel written in blocks to be surrounded by white spaces. In *On Re-Reading Novels* (1922), Woolf argued that the novel was not so much a form but an "emotion which you feel." In *Jacob's Room* (1922) she achieved such emotion, transforming personal grief over the death of Thoby Stephen into a "spiritual shape." Though she takes Jacob from childhood to his early death in war, she leaves out plot, conflict, even character. The emptiness of Jacob's room and the irrelevance of his belongings convey in their minimalism the profound emptiness of loss. Though Jacob's Room is an antiwar novel, Woolf feared that she had ventured too far beyond representation. She vowed to "push on," as she wrote Clive Bell, to graft such experimental techniques onto more-substantial characters.

MAJOR PERIOD

At the beginning of 1924, the Woolfs moved their city residence from the suburbs back to Bloomsbury, where they were less isolated from London society. Soon the aristocratic Vita Sackville-West began to court Virginia, a relationship that would blossom into a lesbian affair. Having already written a story about a Mrs. Dalloway, Woolf thought of a foiling device that would pair that highly sensitive woman with a shell-shocked war victim, a Mr. Smith, so that "the sane and the insane" would exist "side by side." Her aim was to "tunnel" into these two characters until Clarissa Dalloway's affirmations meet Septimus Smith's negations. Also in 1924 Woolf gave a talk at Cambridge called *Character in Fiction*, revised later that year as the Hogarth Press pamphlet *Mr. Bennett and Mrs. Brown*. In it she celebrated the breakdown in patriarchal values that had occurred "in or about December, 1910"—during Fry's exhibit "Manet and the Post-

Impressionists"— and she attacked "materialist" novelists for omitting the essence of character.

In *Mrs. Dalloway* (1925), the boorish doctors presume to understand personality, but its essence evades them. This novel is as patterned as a Post-Impressionist painting but is also so accurately representational that the reader can trace Clarissa's and Septimus's movements through the streets of London on a single day in June 1923. At the end of the day, Clarissa gives a grand party and Septimus commits suicide. Their lives come together when the doctor who was treating (or, rather, mistreating) Septimus arrives at Clarissa's party with news of the death. The main characters are connected by motifs and, finally, by Clarissa's intuiting why Septimus threw his life away.

Woolf wished to build on her achievement in *Mrs. Dalloway* by merging the novelistic and elegiac forms. As an elegy, *To the Lighthouse*—published on May 5, 1927, the 32nd anniversary of Julia Stephen's death—evoked childhood summers at Talland House. As a novel, it broke narrative continuity into a tripartite structure. The first section, "The Window," begins as Mrs. Ramsay and James, her youngest son—like Julia and Adrian Stephen—sit in the French window of the Ramsays' summer home while a houseguest named Lily Briscoe paints them and James begs to go to a nearby lighthouse. Mr. Ramsay, like Leslie Stephen, sees poetry as didacticism, conversation as winning points, and life as a tally of accomplishments. He uses logic to deflate hopes for a trip to the lighthouse, but he needs sympathy from his wife. She is more attuned to emotions than reason. In the climactic dinner-party scene, she inspires such harmony and composure that the moment "partook, she felt, . . . of eternity."

The novel's middle "Time Passes" section focuses on the empty house during a 10-year hiatus and the last-minute housecleaning for the returning Ramsays. Woolf describes the progress of weeds, mold, dust, and gusts of wind, but she merely announces such major events as the deaths of Mrs. Ramsay and a son and daughter. In the novel's third section, "The Lighthouse," Woolf brings Mr. Ramsay, his youngest children (James and Cam), Lily Briscoe, and others from "The Window" back to the house. As Mr. Ramsay and the now-teenage children reach the lighthouse and achieve a moment of reconciliation, Lily completes her painting.

To the Lighthouse melds into its structure questions about creativity and the nature and function of art. Lily argues effectively for nonrepresentational but emotive art, and her painting (in which mother and child are reduced to two shapes with a line between them) echoes the abstract structure of Woolf's profoundly elegiac novel.

In two 1927 essays, *The Art of Fiction* and *The New Biography*, she wrote that fiction writers should be less concerned with naive notions of reality and more with language and design. However restricted by fact, she argued, biographers should yoke truth with imagination, "granite-like solidity" with "rainbow-like intangibility." Their relationship having cooled by 1927, Woolf sought to reclaim Sackville-West through a "biography" that would include Sackville family history. Woolf solved biographical, historical, and personal dilemmas with the story of Orlando, who lives from Elizabethan times through the entire 18th century; he then becomes female, experiences debilitating gender constraints, and lives into the 20th century. Orlando begins writing poetry during the Renaissance, using history and mythology as models, and over the ensuing centuries returns to the poem *The Oak Tree*, revising it according to shifting poetic conventions. Woolf herself writes in mock-heroic imitation of biographical styles that change over the same period of time. Thus, *Orlando: A Biography* (1928) exposes the artificiality of both gender and genre prescriptions. However fantastic, *Orlando* also argues for a novelistic approach to biography.

In 1921 John Maynard Keynes had told Woolf that her memoir "on George," presented to the Memoir Club that year or a year earlier, represented her best writing. Afterward she was increasingly angered by masculine condescension to female talent. In *A Room of One's Own* (1929), Woolf blamed women's absence from history not on their lack of brains and talent but on their poverty. For her 1931 talk *Professions for Women*, Woolf studied the history of women's education and employment and argued that unequal opportunities for women negatively affect all of society. She urged women to destroy the "angel in the house," a reference to Coventry Patmore's poem of that title, the quintessential Victorian paean to women who sacrifice themselves to men.

Having praised a 1930 exhibit of Vanessa Bell's paintings for their wordlessness, Woolf planned a mystical novel that would be similarly impersonal and abstract. In *The Waves* (1931), poetic interludes describe the sea and sky from dawn to dusk. Between the interludes, the voices of six named characters appear in sections that move from their childhood to old age. In the middle section, when the six friends meet at a farewell dinner for another friend leaving for India, the single flower at the centre of the dinner table becomes a "seven-sided flower . . . a whole flower to which every eye brings its own contribution." *The Waves* offers a six-sided shape that illustrates how each individual experiences events—including their friend's death—uniquely. Bernard, the writer in the group, narrates the final section, defying death and a world "without a self." Unique though they are (and their prototypes can be identified in the Bloomsbury group), the characters become one, just as the sea and sky become indistinguishable in the interludes. This oneness with all creation was the primal experience Woolf had felt as a child in Cornwall. In this her most experimental novel, she achieved its poetic equivalent. Through *To the Lighthouse* and *The Waves*, Woolf became, with James Joyce and William Faulkner, one of the three major English-language Modernist experimenters in stream-of-consciousness writing.

Late Work

From her earliest days, Woolf had framed experience in terms of oppositions, even while she longed for a holistic state beyond binary divisions. The "perpetual marriage of granite and rainbow" Woolf described in her essay *The New Biography* typified her approach during the 1930s to individual works and to a balance between writing works of fact and of imagination. Even before finishing *The Waves*, she began compiling a scrapbook of clippings illustrating the horrors of war, the threat of fascism, and the oppression of women. The discrimination against women that Woolf had discussed in *A Room of One's Own* and *Professions for Women* inspired her to plan a book that would trace the story of a fictional family named Pargiter and explain the social conditions affecting family members over a period of time. In *The Pargiters: A Novel-Essay* she would alternate between sections of fiction and of fact. For the fictional historical narrative, she relied upon experiences of friends and family from the Victorian Age to the 1930s. For the essays, she researched that 50-year span of history. The task, however, of moving between fiction and fact was daunting.

Woolf took a holiday from *The Pargiters* to write a mock biography of Flush, the dog of poet Elizabeth Barrett Browning. Lytton Strachey having recently died, Woolf muted her spoof of his biographical method; nevertheless, *Flush* (1933) remains both a biographical satire and a light-hearted exploration of perception, in this case a dog's. In

1935 Woolf completed *Freshwater*, an absurdist drama based on the life of her great-aunt Julia Margaret Cameron. Featuring such other eminences as the poet Alfred, Lord Tennyson, and the painter George Frederick Watts, this riotous play satirizes high-minded Victorian notions of art.

Meanwhile, Woolf feared she would never finish *The Pargiters*. Alternating between types of prose was proving cumbersome, and the book was becoming too long. She solved this dilemma by jettisoning the essay sections, keeping the family narrative, and renaming her book *The Years*. She narrated 50 years of family history through the decline of class and patriarchal systems, the rise of feminism, and the threat of another war. Desperate to finish, Woolf lightened the book with poetic echoes of gestures, objects, colours, and sounds and with wholesale deletions, cutting epiphanies for Eleanor Pargiter and explicit references to women's bodies. The novel illustrates the damage done to women and society over the years by sexual repression, ignorance, and discrimination. Though (or perhaps because) Woolf's trimming muted the book's radicalism, *The Years* (1937) became a best-seller.

When Fry died in 1934, Virginia was distressed; Vanessa was devastated. Then in July 1937 Vanessa's elder son, Julian Bell, was killed in the Spanish Civil War while driving an ambulance for the Republican army. Vanessa was so disconsolate that Virginia put aside her writing for a time to try to comfort her sister. Privately a lament over Julian's death and publicly a diatribe against war, *Three Guineas* (1938) proposes answers to the question of how to prevent war. Woolf connected masculine symbols of authority with militarism and misogyny, an argument buttressed by notes from her clippings about aggression, fascism, and war.

Still distressed by the deaths of Roger Fry and Julian Bell, she determined to test her theories about experimental, novelistic biography in a life of Fry. As she acknowledged in *The Art of Biography* (1939), the recalcitrance of evidence brought her near despair over the possibility of writing an imaginative biography. Against the "grind" of finishing the Fry biography, Woolf wrote a verse play about the history of English literature.

Her next novel, *Pointz Hall* (later retitled *Between the Acts*), would include the play as a pageant performed by villagers and would convey the gentry's varied reactions to it. As another holiday from Fry's biography, Woolf returned to her own childhood with *A Sketch of the Past*, a memoir about her mixed feelings toward her parents and her past and about memoir writing itself. (Here surfaced for the first time in writing a memory of the teenage Gerald Duckworth, her other half brother, touching her inappropriately when she was a girl of perhaps four or five.) Through last-minute borrowing from the letters between Fry and Vanessa, Woolf finished her biography. Though convinced that *Roger Fry* (1940) was more granite than rainbow, Virginia congratulated herself on at least giving back to Vanessa "her Roger."

Woolf's chief anodyne against Adolf Hitler, World War II, and her own despair was writing. During the bombing of London in 1940 and 1941, she worked on her memoir and *Between the Acts*. In her novel, war threatens art and humanity itself, and, in the interplay between the pageant— performed on a June day in 1939 —and the audience, Woolf raises questions about perception and response. Despite *Between the Acts*'s affirmation of the value of art, Woolf worried that this novel was "too slight" and indeed that all writing was irrelevant when England seemed on the verge of invasion and civilization about to slide over a precipice. Facing such horrors, a depressed Woolf found herself unable to write. The demons of self-doubt that she had kept at bay for so long returned to haunt her. On March 28, 1941, fearing that she now lacked the resilience to battle them, she walked behind Monk's House and down to the River Ouse, put stones in her pockets, and drowned herself. *Between the Acts* was published posthumously later that year.

ASSESSMENT

Woolf's experiments with point of view confirm that as Bernard thinks in *The Waves*, "we are not single." Being neither single nor fixed, perception in her novels is fluid, as is the world she presents. While Joyce and Faulkner separate one character's interior monologues from another's, Woolf's narratives move between inner and outer and between characters without clear demarcations. Furthermore, she avoids the self-absorption of many of her contemporaries and implies a brutal society without the explicit details some of her contemporaries felt obligatory. Her nonlinear forms invite reading not for neat solutions but for an aesthetic resolution of "shivering fragments," as she wrote in 1908. While Woolf's fragmented style is distinctly Modernist, her indeterminacy anticipates a postmodern awareness of the evanescence of boundaries and categories.

Woolf's many essays about the art of writing and about reading itself today retain their appeal to a range of, in Samuel Johnson's words, "common" (unspecialized) readers. Woolf's collection of essays *The Common Reader* (1925) was followed by *The Common Reader: Second Series* (1932; also published as *The Second Common Reader*). She continued writing essays on reading and writing, women and history, and class and politics for the rest of her life. Many were collected after her death in volumes edited by Leonard Woolf.

Virginia Woolf wrote far more fiction than Joyce and far more nonfiction than either Joyce or Faulkner. Six volumes of diaries (including her early journals), six volumes of letters, and numerous volumes of collected essays show her deep engagement with major 20th-century issues. Though many of her essays began as reviews, written anonymously to deadlines for money, and many include imaginative settings and whimsical speculations, they are serious inquiries into reading and writing, the novel and the arts, perception and essence, war and peace, class and politics, privilege and discrimination, and the need to reform society.

Woolf's haunting language, her prescient insights into wide-ranging historical, political, feminist, and artistic issues, and her revisionist experiments with novelistic form during a remarkably productive career altered the course of Modernist and postmodernist letters.

COCO CHANEL

(b. Aug. 19, 1883, Saumur, France—d. Jan. 10, 1971, Paris)

The French fashion designer Coco Chanel ruled over Parisian haute couture for almost six decades. Her elegantly casual designs inspired women of fashion to abandon the complicated, uncomfortable clothes—such as petticoats and corsets—that were prevalent in 19th-century dress. Among her now-classic innovations were the Chanel suit, costume jewelry, and the "little black dress."

Gabrielle Bonheur Chanel was born into poverty in the French countryside; her mother died, and her father abandoned her to an orphanage. After a brief stint as a shopgirl and a failed attempt to become a café singer, Chanel engaged in liaisons with a series of wealthy men. In 1913, with financial assistance from one of these men, she opened a tiny millinery shop in Deauville, where she also sold simple sportswear, such as jersey sweaters. Within five years her original use of jersey fabric to create a "poor girl" look had attracted the attention of influential wealthy women seeking relief from the prevalent corseted styles. Faithful to her maxim that "luxury must be comfortable, otherwise it is not luxury," Chanel's designs stressed simplicity and comfort and revolutionized the fashion industry. By the late 1920s the Chanel industries employed 3,500 people and included a couture house, a textile business, perfume laboratories, and a workshop for costume jewelry.

The financial basis of this empire was Chanel No. 5, the phenomenally successful perfume she introduced in 1922 with the help of Ernst Beaux, one of the most talented perfume creators in France. It has been said that the perfume got its name from the series of scents that Beaux created for Chanel to sample—she chose the fifth, a combination of jasmine and several other floral scents that was more complex and mysterious than the single-scented perfumes then on the market. That Chanel was the first major fashion designer to introduce a perfume and that she replaced the typical perfume packaging with a simple and sleek bottle also added to the scent's success. Unfortunately, her partnerships with businessmen Théophile Bader and Pierre Wertheimer, who promised to help her market her fragrance in exchange for a share of the profits, meant that she received only 10 percent of its royalties before World War II and only 2 percent afterward. Despite enacting a series of lawsuits, Chanel failed to regain control of her signature fragrance.

Chanel closed her couture house in 1939 with the outbreak of World War II but returned in 1954 to introduce her highly copied suit design: a collarless, braid-trimmed cardigan jacket with a graceful skirt. She also introduced bell-bottomed pants and other innovations, while always retaining a clean, classic look.

After her death in 1971, Chanel's couture house was led by a series of different designers. This situation stabilized in 1983, when Karl Lagerfeld became chief designer.

ELEANOR ROOSEVELT

(b. Oct. 11, 1884, New York, N.Y., U.S.—d. Nov. 7, 1962, New York City)

Eleanor Roosevelt was an American first lady (1933–45), the wife of Franklin D. Roosevelt, 32nd president of the United States, and a United Nations diplomat and humanitarian. She was, in her time, one of the world's most widely admired and powerful women.

Anna Eleanor Roosevelt was the daughter of Elliott and Anna Hall Roosevelt and the niece of Theodore Roosevelt, 26th president of the United States. She grew up in a wealthy family that attached great value to community service. Both her parents died before she was 10, and she and her surviving brother (another brother died when she was 9) were raised by relatives. The death of Eleanor's father, to whom she had been especially close, was very difficult for her.

At age 15 Eleanor enrolled at Allenswood, a girls' boarding school outside London, where she came under the influence of the French headmistress, Marie Souvestre. Souvestre's intellectual curiosity and her taste for travel and excellence—in everything but sports—awakened similar interests in Eleanor, who later described her three years there as the happiest time of her life. Reluctantly, she returned to New York in the summer of 1902 to prepare for her "coming out" into society that winter. Following family tradition, she devoted time to community service, including teaching in a settlement house on Manhattan's Lower East Side.

EARLY LIFE WITH FRANKLIN

Soon after Eleanor returned to New York, Franklin Roosevelt, her distant cousin, began to court her, and they were married on March 17, 1905, in New York City. His taste for fun contrasted with her own seriousness, and she often commented on how he had to find companions in pleasure elsewhere. Between 1906 and 1916 Eleanor gave birth to six children, one of whom died in infancy.

After Franklin won a seat in the New York Senate in 1911, the family moved to Albany, where Eleanor was initiated into the job of political wife. When Franklin was appointed assistant secretary of the navy in 1913, the family moved to Washington, D.C., and Eleanor spent the next few years performing the social duties expected of an "official wife," including attending formal parties and making social calls in the homes of other government officials. For the most part she found these occasions tedious.

With the entry of the United States into World War I in April 1917, Eleanor was able to resume her volunteer work. She visited wounded soldiers and worked for the Navy–Marine Corps Relief Society and in a Red Cross canteen. This work increased her sense of self-worth, and she wrote later, "I loved it . . . I simply ate it up."

In 1918 Eleanor discovered that Franklin had been having an affair with her social secretary, Lucy Mercer. It was one of the most traumatic events in her life, as she later told Joseph Lash, her friend and biographer. Mindful of his political career and fearing the loss of his mother's financial support, Franklin refused Eleanor's offer of a divorce and agreed to stop seeing Mercer. The Roosevelts' marriage settled into a routine in which both principals kept independent agendas while remaining respectful of and affectionate toward each other. But their relationship had ceased to be an intimate one. Later, Mercer and other glamorous, witty women continued to attract his attention and claim his time, and later in 1945 Mercer, by then the widow of Winthrop Rutherfurd, was with Franklin when he died at Warm Springs, Georgia.

Franklin ran unsuccessfully for vice president on the Democratic ticket in 1920. At this time Eleanor's interest in politics increased, partly as a result of her decision to help in her husband's political career after he was stricken with poliomyelitis in 1921 and partly as a result of her desire to work for important causes. She joined the Women's Trade Union League and became active in the New York state Democratic Party. As a member of the Legislative Affairs Committee of the League of Women Voters, she began studying the Congressional Record and learned to evaluate voting records and debates.

When Franklin became governor of New York in 1929, Eleanor found an opportunity to combine the responsibilities of a political hostess with her own burgeoning career and personal independence. She continued to teach at Todhunter, a girls' school in Manhattan that she and two friends had purchased, making several trips a week back and forth between Albany and New York City.

IN THE WHITE HOUSE

During her 12 years as first lady, the unprecedented breadth of Eleanor's activities and her advocacy of liberal causes made her nearly as controversial a figure as her husband. She instituted regular White House press conferences for women correspondents, and wire services that had not formerly employed women were forced to do so in order to have a representative present in case important news broke. In deference to the president's infirmity, she helped serve as his eyes and ears throughout the nation, embarking on extensive tours and reporting to him on conditions, programs, and public opinion. These unusual excursions were the butt of some criticism and "Eleanor jokes" by her opponents, but many people responded warmly to

Eleanor Roosevelt (top, centre) *visiting with Children of the American Revolution at the White House, 1935.* Encyclopædia Britannica, Inc.

her compassionate interest in their welfare. Beginning in 1936, she also wrote a daily syndicated newspaper column, "My Day."

A widely sought-after speaker at political meetings and at various institutions, she showed particular interest in child welfare, housing reform, and equal rights for women and racial minorities.

In 1939, when the Daughters of the American Revolution (DAR) refused to let Marian Anderson, an African American opera singer, perform in Constitution Hall, Eleanor resigned her membership in the DAR and arranged to hold the concert at the nearby Lincoln Memorial; the event turned into a massive outdoor celebration attended by 75,000 people. On another occasion, when local officials in Alabama insisted that seating at a public meeting be segregated by race, Eleanor carried a folding chair to all sessions and carefully placed it in the centre aisle. Her defense of the rights of African Americans, youth, and the poor helped to bring groups into government that formerly had been alienated from the political process.

LATER YEARS

After President Roosevelt's death in 1945, President Harry S. Truman appointed Eleanor a delegate to the United Nations (UN), where she served as chairman of the Commission on Human Rights (1946–51) and played a major role in the drafting and adoption of the Universal Declaration of Human Rights (1948). In the last decade of her life she continued to play an active part in the Democratic Party, working for the election of Democratic presidential nominee Adlai Stevenson in 1952 and 1956.

In 1961 President John F. Kennedy appointed her chair of his Commission on the Status of Women, and she continued with that work until shortly before her death. She had not initially favoured the Equal Rights Amendment (ERA), saying it would take from women the valuable protective legislation that they had fought to win and still needed, but she gradually embraced it.

An indefatigable traveler, Eleanor Roosevelt circled the globe several times, visiting scores of countries and meeting with most of the world's leaders. She continued to write books and articles, and the last of her "My Day" columns appeared just weeks before her death, from a rare form of tuberculosis, in 1962. She is buried at Hyde Park, her husband's family home on the Hudson River and the site of the Franklin D. Roosevelt Library. In many ways, it was her library too, since she had carved out such an important record as first lady, one against which all her successors would be judged.

KAREN HORNEY

(b. Sept. 16, 1885, Blankenese, near Hamburg, Ger. — d. Dec. 4, 1952, New York, N.Y., U.S.)

Departing from some of the basic principles of Sigmund Freud, the German-born American psychoanalyst Karen Horney proposed an environmental and social basis for the personality and its disorders.

Karen Danielsen married Oscar Horney, a lawyer, in 1909. She studied medicine at the universities of Freiburg, Göttingen, and Berlin, taking an M.D. degree from the last in 1911. After a period of medical practice Karen Horney became interested in psychoanalysis. From 1913 to 1915 she studied and entered analysis with Karl Abraham, a close associate and disciple of Sigmund Freud. From 1915 to 1920 she engaged in clinical and outpatient psychiatric work in connection with Berlin hospitals, and in 1920 she joined the teaching staff of the newly founded Berlin Psychoanalytic Institute.

Although she adhered in the main to the outlines of Freudian theory, Horney early began to disagree with Freud's view of female psychology, which he treated as an offshoot of male psychology. Unaffected by the worshipful awe that held many early Freudians to received dogma, she forthrightly rejected such notions as penis envy and other manifestations of male bias in psychoanalytic theory. She argued instead that the source of much female psychiatric disturbance is located in the very male-dominated culture that had produced Freudian theory. She introduced the concept of womb envy, suggesting that male envy of pregnancy, nursing, and motherhood—of women's primary role in creating and sustaining life—led men to claim their superiority in other fields.

Horney and her husband separated in 1926, and divorced in 1937. During this time, in 1932, she went to the United States to become associate director of the Institute for Psychoanalysis in Chicago. She moved to New York City in 1934 to return to private practice and teach at the New School for Social Research. There she produced her major theoretical works, *The Neurotic Personality of Our Time* (1937) and *New Ways in Psychoanalysis* (1939), in which she argued that environmental and social conditions, rather than the instinctual or biological drives described by Freud, determine much of individual personality and are the chief causes of neuroses and personality disorders. In particular, Horney objected to Freud's concepts of the libido, the death instinct, and the Oedipus complex, which she thought could be more adequately explained by cultural and social conditions. She believed that a primary condition responsible for the later development of neurosis was the infant's experience of basic anxiety, in which the child felt "isolated and helpless in a potentially hostile world." The various strategies the child adopts to cope with this anxiety can eventually become persistent and irrational needs that cause both neurosis and personality disorder.

Many of Horney's ideas, rooted as they were in her wide clinical experience, were translated into a new approach to psychoanalytic therapy. She sought to help patients identify the specific cause of present anxieties, thinking that it was just as important to the goals of psychoanalysis to deal with real-life, present-day problems as it was to reconstruct childhood emotional states and fantasies. In many cases, she suggested that the patient could even learn to psychoanalyze himself.

Her refusal to adhere to strict Freudian theory caused Horney's expulsion from the New York Psychoanalytic

Institute in 1941, which left her free to organize a new group, the Association for the Advancement of Psychoanalysis, and its affiliated teaching centre, the American Institute for Psychoanalysis. Horney founded the association's *American Journal of Psychoanalysis* and served as its editor until her death in 1952. She also continued to write, further expounding her views that neuroses were caused by disturbances in interpersonal relationships in *Our Inner Conflicts* (1945) and *Neurosis and Human Growth* (1950). The Karen Horney Foundation was established in New York the year of her death and gave rise in 1955 to the Karen Horney Clinic. Horney's analysis of the causes and the dynamics of neurosis and her revision of Freud's theory of personality have remained influential. Her ideas on female psychosexual development were given particular attention after *Feminine Psychology*, a collection of her early papers on the subject, was published in 1967.

MARTHA GRAHAM

(b. May 11, 1894, Allegheny county, Pa., U.S.—d. April 1, 1991, New York, N.Y.)

M artha Graham was an influential American dancer, teacher, and choreographer of modern dance, whose ballets and other works were intended to "reveal the inner man." Over 50-plus years she created more than 180 works, from solos to large-scale works, in most of which she herself danced. She gave modern dance new depth as a vehicle for the intense and forceful expression of primal emotions.

EARLY LIFE AND WORKS

Graham was one of three daughters of a physician who was particularly interested in the bodily expression of human behaviour. After some time in the South, her family settled in 1909 in Santa Barbara, California, where she discovered the rhythm of the sea and became acquainted with Oriental art, influences that were to be evident in her choreography throughout her career.

Graham's professional career began in 1916 at Denishawn, the school and dance company founded in Los Angeles by Ruth St. Denis and Ted Shawn, where as a teenager she was introduced to a repertory and curriculum that, for the first time in the United States, explored the world's dances—folk, classical, experimental, Oriental, and American Indian. She was entranced by the religious mysticism of St. Denis, but Shawn was her major teacher; he discovered sources of dramatic power within her and then channeled them into an Aztec ballet, *Xochitl*. The dance was a tremendous success both in vaudeville and in concert performance and made her a Denishawn star.

Graham remained with Denishawn until 1923, and although she ultimately rebelled violently against its eclecticism, she later mirrored in her own works the Orientalism that pervaded the school. She left Denishawn to become a featured dancer in the Greenwich Village Follies revue, where she remained for two years. In 1924 she went to the Eastman School of Music in Rochester, New York, to teach and to experiment.

Graham made her New York City debut as an independent artist in 1926. Though some of the fruits of her experiments were discernible from the first, a good many of her dances, such as *Three Gopi Maidens* and *Danse Languide*, echoed her Denishawn past. The critics found her to be graceful and lyrical. All of that changed with her 1927 concert, and for the next decade and more, the startlingly original dances she performed were to be referred to as ugly, stark, and obscure. The exotic costumes and rich staging of Denishawn were in the past. Among the dances of her 1927 program was *Revolt*, probably the first dance of protest and social comment staged in the United States, which was set to the avant-garde music of Arthur Honegger. The audience was not impressed; dancers and theatregoers, famous and unknown, ridiculed her. Graham herself later referred to this decade as "my period of long woolens," a reference to the plain jersey dress that she wore in many of her dances.

A strong and continuing influence in her life was Louis Horst, musical director at Denishawn, who had left the school two years after Graham. He became her musical director, often composing pieces for her during her first two decades of independence; they remained close until his death in 1964. Among his most noted scores for her were those for the now historic *Frontier* (1935), a solo dance, and *Primitive Mysteries*, written for Graham and a company of female dancers.

Frontier initiated the use of decor in Graham's repertoire and marked the beginning of a long and distinguished collaboration with the noted Japanese-American sculptor Isamu Noguchi, under whose influence she developed one of her most singular stage innovations, the use of sculpture, or three-dimensional set pieces, instead of flats and drops.

MATURITY

For Martha Graham, the dance, like the spoken drama, can explore the spiritual and emotional essence of human beings. Thus, the choreography of *Frontier* symbolized the frontier woman's achievement of mastery over an uncharted domain. In *Night Journey* (1948), a work about the Greek legendary figure Jocasta, the whole dance-drama takes place in the instant when Jocasta learns that she has mated with Oedipus, her own son, and has borne him children. The work treats Jocasta rather than Oedipus as the tragic victim, and shows her reliving the events of her life and seeking justification for her actions. In *Letter to the World* (1940), a work about Emily Dickinson, several characters are used to portray different aspects of the poet's personality.

For more than 10 years Graham's dance company consisted solely of women, but her themes were beginning to call for men as well. She engaged Erick Hawkins, a ballet dancer, to join her company, and he appeared with her in a major work, *American Document* (1938). Though she and Hawkins were married in 1948, the marriage did not last.

In a career spanning more than half a century, Graham created a succession of dances, ranging from solos to large-scale creations of full-program length such as *Clytemnestra* (1958). For her themes she almost always turned to human conflicts and emotions. The settings and the eras vary, but her great gallery of danced portraits never failed to explore the inner emotional life of their characters. She created some dances from American frontier life, the most famous of which is *Appalachian Spring* (1944), with its score by Aaron Copland. Another source was Greek legend, the dances rooted in Classical Greek dramas, stories, and myths. *Cave of the Heart* (1946), based on the figure of *Medea*, with music by Samuel Barber, was not a dance version of the legend but rather an exposure of the Medea latent in every woman who, out of consuming jealousy, not only destroys those she loves but herself as well.

Later works by Graham also borrowed from Greek legend, including *Errand into the Maze* (1947), an investigation of hidden fears presented through the symbols of the Minotaur and the labyrinth; *Alcestis* (1960); *Phaedra* (1962); and *Circe* (1963). Biblical themes and religious figures also inspired her: *Seraphic Dialogue* (1955; Joan of Arc), *Embattled*

Garden (1958; referring to the Garden of Eden), and *Legend of Judith* (1962) and such fanciful abstractions as *Diversion of Angels* (1948) or *Acrobats of God* (1960). Her later works include *The Witch of Endor* (1965), *Cortege of Eagles* (1967), *The Archaic Hours* (1969), *Mendicants of Evening* (1973), *Lucifer* (1975), *The Owl and the Pussycat* (1978), and *Frescoes* (1980). In the early 1980s she created neoclassical dances, beginning with *Acts of Light* (1981). In 1970 she announced her retirement as a dancer, but she continued to create dances and to teach.

ASSESSMENT

Martha Graham created a dance technique that became the first significant alternative to the idiom of classical ballet. As the dancer Alma Guillermoprieto has pointed out, Graham was "the first creator of modern dance to devise a truly universal dance technique out of the movements she developed in her choreography." Her dance language was intended to express shared human emotions and experiences, rather than merely provide decorative displays of graceful movements. The dances were also intended to evoke a visceral response in the audience rather than be comprehended in primarily linear or pictorial terms. Many of her dances feature forceful, angular movements originating in spasms of muscular contraction and release centred in the dancer's pelvis. These expressive contractions help generate the strong sexual tension that is a feature of so many of Graham's works. The resulting dance vocabulary is startlingly unlike that of classical ballet in its jagged and angular lines, and its dislocations and distortions that express intensely felt human emotion. Her technique is the most highly developed body-training method in the entire field of modern dance, requiring both unrelenting discipline and prodigious virtuosity.

Throughout most of her career, Graham maintained a position as the foremost figure in American modern dance. She instructed, or guided, generations of modern dance teachers both in the United States and abroad. She strongly influenced succeeding generations of modern dancers, ballet choreographers, stagers of musicals and operas, and creators of dance-dramas. From the "long woolens" of the 1920s, Graham moved to some of the most opulent productions to be found in modern dance, with an accent on sculptured pieces and brilliant costumes and properties. She was the recipient of many awards and honours, including the Medal of Freedom, the highest civilian award in the United States. In 1973 she published *The Notebooks of Martha Graham*.

SOONG MEI-LING

(b. March 5, 1897, Shanghai, China—d. Oct. 23, 2003, New York, N.Y., U.S.)

Soong Mei-ling (Soong also spelled Sung, Mei-ling also spelled Mayling) was a notable Chinese political figure and second wife of the Nationalist Chinese president Chiang Kai-shek. She is also called Madame Chiang Kai-shek. Her family was successful, prosperous, and well-connected: her sister Soong Ch'ing-ling (Song Qingling) was the wife of Sun Yat-sen, and her brother T. V. Soong was a prominent industrialist and official of the Nationalist Chinese government.

Soong Mei-ling was educated in the United States from 1908 to 1917, when she graduated from Wellesley College, and was thoroughly Americanized. In 1927 she married Chiang Kai-shek, and she helped introduce him to Western

Soong Mei-ling giving a special radio broadcast to thank the American people for their support of China during the Sino-Japanese War (1937–45). Encyclopædia Britannica, Inc.

culture and ideas and worked to publicize his cause in the West. With her husband, she launched in 1934 the New Life Movement, a program that sought to halt the spread of communism by teaching traditional Chinese values. In 1936 Chiang Kai-shek was taken captive by Chang Hsüeh-liang, a warlord who believed the Nationalist government should stop fighting China's communists and instead concentrate on resisting Japanese aggression; Soong Mei-ling played a major role in the negotiations that led to his release.

During World War II she wrote many articles on China for American journals, and in 1943, during a visit to the United States, she became the first Chinese and only the second woman to address a joint session of the U.S. Congress, where she sought increased support for China in its war against Japan. Her efforts resulted in much financial aid, and Soong Mei-ling so impressed the American public that until 1967 her name appeared annually on the U.S. list of the 10 most admired women in the world.

In the mid-1940s civil war broke out in China as Nationalists and communists battled for control of the country. Chiang Kai-shek's forces were defeated in 1949, and Soong Mei-ling and her family moved to Taiwan, where her husband established his government. Still highly influential, she continued to seek support from the United States, and her efforts helped sway the U.S. government's policy toward China and Taiwan. After Chiang Kai-shek's death in 1975, Soong Mei-ling moved to New York, where she lived in semi-seclusion. Following the death in 1988 of Chiang Ching-kuo, Chiang Kai-shek's son from his first marriage and the president of Taiwan, she briefly became involved in Taiwanese politics, but by that time her influence had greatly diminished. Her published works include *This Is Our China* (1940), *The Sure Victory* (1955), and two volumes of selected speeches.

AMELIA EARHART

(b. July 24, 1897, Atchison, Kan., U.S.—disappeared July 2, 1937, near Howland Island, central Pacific Ocean)

One of the world's most celebrated aviators, Amelia Earhart was the first woman to fly alone over the Atlantic Ocean.

Amelia Mary Earhart moved often with her family and completed high school in Chicago in 1916. She worked as a military nurse in Canada during World War I and as a social worker at Denison House in Boston after the war. She learned to fly (against her family's wishes) in 1920–21 and in 1922 bought her first plane, a Kinner Canary. On June 17–18, 1928, she became the first woman to fly across the Atlantic, although she was only a passenger in a plane flown by Wilmer Stutz and Louis Gordon. The same year, her reflections on that flight were published as *20 Hrs., 40 Min.* She married the publisher George Palmer Putnam in 1931 but continued her career under her maiden name.

Determined to justify the renown that her 1928 crossing had brought her, Earhart crossed the Atlantic alone on May 20–21, 1932. Her flight in her Lockheed Vega from Newfoundland to Ireland was completed in the record time of 14 hours 56 minutes. After that flight, she wrote *The Fun of It* (1932). This soon led to a series of flights across the United States and drew her into the movement that encouraged the development of commercial aviation. She also took an active part in efforts to open aviation to women and end male domination in the new field.

In January 1935 she made a solo flight from Hawaii to California, a longer distance than that from the United States to Europe. Earhart was the first person to fly that hazardous route successfully; all previous attempts had ended in disaster. She set out in 1937 to fly around the world, with Fred Noonan as her navigator, in a twin-engine Lockheed Electra. After completing more than two-thirds of the distance, her plane vanished in the central Pacific near the International Date Line. Although her mysterious disappearance has since raised many questions and much speculation about the events surrounding it, the facts remain largely unknown.

IRÈNE JOLIOT-CURIE

(b. Sept. 12, 1897, Paris, France—d. March 17, 1956, Paris)

The French physical chemist Irène Joliot-Curie was awarded, with her husband, the 1935 Nobel Prize for Chemistry for the discovery of new radioactive isotopes prepared artificially. She was the daughter of Nobel Prize winners Pierre and Marie Curie.

Irène Curie from 1912 to 1914 prepared for her *baccalauréat* at the Collège Sévigné and in 1918 became her mother's assistant at the Institut du Radium of the University of Paris. In 1925 she presented her doctoral thesis on the alpha rays of polonium. In the same year she met Frédéric Joliot in her mother's laboratory; they were married the following year (on Oct. 9, 1926). She was to find in him a mate who shared her interest in science, sports, humanism, and the arts. He learned laboratory techniques under Irène's guidance, and beginning in 1928 they signed their scientific work jointly.

In the course of their researches they bombarded boron, aluminum, and magnesium with alpha particles; and they obtained radioactive isotopes of elements not ordinarily radioactive, namely, nitrogen, phosphorus, and aluminum. These discoveries revealed the possibility of using artificially produced radioactive isotopes to follow chemical changes and physiological processes, and such applications were soon successful; the absorption of radio-iodine by the thyroid gland was detected, and the course of radiophosphorus (in the form of phosphates) was traced in the metabolism of the organism. The production of these unstable atomic nuclei afforded further means for the observation of changes in the atom as these nuclei broke down. The Joliot-Curies observed also the production of neutrons and positive electrons in the changes that they studied; and their discovery of artificial radioactive isotopes constituted an important step toward the solution of the problem of releasing the energy of the atom, since the method of Enrico Fermi, using neutrons instead of alpha particles for the bombardments which led to the fission of uranium, was an extension of the method developed by the Joliot-Curies for producing radioelements artificially.

In 1935 Frédéric and Irène Joliot-Curie were awarded the Nobel Prize for Chemistry for the synthesis of new radioactive isotopes. The Joliot-Curies then moved into a home at the edge of the Parc de Sceaux. They left it only for visits to their house in Brittany at Pointe de l'Arcouest, where university families had been meeting together since the time of Marie Curie.

In 1937, Frédéric having been appointed professor at the Collège de France, Irène then devoted her time largely to the upbringing of their children, Hélène and Pierre. But both she and Frédéric had a lofty idea of their human and social responsibilities. They had joined the Socialist Party in 1934 and the Comité de Vigilance des Intellectuels Antifascistes (Vigilance Committee of Anti-Fascist Intellectuals) in 1935. They also took a stand in 1936 on the side of Republican Spain. Irène was one of three women to participate in the Popular Front government of 1936. As undersecretary of state for scientific research, she helped to lay the foundations, with Jean Perrin, for what would later become the Centre National de la Recherche Scientifique (National Centre for Scientific Research).

Anxiety resulting from the rise of Nazism and the awareness of the dangers that could result from the application of chain reactions led them to cease publication. On Oct. 30, 1939, they recorded the principle of nuclear reactors in a sealed envelope, which they deposited at the Académie des Sciences; it remained secret until 1949. Frédéric chose to remain in occupied France with his family and to make certain that the Germans who came into his laboratory could not use his work or his equipment, whose removal to Germany he prevented. The Joliot-Curies continued their research, notably in biology.

In May 1944, Irène and their children took refuge in Switzerland, while Frédéric remained in Paris under an assumed name. After 1945, when General Charles de Gaulle tapped Frédéric for his atomic expertise, Irène devoted her scientific experience and her abilities as an administrator to the acquisition of raw materials, the prospecting for uranium, and the construction of detection installations. In 1946 she was also appointed director of the Institut du Radium. After 1950 they devoted themselves to laboratory work, to teaching, and to various peace movements.

During the 1950s, following several operations, Irène's health began to decline. In 1955 Irène drew up plans for the new nuclear physics laboratories at the Université d'Orsay, south of Paris, where teams of scientists could work with large particle accelerators under conditions less cramped than in the Parisian laboratories. Early in 1956 she was sent into the mountains to recuperate, but her condition did not improve. Wasted away by leukemia as her mother had been, she again entered the Curie Hospital, where she died in 1956.

GOLDA MEIR

(b. May 3, 1898, Kiev [Ukraine]—d. Dec. 8, 1978, Jerusalem, Israel)

Golda Meir was one of the founders of the State of Israel and its fourth prime minister (1969–74).

Born Goldie Mabovitch, Meir and her family immigrated to Milwaukee, Wis., in 1906. She attended the Milwaukee Normal School (now the University of Wisconsin-Milwaukee) and later became a leader in the Milwaukee Labor Zionist Party. In 1921 she and her husband, Morris Myerson, emigrated to Palestine and joined the Merḥavya kibbutz. She became the kibbutz's representative to the Histadrut (General Federation of Labour), the secretary of that organization's Women's Labour Council (1928–32), and a member of its executive committee (1934 until World War II).

Golda Meir helped found the State of Israel. Evening Standard/Hulton Archive/Getty Images

During the war, Meir emerged as a forceful spokesman for the Zionist cause in negotiating with the British mandatory authorities. In 1946, when the British arrested and detained many Jewish activists, including Moshe Sharett, head of the Political Department of the Jewish Agency, she provisionally replaced him and worked for the release of her comrades and the many Jewish war refugees who had violated British immigration regulations by settling in Palestine. Upon his release, Sharett took up diplomatic duties, and she officially took over his former position. She personally attempted to dissuade King Abdullah of Jordan from joining the invasion of Israel decided on by other Arab states.

On May 14, 1948, Meir was a signatory of Israel's independence declaration and that year was appointed minister to Moscow. She was elected to the Knesset (Israeli parliament) in 1949 and served in that body until 1974. As minister of labour (1949–56), she carried out major programs of housing and road construction and vigorously supported the policy of unrestricted Jewish immigration to Israel. Appointed foreign minister in 1956, she Hebraized her name to Golda Meir. She promoted the Israeli policy of assistance to the new African states aimed at enhancing diplomatic support among uncommitted nations. Shortly after retiring from the Foreign Ministry in January 1966, she became secretary general of the Mapai Party and supported Prime Minister Levi Eshkol in intraparty conflicts. After Israel's victory in the Six-Day War (June 1967) against Egypt, Jordan, and Syria, she helped merge Mapai with two dissident parties into the Israel Labour Party.

Upon Eshkol's death on Feb. 26, 1969, Meir, the compromise candidate, became prime minister. She maintained the coalition government that had emerged in June 1967.

Meir pressed for a peace settlement in the Middle East by diplomatic means. She traveled widely, her meetings including those with Nicolae Ceauşescu in Romania (1972) and Pope Paul VI at the Vatican (1973). Also in 1973, Meir's government was host to Willy Brandt, chancellor of West Germany.

Her efforts at forging a peace with the Arab states were halted by the outbreak in October 1973 of the fourth Arab–Israeli war, called the Yom Kippur War. Israel's lack of readiness for the war stunned the nation, and Meir formed a new coalition government only with great difficulty in March 1974 and resigned her post as prime minister on April 10. She remained in power as head of a caretaker government until a new one was formed in June. Although in retirement thereafter, she remained an important political figure. Upon her death it was revealed that she had had leukemia for 12 years. Her autobiography, *My Life*, was published in 1975.

MARLENE DIETRICH

(b. Dec. 27, 1901, Schöneberg (now in Berlin), Germany—d. May 6, 1992, Paris, France)

The German American motion-picture actress Marlene Dietrich, one of the world's most glamorous film stars, was noted for her beauty, voice, aura of sophistication, and languid sensuality.

Dietrich was born Marie Magdalene Dietrich. Her father, Ludwig Dietrich, a Royal Prussian police officer, died when she was very young, and her mother remarried a cavalry officer, Edouard von Losch. Marlene, who as a girl adopted the compressed form of her first and middle names, studied at a private school and learned both English and French by age 12. As a teenager she studied to be a concert violinist, but her initiation into the nightlife of

Weimar Berlin—with its cabarets and notorious demi-monde—made the life of a classical musician unappealing to her. She pretended to have injured her wrist and was forced to seek other jobs acting and modeling to help make ends meet.

In 1921 Dietrich enrolled in Max Reinhardt's Deutsche Theaterschule, and she eventually joined Reinhardt's theatre company. In 1923 she attracted the attention of Rudolf Sieber, a casting director at UFA film studios, who began casting her in small film roles. She and Sieber married the following year, and after the birth of their daughter, Maria, Dietrich returned to work on the stage and in films. Although they did not divorce for decades, the couple separated in 1929.

That same year, director Josef von Sternberg first laid eyes on Dietrich and cast her as Lola-Lola, the sultry and world-weary female lead in *Der blaue Engel* (1930; *The Blue Angel*), Germany's first talking film. The film's success catapulted Dietrich to stardom. Von Sternberg took her to the United States and signed her with Paramount Pictures. With von Sternberg's help, Dietrich began to develop her legend by cultivating a femme fatale film persona in several von Sternberg vehicles that followed—*Morocco* (1930), *Dishonored* (1931), *Shanghai Express* (1932), *Blonde Venus* (1932), *The Scarlet Empress* (1934), and *The Devil Is a Woman* (1935). She showed a lighter side in *Desire* (1936), directed by Frank Borzage, and *Destry Rides Again* (1939).

During the Third Reich and despite Adolf Hitler's personal requests, Dietrich refused to work in Germany, and her films were temporarily banned there. Renouncing Nazism ("Hitler is an idiot," she stated in one wartime interview), Dietrich was branded a traitor in Germany; she was spat upon by Nazi supporters carrying banners that read "Go home Marlene" during her visit to Berlin in 1960. (In 2001, on the 100th anniversary of her birth, the city issued a formal apology for the incident.) Having become a U.S. citizen in 1937, she made more than 500 personal appearances before Allied troops from 1943 to 1946. She later said, "America took me into her bosom when I no longer had a native country worthy of the name, but in my heart I am German—German in my soul."

After the war, Dietrich continued to make successful films, such as *A Foreign Affair* (1948), *The Monte Carlo Story* (1956), *Witness for the Prosecution* (1957), *Touch of Evil* (1958), and *Judgment at Nuremberg* (1961). She was also a popular nightclub performer and gave her last stage performance in 1974. After a period of retirement from the screen, she appeared in the film *Just a Gigolo* (1978). The documentary film *Marlene*, a review of her life and career, which included a voice-over interview of the star by Maximilian Schell, was released in 1986. Her autobiography, *Ich bin, Gott sei Dank, Berlinerin* ("I Am, Thank God, a Berliner"; Eng. trans. *Marlene*), was published in 1987. Eight years after her death, a collection of her film costumes, recordings, written documents, photographs, and other personal items was put on permanent display in the Berlin Film Museum (2000).

Dietrich's persona was carefully crafted, and her films (with few exceptions) were skillfully executed. Although her vocal range was not great, her memorable renditions of songs such as *Falling in Love Again*, *Lili Marleen*, *La Vie en rose*, and *Give Me the Man* made them classics of an era. Her many affairs with both men and women were open secrets, but rather than destroying her career they seemed to enhance it. Her adoption of trousers and other mannish clothes made her a trendsetter and helped launch an American fashion style that persisted into the 21st century. In the words of the critic Kenneth Tynan: "She has sex, but no particular gender. She has the bearing of a man; the characters she plays love power and wear trousers. Her

Marlene Dietrich (left) *in* Der blaue Engel *(1930;* The Blue Angel*).*
Universum Film A.G.; photograph from a private collection

masculinity appeals to women and her sexuality to men."
But her personal magnetism went far beyond her masterful
androgynous image and her glamour; another of her admirers, the writer Ernest Hemingway, said, "If she had nothing
more than her voice, she could break your heart with it."

SIMONE WEIL

(b. Feb. 3, 1909, Paris, France—d. Aug. 24, 1943, Ashford, Kent, Eng.)

The posthumously published works of Simone Weil, a
French mystic, social philosopher, and activist in the
French Resistance during World War II, had particular
influence on French and English social thought.

Intellectually precocious, Weil also expressed social awareness at an early age. At five she refused sugar because the French soldiers at the front during World War I had none, and at six she was quoting the French dramatic poet Jean Racine (1639–99). In addition to studies in philosophy, classical philology, and science, Weil continued to embark on new learning projects as the need arose. She taught philosophy in several girls' schools from 1931 to 1938 and often became embroiled in conflicts with school boards as a result of her social activism, which entailed picketing, refusing to eat more than those on relief, and writing for leftist journals.

To learn the psychological effects of heavy industrial labour, she took a job in 1934–35 in an auto factory, where she observed the spiritually deadening effect of machines on her fellow workers. In 1936 she joined an Anarchist unit near Zaragoza, Spain, training for action in the Spanish Civil War, but after an accident in which she was badly scalded by boiling oil, she went to Portugal to recuperate. Soon thereafter Weil had the first of several mystical experiences, and she subsequently came to view her social concerns as "ersatz Divinity." After the German occupation of Paris during World War II, Weil moved to the south of France, where she worked as a farm servant. She escaped with her parents to the United States in 1942 but then went to London to work with the French Resistance. To identify herself with her French compatriots under German occupation, Weil refused to eat more than the official ration in occupied France. Malnutrition and overwork led to a physical collapse, and during her hospitalization she was found to have tuberculosis. She died after a few months spent in a sanatorium.

Weil's writings, which were collected and published after her death, fill about 20 volumes. Her most important works are *La Pesanteur et la grâce* (1947; *Gravity and Grace*), a collection of religious essays and aphorisms; *L'Enracinement*

(1949; *The Need for Roots*), an essay upon the obligations of the individual and the state; *Attente de Dieu* (1950; *Waiting for God*), a spiritual autobiography; *Oppression et Liberté* (1955; *Oppression and Liberty*), a collection of political and philosophical essays on war, factory work, language, and other topics; and three volumes of *Cahiers* (1951–56; *Notebooks*). Though born of Jewish parents, Weil eventually adopted a mystical theology that came very close to Roman Catholicism. A moral idealist committed to a vision of social justice, Weil in her writings explored her own religious life while also analyzing the individual's relation with the state and God, the spiritual shortcomings of modern industrial society, and the horrors of totalitarianism.

KATHERINE DUNHAM

(b. June 22, 1909, Glen Ellyn, Ill., U.S. — d. May 21, 2006, New York, N.Y.)

The American dancer, choreographer, and anthropologist Katherine Dunham was noted for her innovative interpretations of ritual and ethnic dances.

Dunham early became interested in dance. While a student at the University of Chicago, she formed a dance group that performed in concert at the Chicago World's Fair in 1934 and with the Chicago Civic Opera company in 1935–36. On graduating with a bachelor's degree in anthropology she undertook field studies in the Caribbean and in Brazil. By the time she received an M.A. from the University of Chicago, she had acquired a vast knowledge of the dances and rituals of the black peoples of tropical America. (She later took a Ph.D. in anthropology.) In 1938 she joined the Federal Theatre Project in Chicago and composed a ballet, *L'Ag'Ya*, based on Caribbean dance. Two years later she formed an all-black company, which began touring extensively by 1943. *Tropics* (choreographed 1937) and *Le Jazz Hot* (1938) were among the earliest of many works based on her research.

Dunham was both a popular entertainer and a serious artist intent on tracing the roots of black culture. Many of her students, trained in her studios in Chicago and New York City, became prominent in the field of modern dance. She choreographed for Broadway stage productions and opera—including *Aida* (1963) for the New York Metropolitan Opera. She also choreographed and starred in dance sequences in such films as *Carnival of Rhythm* (1942), *Stormy Weather* (1943), and *Casbah* (1947). In addition, Dunham conducted special projects for African American high school students in Chicago; was artistic and technical director (1966–67) to the president of Senegal; and served as artist-in-residence, and later professor, at Southern Illinois University, Edwardsville, and director of Southern Illinois's Performing Arts Training Centre and Dynamic Museum in East St. Louis, Ill. Dunham was active in human rights causes, and in 1992 she staged a 47-day hunger strike to highlight the plight of Haitian refugees.

Dunham's writings, sometimes published under the pseudonym Kaye Dunn, include *Katherine Dunham's Journey to Accompong* (1946), an account of her anthropological studies in Jamaica; *A Touch of Innocence* (1959), an autobiography; *Island Possessed* (1969); and several articles for popular and scholarly journals. The recipient of numerous awards, Dunham received a Kennedy Center Honor in 1983 and the National Medal of Arts in 1989.

DOROTHY CROWFOOT HODGKIN

(b. May 12, 1910, Cairo, Egypt—d. July 29, 1994, Shipston-on-Stour, Warwickshire, Eng.)

The English chemist Dorothy Crowfoot Hodgkin determined the structure of penicillin and vitamin B_{12}, and her discoveries brought her the 1964 Nobel Prize for Chemistry.

Born Dorothy Mary Crowfoot, Hodgkin was the eldest of four sisters whose parents, John and Molly Crowfoot, worked in North Africa and the Middle East in colonial administration and later as archaeologists. Sent to England for their education, the girls spent much of their childhood apart from their parents. But it was their mother who especially encouraged Dorothy to pursue the passionate interest in crystals that she first displayed at age 10. Educated at a coeducational, state-funded secondary school in the small town of Beccles, Suffolk, Hodgkin fought to be allowed to study science along with the boys. She succeeded and was accepted in 1928 to read for a degree in chemistry at Somerville College, University of Oxford. As an undergraduate, she was one of the first to study the structure of an organic compound using X-ray crystallography.

Hodgkin moved to the University of Cambridge in 1932 to carry out doctoral research with British physicist John Desmond Bernal, who was to be a lifelong influence. In his laboratory, she extended work that he had begun on biological molecules, including sterols (the subject of her thesis), and helped him to make the first X-ray diffraction studies of pepsin, a crystalline protein. She was also highly receptive to his strongly pro-Soviet views and belief in the social function of science. Offered a temporary research fellowship at Somerville, one of Oxford's few colleges for women, she returned there in 1934 and remained until her retirement in 1977. (In the late 1940s the future prime minister Margaret Thatcher was one of her students.) Hodgkin established an X-ray laboratory in a corner of the Oxford University Museum of Natural History (better known for its dinosaur skeletons and mineral collections) and almost immediately began work taking X-ray photographs of insulin.

In 1937 she married the left-wing historian Thomas Hodgkin, who was then teaching adult-education classes in mining and industrial communities in the north of England. As his health was too poor for active military service, he continued this work throughout World War II, returning on weekends to Oxford where his wife remained working on penicillin. They had three children, born in 1938, 1941, and 1946. Thomas Hodgkin subsequently spent extended periods of time in West Africa, where he was an enthusiastic supporter and chronicler of the emerging postcolonial states. Following an infection after the birth of her first child, Dorothy Hodgkin developed chronic rheumatoid arthritis at age 28. This left her hands swollen and distorted, yet she continued to carry out the delicate manipulations necessary to mount and photograph the tiny crystals, smaller than a grain of salt, that she used in her studies.

SCIENTIFIC ACHIEVEMENTS

Hodgkin's insulin research was put to one side in 1939 when Australian pathologist Howard Florey and his colleagues at Oxford succeeded in isolating penicillin and asked her to solve its structure. By 1945 she had succeeded, describing the arrangement of its atoms in three dimensions. Penicillin was at that time the largest molecule to have succumbed to X-ray methods; moreover, the technique had resolved a dispute between eminent organic chemists about its structure. Hodgkin's work on penicillin was recognized by her election to the Royal Society, Britain's premier scientific academy, in 1947, only two years after a woman had been elected for the first time.

In the mid-1950s, Hodgkin discovered the structure of vitamin B_{12}; notably, she made extensive use of computers to carry out the complex computations involved. Her achievements led to her election in 1960 as the first Wolfson Research Professor of the Royal Society, a post she held while remaining in Oxford. Nominated more than once for the Nobel Prize, she won in 1964 for her work on penicillin and vitamin B_{12}. The following year she was made a member of the Order of Merit, Britain's highest honour for achievement in science, the arts, and public life.

Hodgkin never gave up on discovering the structure of insulin, a large, complex protein molecule that could not be understood until both the techniques of X-ray diffraction and high-speed computing were sufficiently advanced. Eventually her patience was rewarded: working with an international team of young researchers, she discovered its structure in 1969, 34 years after she had taken her first X-ray photograph of an insulin crystal.

SOCIAL ACTIVISM

Hodgkin devoted much of the latter part of her life to the cause of scientists in developing countries, especially China and India, and to improved East-West relations and disarmament. From 1975 to 1988 she was president of the Pugwash Conferences on Science and World Affairs, an organization that brings together scientists from around the world to discuss peaceful progress toward international security and development. She also accepted the post of chancellor of the University of Bristol (1970–88), an honorary position in which she nevertheless fought vigorously for improved education funding at a time of government cutbacks. Only the steadily increasing pain and infirmity from her arthritis eventually forced her to curtail her public activities.

Hodgkin's soft-spoken, gentle, and modest demeanour hid a steely determination to achieve her ends, whatever obstacles might stand in her way. She inspired devotion in her students and colleagues, even the most junior of whom knew her simply as Dorothy. Her structural studies of biologically important molecules set standards for a field that was very much in development during her working life, and she made fundamental contributions to our understanding of how these molecules carry out their tasks in living systems.

MOTHER TERESA

(baptized Aug. 27, 1910, Skopje, Macedonia, Ottoman Empire [now in Republic of Macedonia]—d. Sept. 5, 1997, Calcutta [Kolkata], India; beatified Oct. 19, 2003)

Mother Teresa of Calcutta was the founder of the Order of the Missionaries of Charity, a Roman Catholic congregation of women dedicated to the poor, particularly to the destitute of India. She was the recipient of numerous honours, including the 1979 Nobel Prize for Peace.

Mother Teresa was born Agnes Gonxha Bojaxhiu, the daughter of an ethnic Albanian grocer. In 1928 she went to Ireland to join the Sisters of Loretto at the Institute of the Blessed Virgin Mary and sailed only six weeks later to India as a teacher. She taught for 17 years at the order's school in Calcutta (Kolkata).

In 1946 Sister Teresa experienced her "call within a call," which she considered divine inspiration to devote herself to caring for the sick and poor. She then moved into the slums she had observed while teaching. Municipal authorities, upon her petition, gave her a pilgrim hostel, near the sacred temple of Kali, where she founded her order in 1948. Sympathetic companions soon flocked to her aid. Dispensaries and outdoor schools were organized. Mother Teresa adopted Indian citizenship, and her Indian nuns all donned the sari as their habit. In 1950 her order received canonical sanction from Pope Pius XII, and in 1965 it became a pontifical congregation (subject only to the pope). In 1952 she established Nirmal Hriday ("Place for the Pure of Heart"), a hospice where the terminally ill could die with dignity. Her order also opened numerous centres serving the blind, the aged, and the disabled. Under Mother Teresa's guidance, the Missionaries of Charity built a leper colony, called Shanti Nagar ("Town of Peace"), near Asansol, India.

In 1963 the Indian government awarded Mother Teresa the title Padmashri ("Lord of the Lotus") for her services to the people of India. In 1964, on his trip to India, Pope Paul VI gave her his ceremonial limousine, which she immediately raffled to help finance her leper colony. In 1968 she was summoned to Rome to found a home there, staffed primarily with Indian nuns. In recognition of her apostolate, she was honoured on Jan. 6, 1971, by Pope Paul, who awarded her the first Pope John XXIII Peace Prize. In 1979 she received the Nobel Peace Prize for her humanitarian work.

In her later years Mother Teresa spoke out against divorce, contraception, and abortion. She also suffered ill health and had a heart attack in 1989. In 1990 she resigned as head of the order but was returned to office by a near unanimous vote—the lone dissenting voice was her own. A worsening heart condition forced her retirement, and the order chose the Indian-born Sister Nirmala as her successor in 1997. At the time of Mother Teresa's death, her order included hundreds of centres in more than 90 countries with some 4,000 nuns and hundreds of thousands of lay workers. Within two years of Mother Teresa's death, the process to declare her a saint was begun, and Pope John Paul II issued a special dispensation to expedite the process of canonization. She was beatified on Oct. 19, 2003, reaching the ranks of the blessed in the shortest time in the history of the church.

Although Mother Teresa displayed cheerfulness and a deep commitment to God in her daily work, her letters (which were collected and published in 2007) indicate that she did not feel God's presence in her soul during the last 50 years of her life. The letters reveal the suffering she endured and her feeling that Jesus had abandoned her at the start of her mission. Continuing to experience a spiritual darkness, she came to believe that she was sharing in Christ's Passion, particularly the moment in which Christ asks, "My God, my God, why have you forsaken me?" Despite this hardship, Mother Teresa integrated the feeling of absence into her daily religious life and remained committed to her faith and her work for Christ.

LUCILLE BALL

(b. Aug. 6, 1911, Celoron, near Jamestown, N.Y., U.S.—d. April 26, 1989, Los Angeles, Calif.)

The radio and motion-picture actress Lucille Ball (in full Lucille Désirée Ball) was a longtime comedy star of American television, best remembered for her classic television comedy series *I Love Lucy*.

Ball determined at an early age to become an actress and left high school at age 15 to enroll in a drama school in New York City. Her early attempts to find a place in the theatre all met with rebuffs, and she took a job as a model under the name Diane Belmont. She was moderately successful as a model. A poster on which she appeared brought her to the attention of the Hollywood studios and won her spots in *Roman Scandals* (1933), *Blood Money* (1933), *Kid Millions* (1934), and other movies.

Ball remained in Hollywood and appeared in increasingly larger roles in a succession of movies—*Carnival* (1935), *Stage Door* (1937), *Room Service* (1938), *Five Came Back* (1939). In 1940, she starred in *Too Many Girls*, which also featured the popular Cuban bandleader and actor Desi Arnaz, whom she married in 1940. For 10 years they conducted

Lucille Ball and Bob Hope in Fancy Pants *(1950)*. © 1950 Paramount
Pictures Corporation; photograph from a private collection

separate careers, he as a bandleader and she as a movie actress who was usually seen in B-grade comedies. She won major roles in *The Big Street* (1942) with Henry Fonda, *Du Barry Was a Lady* (1943), *Without Love* (1945), *Ziegfeld Follies* (1946), and *Sorrowful Jones* (1949) and *Fancy Pants* (1950), both with Bob Hope. All of her comedies were box office successes, but they failed to make the most of her wide-ranging talents.

In 1950 Ball and her husband formed Desilu Productions, which, after experimenting with a radio program, launched in October 1951 a television comedy series entitled *I Love Lucy*. Starring the two of them in a comedy version of their real lives, the show was an instant hit. For the six years (1951–56 and, under the title *The Lucille Ball-Desi Arnaz Show*, 1957–58) during which fresh episodes were produced, it remained at or near the top of the TV ratings. *I Love Lucy* proved to be an outstanding vehicle for Ball's exceptional comedic talents. As the character Lucy, a wise-cracking housewife who regularly concocted schemes to get herself out of the house, Ball showcased her expertise for timing, physical comedy, and range of characterization. The show also introduced several technical innovations to television broadcasting (notably the use of three cameras to film the show) and set the standard for situation comedies, thriving in reruns for decades.

Meanwhile Desilu acquired RKO Pictures, began producing other shows for television, and became one of the major companies in a highly competitive field. Ball and Arnaz were divorced in 1960, and two years later she succeeded him as president of Desilu, becoming the only woman at that time to lead a major Hollywood production company.

After starring in the Broadway show *Wildcat* in 1961, Ball returned to television in *The Lucy Show* (1962–68). She resumed movie work with *Yours, Mine and Ours* (1968) and

Mame (1974). In 1967 she sold Desilu and formed her own company, Lucille Ball Productions, which produced her third television series, *Here's Lucy* (1968–74). She continued to appear thereafter in special productions and as a guest star. In 1985 she played a Manhattan bag lady in the television film *Stone Pillow*. Her fourth television series, *Life with Lucy*, aired for two months in 1986.

ROSA PARKS

(b. Feb. 4, 1913, Tuskegee, Ala., U.S.—d. Oct. 24, 2005, Detroit, Mich.)

The African American civil rights activist Rosa Parks refused to relinquish her seat on a public bus to a white man, precipitating the 1955–56 Montgomery bus boycott in Alabama. Her act is recognized as the spark that ignited the U.S. civil rights movement.

In 1932 Rosa Louise McCauley married Raymond Parks, who encouraged her to return to high school and earn a diploma. She later made her living as a seamstress. In 1943 Rosa Parks became a member of the Montgomery chapter of the National Association for the Advancement of Colored People (NAACP), and she served as its secretary until 1956. On Dec. 1, 1955, she was arrested for refusing to give her bus seat to a white man, a violation of the city's racial segregation ordinances.

Under the aegis of the Montgomery Improvement Association and the leadership of the young pastor of the Dexter Avenue Baptist Church, Martin Luther King, Jr., a boycott of the municipal bus company was begun on December 5. (African Americans constituted some 70 percent of the ridership.) On Nov. 13, 1956, the U.S. Supreme Court upheld a lower court's decision declaring Montgomery's segregated seating unconstitutional, and the court order was served on December 20; the boycott ended the following day. For her role in igniting the successful campaign, which brought King to national prominence, Parks became known as the "mother of the civil rights movement."

In 1957 Parks moved with her husband and mother to Detroit, where, from 1965 to 1988, she was a member of the staff of Michigan Congressman John Conyers, Jr. She also remained active in the NAACP. The Southern Christian Leadership Conference established the annual Rosa Parks Freedom Award in her honour. In 1987 she cofounded the Rosa and Raymond Parks Institute for Self Development to provide career training for young people. She was the recipient of numerous awards, including the Presidential Medal of Freedom (1996) and the Congressional Gold Medal (1999).

JIANG QING

(b. March 1914, Zhucheng, Shandong province, China—d. May 14, 1991)

Jiang Qing, born Li Jinhai, was the third wife of Chinese communist leader Mao Zedong and the most influential woman in the People's Republic of China for a while until her downfall in 1976, after Mao's death. As a member of the Gang of Four she was convicted in 1981 of "counter-revolutionary crimes" and imprisoned.

Jiang, who was reared by her relatives, became a member of a theatrical troupe in 1929. Her activity in a communist-front organization in 1933 led to her arrest and detainment. Upon her release she went to Shanghai. She was arrested again in Shanghai in 1934 and left for Beijing after her release, but she later returned to Shanghai, where she played minor roles for the left-wing Diantong Motion Pictures Company under her new stage name, Lan Ping.

When the Japanese attacked Shanghai in 1937, Jiang fled to the Chinese Nationalist wartime capital at Chongqing, where she worked for the government-controlled Central

Jiang Qing and Mao Zedong, 1945. Library of Congress, Washington, D.C. (neg. no. LC-USZ62-126856)

Movie Studio until she crossed the Nationalist lines. She went through Xi'an to join the communist forces in Yan'an and started to use the name Jiang Qing. While a drama instructor at the Lu Xun Art Academy, she met Mao for the first time when he gave a talk at the school. They were married in 1939 (technically, she was Mao's fourth wife; he had an arranged marriage in his youth but never acknowledged it). The marriage was criticized by many party members, especially since the woman whom Mao divorced (one of the few women to survive the communists' Long March of 1934–35) was then hospitalized in Moscow. Party leaders agreed to the marriage on condition that Jiang stay out of politics for the next 20 years.

After the establishment of the People's Republic of China in 1949, Jiang remained out of public view except to serve as Mao's hostess for foreign visitors or to sit on various cultural committees. In 1963, however, she became more politically active, sponsoring a movement in the theatrical form *jingxi* (Peking opera) and in ballet aimed at infusing traditional Chinese art forms with proletarian themes. Jiang's cultural reform movement gradually grew into a prolonged attack on many of the leading cultural and intellectual figures in China and culminated in the Cultural Revolution that by 1966 had begun to sweep the country.

Jiang reached the height of her power and influence in 1966, winning renown for her fiery speeches to mass gatherings and her involvement with the radical young Red Guard groups of the revolution. One of the few people whom Mao trusted, she became the first deputy head of the Cultural Revolution and acquired far-reaching powers over China's cultural life. She oversaw the total suppression of a wide variety of traditional cultural activities during the decade of the revolution. As the revolution's initial fervour waned in the late 1960s, however, so did Jiang's prominence. She reemerged in 1974 as a cultural leader and spokeswoman for Mao's new policy of "settling down."

Mao died on Sept. 9, 1976, and the radicals in the party lost their protector. A month later, wall posters appeared attacking Jiang and three other radicals as the Gang of Four, and the attacks grew progressively more hostile. Jiang and the other members of the Gang of Four were soon afterward arrested. She was expelled from the Communist Party in 1977. In 1980–81 at her public trial as a member of the Gang of Four, Jiang was accused of fomenting the widespread civil unrest that had gripped China during the Cultural Revolution, but she refused to confess her guilt; instead, she denounced the court and the country's leaders. She received a suspended death sentence, but in 1983 it was commuted to life imprisonment. Her death in prison was officially reported as a suicide.

ELIZABETH STERN

(b. Sept. 19, 1915, Cobalt, Ont., Can.—d. Aug. 18, 1980, Los Angeles, Calif., U.S.)

The Canadian-born American pathologist Elizabeth Stern is noted for her work on the stages of a cell's progression from a normal to a cancerous state.

Stern received a medical degree from the University of Toronto in 1939 and the following year went to the United States, where she became a naturalized citizen in 1943. She received further medical training at the Pennsylvania Medical School and at the Good Samaritan and Cedars of Lebanon hospitals in Los Angeles. She was one of the first specialists in cytopathology, the study of diseased cells. From 1963 she was professor of epidemiology in the School of Public Health at the University of California, Los Angeles.

While at UCLA, Stern became interested in cervical cancer, and she began to focus her research solely on its causes and progression. The discoveries she made during this period led her to publish in 1963 what is believed to be the first case report linking a specific virus (herpes simplex virus) to a specific cancer (cervical cancer). For another phase of her research she studied a group of more than 10,000 Los Angeles county women who were clients of the county's public family planning clinics.

In a 1973 article in the journal *Science*, Stern became the first person to report a definite link between the prolonged use of oral contraceptives and cervical cancer. Her research connected the use of contraceptive pills containing steroids with cervical dysplasia, which is often a precursor of cervical cancer. In her most noted work in this field, Stern studied cells cast off from the lining of the cervix and discovered that a normal cell goes through 250 distinct stages of cell progression before reaching an advanced stage of cervical cancer. This prompted the development of diagnostic techniques and screening instruments to detect the cancer in its early stages. Her research helped make cervical cancer, with its slow rate of metastasis, one of the types of cancer that can be successfully treated by prophylactic measures (i.e., excision of abnormal tissue).

Stern continued her teaching and research into the late 1970s, despite undergoing chemotherapy for stomach cancer. She died of the disease in 1980.

SIRIMAVO R. D. BANDARANAIKE

(b. April 17, 1916, Ratnapura, Ceylon [now Sri Lanka]—d. Oct. 10, 2000, Colombo, Sri Lanka)

Upon her party's victory in the 1960 Ceylon general election, Sirimavo Ratwatte Dias Bandaranaike became the world's first woman prime minister. She left office in 1965 but returned to serve two more terms (1970–77, 1994–2000) as prime minister. The family she founded with her late husband, S.W.R.D. Bandaranaike, rose to great prominence in Sri Lankan politics.

Born into a wealthy family, she married the politician S.W.R.D. Bandaranaike in 1940 and began to interest herself in social welfare. After her husband, who became prime minister in 1956, was assassinated in 1959, she was induced by his Sri Lanka Freedom Party (SLFP) to become the party's leader. The SLFP won a decisive victory at the general election in July 1960, and she became prime minister.

Bandaranaike carried on her husband's program of socialist economic policies, neutrality in international relations, and the active encouragement of the Buddhist religion and of the Sinhalese language and culture. Her government nationalized various economic enterprises and enforced a law making Sinhalese the sole official language. By 1964 a deepening economic crisis and the SLFP's coalition with the Marxist Lanka Sama Samaja Party ("Ceylon Socialist Party") had eroded popular support for her government, which was resoundingly defeated in the general election of 1965. In 1970, however, her socialist coalition, the United Front, regained power.

As prime minister, Bandaranaike pursued more radical policies. Her government further restricted free enterprise, nationalized industries, carried out land reforms, and promulgated a new constitution that created an executive presidency and made Ceylon into a republic named Sri Lanka. While reducing inequalities of wealth, Bandaranaike's socialist policies had once again caused economic stagnation, and her government's support of Buddhism and the Sinhalese language had helped alienate the country's large Tamil minority. The failure to deal with ethnic rivalries and economic distress led, in the election of July 1977, to the SLFP's retaining only 8 of the 168 seats in the National Assembly, and Bandaranaike was replaced as prime minister.

In 1980 the Sri Lanka parliament stripped Bandaranaike of her political rights and barred her from political office, but in 1986 President J. R. Jayawardene granted her a pardon that restored her rights. She ran unsuccessfully as the SLFP's candidate for president in 1988, and after regaining a seat in parliament in 1989 she became the leader of the opposition.

Bandaranaike's children, in the meantime, had become major political figures within the SLFP. Her son, Anura P.S.D. Bandaranaike (b. 1949), was first elected to parliament in 1977 and had become the leader of the SLFP's right-wing faction by 1984. He was frustrated in his bid to become the party's leader, however, by his sister Chandrika Bandaranaike Kumaratunga (b. 1945), who held left-wing views and was favoured by their mother for the leadership. In response, Anura defected from the SLFP and joined the rival United National Party (UNP) in 1993.

Chandrika had been active in the SLFP before marrying the film actor Vijaya Kumaratunga in 1978, and after his assassination in 1988 she rejoined her mother's party. She soon came to head its left-wing faction, and a string of electoral victories propelled her to the leadership of an SLFP-based coalition that won the parliamentary elections of August 1994. Chandrika became prime minister, and in November of that year she won the presidential election over the UNP candidate. Chandrika appointed her mother, Sirimavo Bandaranaike, to serve as prime minister in her new government, which mounted a major military campaign against Tamil separatists in 1995. Failing health forced Bandaranaike to resign her post in August 2000. Shortly after voting in the October parliamentary elections, she suffered a heart attack and died.

INDIRA GANDHI

(b. Nov. 19, 1917, Allahabad, India—d. Oct. 31, 1984, New Delhi)

Indira Gandhi served as prime minister of India for three consecutive terms (1966–77) and a fourth term (1980–84). She was assassinated by Sikh extremists.

Indira Priyadarshini Nehru was the only child of Jawaharlal Nehru, the first prime minister of independent India. She attended Visva-Bharati University, West Bengal, and the University of Oxford, and in 1942 she married Feroze Gandhi (died 1960), a fellow member of the Indian National Congress (Congress Party). She was a member of the working committee of the ruling Congress Party from 1955, and in 1959 she was elected to the largely honorary post of party president. Lal Bahadur Shastri, who succeeded Nehru as prime minister in 1964, named her minister of information and broadcasting in his government.

On Shastri's sudden death in January 1966, Gandhi became leader of the Congress Party—and thus also prime minister—in a compromise between the right and left wings of the party. Her leadership, however, came under continual challenge from the right wing of the party, led by a former minister of finance, Morarji Desai. In the election of 1967 she won a slim majority and had to accept Desai as deputy prime minister. In 1971, however, she won a sweeping electoral victory over a coalition of conservative parties. Gandhi strongly supported East Bengal (now Bangladesh) in its secessionist conflict with Pakistan in late 1971, and India's armed forces achieved a swift and decisive victory over Pakistan that led to the creation of Bangladesh.

In March 1972, buoyed by the country's success against Pakistan, Gandhi again led her new Congress Party to a landslide victory in national elections. Shortly afterward her defeated Socialist Party opponent charged that she had violated the election laws. In June 1975 the High Court of Allahabad ruled against her, which meant that she would be deprived of her seat in Parliament and would have to stay out of politics for six years. In response, she declared a state of emergency throughout India, imprisoned her political opponents, and assumed emergency powers, passing many laws limiting personal freedoms. During this period she implemented several unpopular policies, including large-scale sterilization as a form of birth control. When long-postponed national elections were held in 1977, Gandhi and her party were soundly defeated, whereupon she left office. The Janata Party took over the reins of government.

Early in 1978 Gandhi's supporters split from the Congress Party and formed the Congress (I) Party—the "I" signifying Indira. She was briefly imprisoned (October 1977 and December 1978) on charges of official corruption. Despite these setbacks, she won a new seat in Parliament in November 1978, and her Congress (I) Party began to gather strength. Dissension within the ruling Janata Party led to the fall of its government in August 1979. When new elections for the Lok Sabha (lower house of Parliament) were held in January 1980, Gandhi

During her four terms as India's prime minister, Indira Gandhi faced challenges from outside the country and inside her own party. Keystone/Hulton Archive/Getty Images

and her Congress (I) Party were swept back into power in a landslide victory. Her son Sanjay Gandhi, who had become her chief political adviser, also won a seat in the Lok Sabha. All legal cases against Indira, as well as against her son, were withdrawn.

Sanjay Gandhi's death in an airplane crash in June 1980 eliminated Indira's chosen successor from the political leadership of India. After Sanjay's death, she groomed her other son, Rajiv, for the leadership of her party. Indira Gandhi adhered to the quasi-socialist policies of industrial development that had been begun by her father. She established closer relations with the Soviet Union, depending on that nation for support in India's long-standing conflict with Pakistan.

During the early 1980s Gandhi was faced with threats to the political integrity of India. Several states sought a larger measure of independence from the central government, and Sikh extremists in Punjab state used violence to assert their demands for an autonomous state. In response, Gandhi ordered an army attack in June 1984 on the Harimandir (Golden Temple) at Amritsar, the Sikhs' holiest shrine, which led to the deaths of more than 450 Sikhs. Five months later Gandhi was killed in her garden by a fusillade of bullets fired by two of her own Sikh bodyguards in revenge for the attack on the Golden Temple.

EVA PERÓN

(b. May 7, 1919, Los Toldos, Arg. — d. July 26, 1952, Buenos Aires)

Eva Duarte de Perón was the second wife of Argentine president Juan Perón. During her husband's first term as president (1946–52), she became a powerful though unofficial political leader, revered by the lower economic classes, who knew her as Evita.

Eva Duarte (in full María Eva Duarte) married Col. Juan Perón, a widower, in 1945 after an undistinguished career as a stage and radio actress. She participated in her husband's 1945–46 presidential campaign, winning the adulation of the masses, whom she addressed as *los descamisados* (Spanish: "the shirtless ones").

Although she never held any government post, Evita acted as de facto minister of health and labour, awarding generous wage increases to the unions, who responded with political support for Perón. After cutting off government subsidies to the traditional Sociedad de Beneficencia (Spanish: "Aid Society"), thereby making more enemies among the traditional elite, she replaced it with her own Eva Perón Foundation, which was supported by "voluntary" union and business contributions plus a substantial cut of the national lottery and other funds. These resources were used to establish thousands of hospitals, schools, orphanages, homes for the aged, and other charitable institutions. Evita was largely responsible for the passage of the woman suffrage law and formed the Peronista Feminist Party in 1949. She also introduced compulsory religious education into all Argentine schools. In 1951, although dying of cancer, she obtained the nomination for vice president, but the army forced her to withdraw her candidacy.

After her death, Evita remained a formidable influence in Argentine politics. Her working-class followers tried unsuccessfully to have her canonized, and her enemies, in an effort to exorcise her as a national symbol of Peronism, stole her embalmed body in 1955 after Juan Perón was overthrown and secreted it in Italy for 16 years. In 1971 the military government, bowing to Peronist demands, turned over her remains to her exiled widower in Madrid. After Juan Perón died in office in 1974, his third wife, Isabel Perón, hoping to gain favour among the populace, repatriated the remains and installed them next to the deceased leader in a crypt in the presidential palace. Two years later a new military junta hostile to Peronism removed the bodies; Evita's remains were finally interred in the Duarte family crypt in Recoleta cemetery.

ROSALIND FRANKLIN
(b. July 25, 1920, London, Eng.—d. April 16, 1958, London)

The British scientist Rosalind Franklin was an unacknowledged contributor to the discovery of the molecular structure of deoxyribonucleic acid (DNA), a constituent of chromosomes that serves to encode genetic information.

Rosalind Elsie Franklin attended St. Paul's Girls' School before studying physical chemistry at Newnham College, Cambridge. After graduating in 1941, she received a fellowship to conduct research in physical chemistry at Cambridge. But the advance of World War II changed her course of action: not only did she serve as a London air raid warden, but in 1942 she gave up her fellowship in order to work for the British Coal Utilisation Research Association, where she investigated the physical chemistry of carbon and coal for the war effort. Nevertheless, she was able to use this research for her doctoral thesis, and in 1945 she received a doctorate from Cambridge. From 1947 to 1950 she worked with Jacques Méring at the State Chemical Laboratory in Paris, studying X-ray diffraction technology. That work led to her research on the structural changes caused by the formation of graphite in heated carbons—work that proved valuable for the coking industry.

In 1951 Franklin joined the Biophysical Laboratory at King's College, London, as a research fellow. There she applied X-ray diffraction methods to the study of DNA. When she began her research at King's College, very little was known about the chemical makeup or structure of DNA. However, she soon discovered the density of DNA and, more important, established that the molecule existed in a helical conformation. Her work to make clearer X-ray patterns of DNA molecules laid the foundation for James Watson and Francis Crick to suggest in 1953 that the structure of DNA is a double-helix polymer, a spiral consisting of two DNA strands wound around each other.

From 1953 to 1958 Franklin worked in the Crystallography Laboratory at Birkbeck College, London. While there she completed her work on coals and on DNA and began a project on the molecular structure of the tobacco mosaic virus. She collaborated on studies showing that the ribonucleic acid (RNA) in that virus was embedded in its protein rather than in its central cavity and that this RNA was a single-strand helix, rather than the double helix found in the DNA of bacterial viruses and higher organisms. Franklin's involvement in cutting-edge DNA research was halted by her untimely death from cancer in 1958.

ROSALYN S. YALOW

(b. July 19, 1921, New York, N.Y., U.S.)

The American medical physicist Rosalyn Sussman Yalow was a joint recipient (with Andrew V. Schally and Roger Guillemin) of the 1977 Nobel Prize for Physiology or Medicine, awarded for her development of the radioimmunoassay (RIA), an extremely sensitive technique for measuring minute quantities of biologically active substances.

Yalow graduated with honours from Hunter College of the City University of New York in 1941 and four years later received her Ph.D. in physics from the University of Illinois. From 1946 to 1950 she lectured on physics at Hunter, and in 1947 she became a consultant in nuclear physics to the Bronx Veterans Administration Hospital, where from 1950 to 1970 she was physicist and assistant chief of the radioisotope service.

With a colleague, the American physician Solomon A. Berson, Yalow began using radioactive isotopes to examine and diagnose various disease conditions. Yalow and Berson's investigations into the mechanism underlying type II diabetes led to their development of RIA. In the 1950s it was known that individuals treated with injections of animal insulin developed resistance to the hormone and so required greater amounts of it to offset the effects of the disease; however, a satisfactory explanation for this phenomenon had not been put forth. Yalow and Berson theorized that the foreign insulin stimulated the production of antibodies, which became bound to the insulin and prevented the hormone from entering cells and carrying out its function of metabolizing glucose. In order to prove their hypothesis to a skeptical scientific community, the researchers combined techniques from immunology and radioisotope tracing to measure minute amounts of these antibodies, and the RIA was born. It was soon apparent that this method could be used to measure hundreds of other biologically active substances, such as viruses, drugs, and other proteins. This made possible such practical applications as the screening of blood in blood banks for hepatitis virus and the determination of effective dosage levels of drugs and antibiotics.

In 1970 Yalow was appointed chief of the laboratory later renamed the Nuclear Medical Service at the Veterans Administration Hospital. In 1976 she was the first female recipient of the Albert Lasker Basic Medical Research Award. Yalow became a distinguished professor at large at the Albert Einstein College of Medicine at Yeshiva University in 1979 and left in 1985 to accept the position of Solomon A. Berson Distinguished Professor at Large at the Mount Sinai School of Medicine. She was awarded the National Medal of Science in 1988.

NADINE GORDIMER

(b. Nov. 20, 1923, Springs, Transvaal, S.Af.)

The South African novelist and short-story writer Nadine Gordimer examined the theme of exile and alienation in her works; she received the Nobel Prize for Literature in 1991.

Gordimer was born into a privileged white middle-class family and began reading at an early age. By the age of 9 she was writing, and she published her first story in a magazine when she was 15. Her wide reading informed her about the world on the other side of apartheid—the official South African policy of racial segregation—and that discovery in time developed into strong political opposition to apartheid. Never an outstanding scholar, she attended the University of Witwatersrand for one year. In addition to writing, she lectured and taught at various schools in the United States during the 1960s and '70s.

Gordimer's first book was *The Soft Voice of the Serpent* (1952), a collection of short stories. In 1953 a novel, *The Lying Days*, was published. Both exhibit the clear, controlled, and unsentimental technique that became her hallmark. Her stories concern the devastating effects of apartheid on the lives of South Africans—the constant tension between personal isolation and the commitment to social justice, the numbness caused by the unwillingness to accept apartheid, the inability to change it, and the refusal of exile.

In 1974 Gordimer won the Booker Prize for *The Conservationist* (1974). Later novels include *Burger's Daughter* (1979), *July's People* (1981), *A Sport of Nature* (1987), and *My*

Son's Story (1990). Gordimer addressed environmental issues in *Get a Life* (2005), the story of a South African ecologist who, after receiving thyroid treatment, becomes radioactive to others. She also wrote a number of short-story collections, including *A Soldier's Embrace* (1980), *Crimes of Conscience* (1991), and *Loot and Other Stories* (2003). *Living in Hope and History: Notes from Our Century* (1999) is a collection of essays, correspondence, and reminiscences. In 2007 Gordimer was awarded the French Legion of Honour.

ELIZABETH II

(b. April 21, 1926, London, Eng.)

Elizabeth II reigned as the queen of the United Kingdom of Great Britain and Northern Ireland from Feb. 6, 1952.

Elizabeth II, born Elizabeth Alexandra Mary, was the elder daughter of Albert, duke of York, and his wife, Lady Elizabeth Bowes-Lyon. As the child of a younger son of King George V, the young Elizabeth had little prospect of acceding to the throne until her uncle, Edward VIII (afterward duke of Windsor), abdicated in her father's favour on Dec. 11, 1936, at which time her father became King George VI and she became heir presumptive. The princess's education was supervised by her mother, who entrusted her daughters to a governess, Marion Crawford; the princess was also grounded in history by C.H.K. Marten, afterward provost of Eton College, and had instruction from visiting teachers in music and languages. During World War II she and her sister, Princess Margaret Rose, perforce spent much of their time safely away from the London blitz and separated from their parents, living mostly at Balmoral Castle in Scotland and at the Royal Lodge, Windsor, and Windsor Castle.

Early in 1947 Princess Elizabeth went with the king and queen to South Africa. After her return there was an announcement of her betrothal to her distant cousin Lieutenant Philip Mountbatten of the Royal Navy, formerly Prince Philip of Greece and Denmark. The marriage took place in Westminster Abbey on Nov. 20, 1947. On the eve of the wedding her father, the king, conferred upon the bridegroom the titles of duke of Edinburgh, earl of Merioneth, and Baron Greenwich. They took residence at Clarence House in London. Their first child, Prince Charles (Charles Philip Arthur George), was born Nov. 14, 1948, at Buckingham Palace.

In the summer of 1951 the health of King George VI entered into a serious decline, and Princess Elizabeth represented him at the Trooping the Colour and on

Elizabeth II and coronation guests, June 2, 1953. Encyclopædia Britannica, Inc.

various other state occasions. On October 7 she and her husband set out on a highly successful tour of Canada and Washington, D.C. After Christmas in England she and the duke set out in January 1952 for a tour of Australia and New Zealand, but en route, at Sagana, Kenya, news reached them of the king's death on Feb. 6, 1952. Elizabeth, now queen, at once flew back to England. The first three months of her reign, the period of full mourning for her father, were passed in comparative seclusion. But in the summer, after she had moved from Clarence House to Buckingham Palace, she undertook the routine duties of the sovereign and carried out her first state opening of Parliament on Nov. 4, 1952. Her coronation was held at Westminster Abbey on June 2, 1953.

Beginning in November 1953, the queen and the duke of Edinburgh made a six-month round-the-world tour of the Commonwealth, which included the first visit to Australia and New Zealand by a reigning British monarch. In 1957, after state visits to various European nations, she and the duke visited Canada and the United States. In 1961 she made the first royal British tour of the Indian subcontinent in 50 years, and she was also the first reigning British monarch to visit South America (in 1968) and the Persian Gulf countries (in 1979). During her "Silver Jubilee" in 1977, she presided at a London banquet attended by the leaders of the 36 members of the Commonwealth, traveled all over Britain and Northern Ireland, and toured overseas in the South Pacific and Australia, in Canada, and in the Caribbean.

On the accession of Queen Elizabeth, her son Prince Charles became heir apparent; he was named prince of Wales on July 26, 1958, and was so invested on July 1, 1969. The queen's other children were Princess Anne (Anne Elizabeth Alice Louise), born Aug. 15, 1950; Prince Andrew (Andrew Albert Christian Edward), born Feb. 19, 1960, and created duke of York in 1986; and Prince Edward (Edward Anthony Richard Louis), born March 10, 1964. All these children have the surname "of Windsor," but in 1960 Elizabeth decided to create the hyphenated name Mountbatten-Windsor for other descendants not styled prince or princess and royal highness. Elizabeth's first grandchild (Princess Anne's son) was born on Nov. 15, 1977.

The queen seemed increasingly aware of the modern role of the monarchy, allowing, for example, the televising of the royal family's domestic life in 1970 and condoning the formal dissolution of her sister's marriage in 1978. However, after the failed marriage of her son and Diana, princess of Wales, and Diana's death in 1997, popular feeling in Britain turned against the royal family, which was thought to be out of touch with contemporary British life. In line with her earlier attempts at modernizing the monarchy, the queen, after 1997, sought to present a less-stuffy and less-traditional image of the monarchy. These attempts have met with mixed success.

Queen Elizabeth has been known to favour simplicity in court life and take a serious and informed interest in government business, aside from the traditional and ceremonial duties. Privately she has become a keen horsewoman; she has kept racehorses, frequently attended races, and periodically visited the Kentucky stud farms in the United States. Her financial and property holdings have made her one of the world's richest women.

ANNE FRANK

(b. June 12, 1929, Frankfurt am Main, Ger. — d. March 1945, Bergen-Belsen concentration camp, near Hannover)

Anne Frank, a young Jewish girl who wrote a diary of her family's two years in hiding during the German occupation of The Netherlands, personalized the Holocaust for generations of readers. *The Diary of a Young Girl* (published posthumously) has become a classic of war literature.

Early in the Nazi regime of Adolf Hitler, Anne's father, Otto Frank (1889–1980), a German businessman, took his wife and two daughters to live in Amsterdam. In 1941, after German forces occupied The Netherlands, Anne was compelled to transfer from a public to a Jewish school. Faced with deportation (supposedly to a forced-labour camp), the Franks went into hiding on July 9, 1942, with four other Jews in the back-room office and warehouse of Otto Frank's food-products business. With the aid of a few non-Jewish friends who smuggled in food and other supplies, they lived confined to their secret annex until Aug. 4, 1944, when the Gestapo, acting on a tip from Dutch informers, discovered them.

The family was transported to Westerbork, a transit camp in The Netherlands, and from there to Auschwitz in German-occupied Poland on Sept. 3, 1944, on the last transport to leave Westerbork for Auschwitz. Anne (in full Annelies Marie) and her sister Margot were transferred to Bergen-Belsen the following month. Anne's mother died in early January, just before the evacuation of Auschwitz on Jan. 18, 1945. Both Anne and Margot died in a typhus epidemic in March 1945, only weeks before the liberation of Bergen-Belsen. Otto Frank was found hospitalized at Auschwitz when it was liberated by Russian troops on Jan. 27, 1945.

Friends who had searched the family's hiding place after their capture later gave Otto Frank the papers left behind by the Gestapo. Among them he found Anne's diary, which was published as *The Diary of a Young Girl* (originally in Dutch, 1947). Precocious in style and insight, it traces her emotional growth amid adversity. In it she wrote, "In spite of everything I still believe that people are really good at heart."

The diary has been translated into more than 65 languages and is the most widely read diary of the Holocaust, and Anne is probably the best-known of Holocaust victim. A new English translation, published in 1995, contained material edited out of the original version, making the new work nearly one-third longer. The Frank family's hiding place on the Prinsengracht—a canal in Amsterdam—has become a museum.

VIOLETA BARRIOS DE CHAMORRO
(b. Oct. 18, 1929, Rivas, Nic.)

Newspaper publisher and politician Violeta Barrios de Chamorro was Central America's first woman president and served as leader of Nicaragua from 1990 to 1997.

Violeta Barrios was born into a wealthy Nicaraguan family (her father was a cattle rancher). She received much of her early education in the U.S. states of Texas and Virginia. In 1950, shortly after the death of her father, she returned to Nicaragua, where she married Pedro Joaquim Chamorro Cardenal, editor of the newspaper *La Prensa*, which was often critical of the Somoza family dictatorship. The Chamorros were forced into exile in 1957 and lived in Costa Rica for several years before returning to Nicaragua after the Somoza government declared an amnesty.

On Jan. 10, 1978, Pedro Chamorro, who had continued to criticize the Somozas and had been imprisoned several times during the 1960s and '70s, was assassinated. His death helped to spark a revolution, led by the Sandinista National Liberation Front, which toppled the government of Anastasio Somoza Debayle in July 1979. A member of the Sandinista ruling junta in 1979–80, Violeta Chamorro soon became disillusioned with the Sandinistas' Marxist policies, and later she became an outspoken foe. She took over *La Prensa*, which was frequently shut down during the 1980s and was banned completely for a period in 1986–87. During the 1980s she was accused by the Sandinistas of accepting money from the U.S. Central Intelligence Agency, which was then providing support to opposition groups and directing the Contra rebels in their guerrilla war against the Sandinista government.

An end to the guerrilla war was negotiated in the late 1980s, and free elections were scheduled for 1990. Chamorro, drafted as the presidential candidate of the 14-party National Opposition Union (Unión Nacional Opositor; UNO) alliance, won a surprisingly easy victory over President Daniel Ortega Saavedra, head of the Sandinistas. She was inaugurated on April 25, 1990, becoming Central America's first woman president.

During her presidency Chamorro reversed a number of Sandinista policies. Several state-owned industries were privatized, censorship was lifted, and the size of the army was reduced. At the same time, she retained a number of Sandinistas in the government and attempted to reconcile the country's various political factions. Many credit her conciliatory policies with helping to maintain the fragile peace that had been negotiated. Barred from running for a second term, she retired from politics after her term ended in January 1997.

SANDRA DAY O'CONNOR

(b. March 26, 1930, El Paso, Texas, U.S.)

Sandra Day O'Connor was an associate justice of the Supreme Court of the United States from 1981 to

2006. She was the first woman to serve on the Supreme Court. A moderate conservative, she was known for her dispassionate and meticulously researched opinions.

O'Connor grew up on a large family ranch near Duncan, Arizona. She received undergraduate (1950) and law (1952) degrees from Stanford University, where she met the future chief justice of the United States William Rehnquist. Upon her graduation she married a classmate, John Jay O'Connor III. Unable to find employment in a law firm because she was a woman—despite her academic achievements, one firm offered her a job as a secretary—she became a deputy district attorney in San Mateo county, California. After a brief tenure, she and her husband, a member of the U.S. Army Judge Advocate General Corps, moved to Germany, where she served as a civil attorney for the army (1954–57).

Upon her return to the United States, O'Connor pursued private practice in Maryville, Arizona, becoming an assistant attorney general for the state (1965–69). In 1969 she was elected as a Republican to the Arizona Senate (1969–74), rising to the position of majority leader—the first woman in the United States to occupy such a position. In 1974 she was elected a Superior Court judge in Maricopa county, and in 1979 she was appointed to the Arizona Court of Appeals in Phoenix. In July 1981 President Ronald Reagan nominated her to fill the vacancy left on the Supreme Court by the retirement of Justice Potter Stewart. Described by Reagan as a "person for all seasons," O'Connor was confirmed unanimously by the Senate and was sworn in as the first female justice on Sept. 25, 1981.

O'Connor quickly became known for her pragmatism and was considered, with Justice Anthony Kennedy, a decisive swing vote in the Supreme Court's decisions. In such disparate fields as election law and abortion rights, she attempted to fashion workable solutions to major constitutional questions, often over the course of several cases. In her decisions in election law she emphasized the importance of equal-protection claims (*Shaw v. Reno*, [1993]), declared unconstitutional district boundaries that are "unexplainable on grounds other than race" (*Bush v. Vera*, [1996]), and sided with the court's more liberal members in upholding the configuration of a congressional district in North Carolina created on the basis of variables including but not limited to race (*Easley v. Cromartie*, [2001]).

In similar fashion, O'Connor's views on abortion rights were articulated gradually. In a series of rulings, she signaled a reluctance to support any decision that would deny women the right to choose a safe and legal abortion. By "defecting" in part from the conservative majority in *Webster v. Reproductive Health Services* (1989)—in which the court upheld a Missouri law that prohibited public employees from performing or assisting in abortions not necessary to save a woman's life and that required doctors to determine the viability of a fetus if it was at least 20 weeks old—she reduced the court's opinion to a plurality. Through her stewardship in *Planned Parenthood of Southeastern Pennsylvania v. Casey* (1992), the court refashioned its position on the right to abortion. The court's opinion, which O'Connor wrote with Justices Anthony Kennedy and David Souter, reaffirmed the constitutionally protected right to abortion established in *Roe v. Wade* (1973) but also lowered the standard that legal restrictions on abortion must meet in order to pass constitutional muster. After *Casey*, such laws would be considered unconstitutional only if they constituted an "undue burden" on women seeking to obtain an abortion.

In 2006 O'Connor retired from the Supreme Court and was replaced by Samuel Alito.

ELLEN JOHNSON-SIRLEAF
(b. Oct. 29, 1938, Monrovia, Liberia)

The Liberian politician and economist Ellen Johnson-Sirleaf was president of Liberia from 2006. She was the first woman to be elected head of state of an African country.

Of mixed Gola and German heritage, Ellen Johnson was the daughter of the first indigenous Liberian to sit in the national legislature. At age 17 she married James Sirleaf (they were later divorced). In 1961 Johnson-Sirleaf went to the United States to study economics and business administration. After obtaining a master's degree (1971) in public administration from Harvard University, she entered government service in Liberia.

She served as assistant minister of finance (1972–73) under President William Tolbert and as finance minister (1980–85) in Samuel K. Doe's military dictatorship. Johnson-Sirleaf became known for her personal financial integrity and clashed with both heads of state.

During Doe's regime she was imprisoned twice and narrowly avoided execution. In the 1985 national election she campaigned for a seat in the Senate and openly criticized the military government, which led to her arrest and a 10-year prison sentence. She was released after a short time and allowed to leave the country. During 12 years of exile in Kenya and the United States, she became an influential economist for the World Bank, Citibank, and other international financial institutions. From 1992 to 1997 she was the director of the Regional Bureau for Africa of the United Nations Development Programme.

Johnson-Sirleaf ran for president in the 1997 election, representing the Unity Party. She finished second to Charles Taylor and was forced back into exile when his government charged her with treason. By 1999 Liberia

Ellen Johnson-Sirleaf's influence on Liberian politics stemmed from terms as finance minister and her election as president in 2006. Jim Watson/AFP/ Getty Images

had collapsed into civil war. After Taylor went into exile in 2003, Johnson-Sirleaf returned to Liberia to chair the Commission on Good Governance, which oversaw preparations for democratic elections. In 2005 she again ran for president, vowing to end civil strife and corruption, establish unity, and rebuild the country's devastated infrastructure. Known as the "Iron Lady," she placed second in the first round of voting, and on Nov. 8, 2005, she won the runoff election, defeating football (soccer) legend George Weah. Johnson-Sirleaf was sworn in as president of Liberia on Jan. 16, 2006.

With more than 15,000 United Nations peacekeepers in the country and unemployment running at 80 percent,

Johnson-Sirleaf faced serious challenges. She immediately sought debt amelioration and aid from the international community. In addition, she established a Truth and Reconciliation Committee to probe corruption and heal ethnic tensions.

GRO HARLEM BRUNDTLAND
(b. April 20, 1939, Oslo, Nor.)

Having served three terms as prime minister of Norway in the 1980s and '90s, Gro Harlem Brundtland later was director general of the World Health Organization (WHO; 1998–2003). Trained as a physician, she became identified with public health and environmental issues and with the rights of women.

The daughter of a physician and politician, she received an M.D. degree from the University of Oslo in 1963 and a master's degree in public health from Harvard University in 1965. She then worked as a public health officer for the city of Oslo and for Oslo schools. A member of the Labour Party, she was minister of the environment from 1974 to 1979, and she was first elected to the Storting (parliament) in 1977. In 1975 she was elected deputy leader of the party and in 1981 its leader.

When the Labour prime minister resigned in 1981, Brundtland was appointed to the post, the youngest person and first woman to become prime minister of Norway. She served for only nine months, because Labour lost the elections held later that year. She returned as prime minister in 1986–89 and served again in 1990–96 until her resignation. Brundtland never had fewer than 8 women in her 18-member cabinet and, overall, is credited with securing better educational and economic opportunities for women in Norway. In 1983 she became chair of the UN World Commission on Environment and Development, which in 1987 issued *Our Common Future*, the report that introduced the idea of "sustainable development" and led to the first Earth Summit. In 1998 she became director general of the WHO, where she tackled global pandemics such as AIDS and SARS; her term ended in 2003. In 2007, together with Han Seung-soo, former minister of foreign affairs of South Korea, and Ricardo Lagos Escobar, a former president of Chile, she was appointed a special envoy on climate change to Ban Ki-moon, the secretary-general of the United Nations.

WANGARI MAATHAI

(b. April 1, 1940, Nyeri, Kenya)

I n 2004 the Kenyan politician and environmental activist Wangari Muta Maathai was awarded the 2004 Nobel Prize for Peace, becoming the first black African woman to win the award. Her work often has been considered both unwelcome and subversive in her own country, where her outspokenness has constituted stepping far outside traditional gender roles.

Maathai was educated in the United States at Mount St. Scholastica College (now Benedictine College; B.S. in biology, 1964) and at the University of Pittsburgh (M.S., 1966). In 1971 she received a Ph.D. at the University of Nairobi, effectively becoming the first woman in either East or Central Africa to earn a doctorate. She began teaching in the Department of Veterinary Anatomy at the University of Nairobi after graduation, and in 1977 she became chair of the department.

While working with the National Council of Women of Kenya, Maathai developed the idea that village women could improve the environment by planting trees to provide a fuel source and to slow the processes of deforestation and desertification. The Green Belt Movement, an organization she founded in 1977, had by the early 21st century planted some 30 million trees. Leaders of the Green Belt Movement established the Pan African Green Belt Network in 1986 in order to educate world leaders about conservation and environmental improvement. As a result of the movement's activism, similar initiatives were begun in other African countries, including Tanzania, Ethiopia, and Zimbabwe.

In addition to her conservation work, Maathai also has been an advocate for human rights, AIDS prevention, and women's issues, and she frequently represented these concerns at meetings of the United Nations General Assembly. She was elected to Kenya's National Assembly in 2002 with 98 percent of the vote, and in 2003 she was appointed assistant minister of environment, natural resources, and wildlife. When she won the Nobel Prize in 2004, the committee commended her "holistic approach to sustainable development that embraces democracy, human rights, and women's rights in particular."

Her first book, *The Green Belt Movement: Sharing the Approach and the Experience* (1988; rev. ed. 2003), detailed the history of the organization. She published an auto-biography, *Unbowed*, in 2007. Another volume, *The Challenge for Africa* (2009), criticized Africa's leadership as ineffectual and urged Africans to try to solve their problems without Western assistance. Maathai also has been a frequent contributor to international publications such as the *Los Angeles Times* and the *Guardian*.

MARTHA STEWART

(b. Aug. 3, 1941, Jersey City, N.J., U.S.)

Martha Stewart, an American entrepreneur and domestic lifestyle innovator, built a catering business into an international media and home furnishing corporation, Martha Stewart Living Omnimedia, Inc.

Raised in Nutley, N.J., Martha Helen Kostyra grew up in a Polish American household where the traditional arts of cooking, sewing, canning and preserving, house-keeping, and gardening were practiced. She started planning birthday parties for neighbour children while she was in grammar school, and she paid her college tuition by taking modeling jobs in New York City. She married law student Andrew Stewart (1961; they divorced in 1990) while studying at Barnard College (B.A., European history and architectural history, 1963); their daughter, Alexis, was born in 1965. Stewart worked as a stockbroker at a small Wall Street firm (1965–72) until she and her family moved to Westport, Connecticut, and turned their ambitions toward restoring Turkey Hill, a Federal-style farmhouse. With yeoman labour they gardened, restored, and deco-rated, acquiring the skills and the setting for books and TV shows.

After launching a catering business (1976) with a partner, Norma Collier, Stewart's talent for innovation and presentation attracted a string of prestigious clients. Her first book, *Entertaining* (1982; with Elizabeth Hawes), set the tone for subsequent publications: superb art direction, gorgeous settings, labour-intensive recipes and decorating projects. In addition, she oversaw the *CBS Masterworks Dinner Classics*, a series of music compilations that could provide the appropriate background music for a picnic, cocktail party, Sunday brunch, or exotic meal.

Following continued success with such books as *Martha Stewart's Hors d'Oeuvres* (1984) and *Weddings* (1987), Time Publishing Ventures, Inc., teamed with Stewart (1990) to publish a monthly magazine, *Martha Stewart Living*, with Stewart not only as editor in chief but as the

featured personality within its pages. She began a syndicated television show of the same name (1993) and
eventually bought the magazine from Time Warner Inc.
(1997), funding the purchase with proceeds from her
merchandising arrangement with Kmart, which debuted
as the Martha Stewart Everyday line of household furnish-
ings. Each of these business moves took her closer to her
ultimate goal of creating a multichannel media and
marketing firm. That goal was fully realized when Martha
Stewart Living Omnimedia was listed on the New York
Stock Exchange (1999), with Stewart as chairman and
chief executive officer (CEO). She became a billionaire,
however briefly, with the public launch of her company.

In December 2001 Stewart ordered the sale of 4,000
shares of ImClone Systems, a biomedical firm owned by
family friend Samuel Waksal. The sale of her shares, occur-
ring one day before public information about ImClone
caused the stock price to drop, sparked accusations of
insider trading. Stewart stepped down as CEO of her firm
in 2003, assuming the title of chief creative officer and
appearing to distance herself from daily operations as she
focused on defending herself against charges of lying and
obstructing justice. Convicted in 2004 and sentenced to
serve five months in prison followed by five months of
home detention, Stewart urged her fans to continue supporting her company.

As she built her business, Stewart's perfectionism,
comprehensive knowledge, and bottomless capacity for work
were not universally admired. She was censured for setting
an impossible model for harried working mothers, and her
glorification of a home-centred existence seemed to some
a step backward for women. But her fans were legion, and
many criticisms were swept away by the personal appeal
that made her company a commercial success.

CHRISTIANE NÜSSLEIN-VOLHARD

(b. Oct. 20, 1942, Magdeburg, Ger.)

The German developmental geneticist Christiane Nüsslein-Volhard was jointly awarded the 1995 Nobel Prize for Physiology or Medicine with geneticists Eric F. Wieschaus and Edward B. Lewis for their research concerning the mechanisms of early embryonic development. Nüsslein-Volhard, working in tandem with Wieschaus, expanded upon the pioneering work of Lewis, who used the fruit fly, or vinegar fly (*Drosophila melanogaster*), as an experimental subject. Her work has relevance to the development of all multicellular organisms, including humans.

At Eberhard-Karl University of Tübingen, Nüsslein-Volhard received a diploma in biochemistry in 1968 and a doctorate in genetics in 1973. After holding fellowships in Basel and Freiburg, she joined Wieschaus as a group leader at the European Molecular Biology Laboratory in Heidelberg in 1978. In 1981 she returned to Tübingen, where, in 1985, she became director of the Max Planck Institute for Developmental Biology.

At Heidelberg, Nüsslein-Volhard and Wieschaus spent more than a year crossbreeding 40,000 fruit fly families and systematically examining their genetic makeup at a dual microscope. Their trial-and-error methods resulted in the discovery that of the fly's 20,000 genes, about 5,000 are deemed important to early development and about 140 are essential. They assigned responsibility for the fruit fly's embryonic development to three genetic categories: gap genes, which lay out the head-to-tail body plan; pair-rule genes, which determine body segmentation; and segment-polarity genes, which establish repeating structures within each segment.

In the early 1990s Nüsslein-Volhard began studying genes that control development in the zebra fish *Danio rerio*. These organisms are ideal models for investigations into developmental biology because they have clear embryos, have a rapid rate of reproduction, and are closely related to other vertebrates. Nüsslein-Volhard studied the migration of cells from their sites of origin to their sites of destination within zebra fish embryos. Her investigations in zebra fish have helped elucidate genes and other cellular substances involved in human development and in the regulation of normal human physiology.

In addition to the Nobel Prize, Nüsslein-Volhard received the Leibniz Prize (1986) and the Albert Lasker Basic Medical Research Award (1991). She also published several books, including *Zebrafish: A Practical Approach* (2002; written with Ralf Dahm) and *Coming to Life: How Genes Drive Development* (2006).

BILLIE JEAN KING

(b. Nov. 22, 1943, Long Beach, Calif., U.S.)

The American athlete and tennis player Billie Jean King (née Billie Jean Moffitt) is noteworthy for having elevated the status of women's professional tennis through her influence and playing style, beginning in the late 1960s. In her career she won 39 major titles, competing in both singles and doubles.

King was athletically inclined from an early age. She first attracted international attention in 1961 by winning the Wimbledon doubles championship with Karen Hantz; theirs was the youngest team to win. She went on to capture a record 20 Wimbledon titles (singles 1966–68, 1972–73, and 1975; women's doubles 1961–62, 1965, 1967–68, 1970–73, 1979; mixed doubles 1967, 1971, 1973–74), in addition

In addition to winning many titles, Billie Jean King made women's tennis a sport distinct from the men's game and increased winners' purses on the ladies' tour. Bentley Archive/Popperfoto/Getty Images

to U.S. singles (1967, 1971–72, 1974), French singles (1972), and the Australian title (1968); her Wimbledon record was tied by Martina Navratilova in 2003. She was perhaps one of the greatest doubles players in the history of tennis, winning 27 major titles. With her victories in 1967, she was the first woman since 1938 to sweep the U.S. and British singles, doubles, and mixed doubles titles in a single year.

King turned professional after 1968 and became the first woman athlete to win more than $100,000 in one season (1971). In 1973 she beat the aging Bobby Riggs in a much-publicized "Battle of the Sexes" match. The match set a record for the largest tennis audience and the largest purse awarded up to that time. She pushed relentlessly for the rights of women players, helped to form a separate women's tour, and obtained financial backing from commercial sponsors. She was one of the founders and the first president (1974) of the Women's Tennis Association.

King and her husband, Larry King (married 1965), were part of a group that founded World Team Tennis (WTT) in 1974. King served as the player-coach of the Philadelphia Freedoms, thus becoming one of the first women to coach professional male athletes. The WTT folded after 1978 because of financial losses, but King revived the competition in 1981.

King retired from competitive tennis in 1984 and the same year became the first woman commissioner in professional sports in her position with the World Team Tennis League. She was inducted into the Women's Sports Hall of Fame in 1980, the International Tennis Hall of Fame in 1987, and the National Women's Hall of Fame in 1990. King remained active in tennis and since the mid-1990s served as coach for several Olympic and Federation Cup teams. The United States Tennis Association honoured King in August 2006, when it renamed the National Tennis Center, home of the U.S.

Open, the Billie Jean King National Tennis Center. She published two autobiographies, *Billie Jean* (1974; with Kim Chapin) and *The Autobiography of Billie Jean King* (1982; with Frank Deford), as well as *We Have Come a Long Way: The Story of Women's Tennis* (1988; with Cynthia Starr) and *Pressure Is a Privilege: Lessons I've Learned from Life and the Battle of the Sexes* (2008; with Christine Brennan).

MARY ROBINSON

(b. May 21, 1944, Ballina, County Mayo, Ire.)

The Irish lawyer, politician, and diplomat Mary Robinson served as president of Ireland (1990–97) and as United Nations High Commissioner for Human Rights (UNHCHR; 1997–2002).

Robinson, born Mary Teresa Winifred Bourke, was educated at Trinity College and King's Inns in Dublin and at Harvard University in the United States. She served at Trinity College (University of Dublin) as Reid Professor of penal legislation, constitutional and criminal law, and the law of evidence (1969–75) and lecturer in European Community law (1975–90). In 1988 she established (with her husband) at Trinity College the Irish Centre for European Law. A distinguished constitutional lawyer and a renowned supporter of human rights, she was elected to the Royal Irish Academy and was a member of the International Commission of Jurists in Geneva (1987–90). She sat in the Seanad (upper chamber of Parliament) for the Trinity College constituency (1969–89) and served as whip for the Labour Party until resigning from the party over the Anglo-Irish Agreement of 1985, which she felt ignored unionist objections. She was also a member of the Dublin City Council (1979–83) and ran unsuccessfully in 1977 and 1981 for Dublin parliamentary constituencies.

Nominated by the Labour Party and supported by the Green Party and the Workers' Party, Robinson became Ireland's first woman president in 1990 by mobilizing a liberal constituency and merging it with a more conservative constituency opposed to the Fianna Fáil party. As president, Robinson adopted a much more prominent role than her predecessors, and she did much to communicate a more modern image of Ireland. Strongly committed to human rights, she was the first head of state to visit Somalia after it suffered from civil war and famine in 1992 and the first to visit Rwanda after the genocide in that country in 1994. Shortly before her term as president expired, she took up the post of UNHCHR. As high commissioner, Robinson changed the priorities of her office to emphasize the promotion of human rights at the national and regional levels; she was the first UNHCHR to visit China, and she also helped to improve the monitoring of human rights in Kosovo. In 2001 Robinson served as secretary-general of the World Conference against Racism, Racial Discrimination, Xenophobia and Related Intolerance, held in Durban, South Africa. In 1998 she was elected chancellor of Trinity College.

After leaving her post at the UN, Robinson founded the nongovernmental organization Realizing Rights: The Ethical Globalization Initiative, in 2002. Its central concerns included equitable international trade, access to health care, migration, women's leadership, and corporate responsibility. She was also a founding member of the Council of Women World Leaders, served as honorary president of Oxfam International (a private organization that provides relief and development aid to impoverished or disaster-stricken communities worldwide), and was a member of the Club of Madrid (which promotes democracy). In 2004 Amnesty International awarded her its Ambassador of Conscience award for her human rights work.

AUNG SAN SUU KYI

(b. June 19, 1945, Rangoon, Burma [now Yangon, Myanmar])

The Myanmar opposition leader Aung San Suu Kyi is the daughter of Aung San (a martyred national hero of independent Burma) and Khin Kyi (a prominent Burmese diplomat), and winner in 1991 of the Nobel Prize for Peace.

Aung San Suu Kyi was 2 years old when her father, then the de facto prime minister of what would shortly become independent Burma, was assassinated. She attended schools in Burma until 1960, when her mother was appointed ambassador to India. After further study in India, she attended the University of Oxford, where she met her future husband. She had two children and lived a rather quiet life until 1988, when she returned to Burma to nurse her dying mother. There the mass slaughter of protesters against the brutal and unresponsive rule of the military strongman U Ne Win led her to speak out against him and to begin a nonviolent struggle for democracy and human rights.

In July 1989 the military government of the newly named Union of Myanmar placed Aung San Suu Kyi under house arrest and held her incommunicado. The military offered to free her if she agreed to leave Myanmar, but she refused to do so until the country was returned to civilian government and political prisoners were freed. The newly formed group with which she became affiliated, the National League for Democracy (NLD), won more than 80 percent of the parliamentary seats that were contested in 1990, but the results of that election were ignored by the military government.

Aung San Suu Kyi was freed from house arrest in July 1995. The following year she attended the NLD party congress, but the military government continued to harass both her and her party. In 1998 she announced the formation of a representative committee that she declared was the country's legitimate ruling parliament. The military junta once again placed her under house arrest from September 2000 to May 2002. Following clashes between the NLD and pro-government demonstrators in 2003, the government returned her to house arrest. Calls for her release continued throughout the international community in the face of her sentence's annual renewal. In August 2009, she was convicted of breaching the terms of her house arrest and sentenced to an additional 18 months. It is widely believed that the new conviction was designed to prevent Aung from participating in elections scheduled for 2010.

SHIRIN EBADI

(b. June 21, 1947, Hamadan, Iran)

For her efforts to promote democracy and human rights, especially those of women and children in Iran, Shirin Ebadi received the Nobel Prize for Peace in 2003. She was the first Muslim woman and the first Iranian to receive the award.

Ebadi was born into an educated Iranian family; her father was an author and a lecturer in commercial law. When she was an infant, her family moved to Tehrān. Ebadi attended Anoshiravn Dadgar and Reza Shah Kabir schools before earning a law degree, in only three and a half years, from the University of Tehrān (1969). That same year she took an apprenticeship at the Department of Justice and became one of the first women judges in Iran. While serving as a judge, she also earned a doctorate in private law from the University of Tehrān (1971). From 1975 to 1979 she was head of the city court of Tehrān.

After the 1979 revolution and the establishment of an Islamic republic, women were deemed unsuitable to serve as judges because the new leaders believed that Islam forbids it. Ebadi was subsequently forced to become a clerk of the court. After she and other female judges protested this action, they were given higher roles within the Department of Justice but were still not allowed to serve as judges. Ebadi resigned in protest. She then chose to practice law but was initially denied a lawyer's license. In 1992, after years of struggle, she finally obtained a license to practice law and began to do so. She also taught at the University of Tehrān and became an advocate for civil rights.

In court Ebadi defended women and dissidents and represented many people who, like her, had run afoul of the Iranian government. She also distributed evidence implicating government officials in the 1999 murders of students at the University of Tehrān, for which she was jailed for three weeks in 2000. Found guilty of "disturbing public opinion," she was given a prison term, barred from practicing law for five years, and fined, although her sentence was later suspended.

Ebadi wrote a number of books on the subject of human rights. These include *The Rights of the Child: A Study of Legal Aspects of Children's Rights in Iran* (1994), *History and Documentation of Human Rights in Iran* (2000), and *The Rights of Women* (2002). She also was founder and head of the Association for Support of Children's Rights in Iran. In addition to writing books on human rights, Ebadi reflected on her own experiences in *Iran Awakening: From Prison to Peace Prize, One Woman's Struggle at the Crossroads* (2006; with Azadeh Moaveni; also published as *Iran Awakening: A Memoir of Revolution and Hope*).

HILLARY RODHAM CLINTON

(b. Oct. 26, 1947, Chicago, Ill., U.S.)

The American lawyer and politician Hillary Rodham Clinton served as a U.S. senator (2001–09) and secretary of state (2009–) in the administration of Pres. Barack Obama. She also served as first lady (1993–2001) during the administration of her husband, Bill Clinton, 42nd president of the United States.

The first president's wife born after World War II, Hillary Diane Rodham was the eldest child of Hugh and Dorothy Rodham. She grew up in Park Ridge, Illinois, a Chicago suburb, where her father's textile business provided the family with a comfortable income. Her parents' emphasis on hard work and academic excellence set high standards.

A student leader in public schools, she was active in youth programs at the First United Methodist Church. Although she later became associated with liberal causes, during this time she adhered to the Republican Party of her parents. She campaigned for Republican presidential candidate Barry Goldwater in 1964 and chaired the local chapter of the Young Republicans. A year later, after she enrolled at Wellesley College, her political views began to change. Influenced by the assassinations of Malcolm X, Robert F. Kennedy, and Martin Luther King, Jr., she joined the Democratic Party and volunteered in the presidential campaign of antiwar candidate Eugene McCarthy.

After her graduation from Wellesley in 1969, Clinton entered Yale Law School, where she came under the influence of Yale alumna Marian Wright Edelman, a lawyer and children's rights advocate. Through her work with Edelman, she developed a strong interest in family law and issues affecting children.

Although Hillary met Bill Clinton at Yale, they took separate paths after graduation in 1973. He returned to his native Arkansas, and she worked with Edelman in Massachusetts for the Children's Defense Fund. In 1974 Hillary participated in the Watergate inquiry into the possible impeachment of President Richard M. Nixon. When her assignment ended with Nixon's resignation in August 1974, she made what some people consider the crucial decision of her life—she moved to Arkansas. She taught at the University of Arkansas School of Law, and, following her marriage to Bill Clinton on Oct. 11, 1975, she joined the prominent Rose Law Firm in Little Rock, Arkansas, where she later became a partner.

After Bill was elected governor of Arkansas in 1978, she continued to pursue her career and retained her maiden name (until 1982), bringing considerable criticism from voters who felt that her failure to change her name indicated a lack of commitment to her husband. Their only child, Chelsea Victoria, was born in 1980.

Throughout Bill's tenure as governor (1979–81, 1983–92), Hillary worked on programs that aided children and the disadvantaged; she also maintained a successful law practice. She served on the boards of several high-profile corporations and was twice named one of the nation's 100 most influential lawyers (1988, 1991) by the *National Law Journal*. She also served as chair of the Arkansas Education Standards Committee and founded the Arkansas Advocates for Children and Families. She was named Arkansas Woman of the Year in 1983 and Arkansas Young Mother of the Year in 1984.

In Bill's 1992 presidential campaign, Hillary played a crucial role by greeting voters, giving speeches, and serving as one of her husband's chief advisers. Her appearance with him on the television news program *60 Minutes* in

January 1992 made her name a household word. Responding to questions about Bill's alleged 12-year sexual relationship with an Arkansas woman, Gennifer Flowers, Bill and Hillary discussed their marital problems, and Hillary told voters to judge her husband by his record—adding that, if they did not like what they saw, then, "heck, don't vote for him."

With a professional career unequaled by any previous presidential candidate's wife, Hillary was heavily scrutinized. Conservatives complained that she had her own agenda, because she had worked for some liberal causes. During one campaign stop, she defended herself from such criticism by asserting that she could have "stayed home and baked cookies." This impromptu remark was picked up by the press and used by her critics as evidence of her lack of respect for women who are full-time homemakers.

Some of Hillary's financial dealings raised suspicions of impropriety and led to major investigations after she became first lady. Her investment in Whitewater, a real estate development in Arkansas, and her commodities trading in 1978–79 — through which she reportedly turned a $1,000 investment into $100,000 in a few months — came under close scrutiny.

During the 1992 campaign, Bill Clinton sometimes spoke of a "twofer" ("two for the price of one") presidency, implying that Hillary would play an important role in his administration. Early indications from the Clinton White House supported this interpretation. She appointed an experienced staff and set up her own office in the West Wing, an unprecedented move. Her husband appointed her to head the Task Force on National Health Care, a centrepiece of his legislative agenda. She encountered sharp criticism when she closed the sessions of the task force to the public, and doctors and other health care professionals objected that she was not a "government official" and had no right to bar them from the proceedings. An appeals court later supported her stand, ruling that presidents' wives have "a longstanding tradition of public service . . . act[ing] . . . as advisers and personal representatives of their husbands."

To promote the findings of the task force, she appeared before five congressional committees and received considerable and mostly favourable press coverage for her expertise on the subject. But Congress ultimately rejected the task force's recommendations, and her role in the health care debate galvanized conservatives and helped Republicans recapture Congress in the 1994 elections.

Hillary was criticized on other matters as well, including her role in the firing of seven staff members from the White House travel office ("Travelgate") and her involvement in legal maneuvering by the White House during the Whitewater investigation. As the 1996 election approached, she was less visible and played a more traditional role as first lady. Her first book, *It Takes a Village: And Other Lessons Children Teach Us* (1996), described her views on child rearing and prompted accolades from supporters and stark criticism from her opponents.

Revelations about President Clinton's affair with White House intern Monica Lewinsky brought the first lady back into the spotlight in a complex way. She stood faithfully by her husband during the scandal—in which her husband first denied and then admitted to having had a sexual relationship with Lewinsky—and throughout his ensuing impeachment and trial in the Senate.

In 1999 Hillary made history of a different sort when she launched her candidacy for the U.S. Senate seat from New York being vacated by Daniel Patrick Moynihan. To meet the state's residency requirement, she moved out of Washington, D.C., on Jan. 5, 2000, to a house that she and the president purchased in Chappaqua, New York. After a bitter campaign, she defeated Republican Rick Lazio by a substantial margin to become the first first lady to win elective office. Although often a subject of controversy, Hillary showed that the ceremonial parts of the first lady's job could be merged with a strong role in public policy and that the clout of the first lady could be converted into a personal political power base.

Sworn into office on Jan. 3, 2001, Hillary continued to push for health care reform, and she remained an advocate for children. She served on several senatorial committees, including the Committee for Armed Services. Following the September 11 attacks in 2001, she supported the U.S.-led invasion of Afghanistan but grew highly critical of

Hillary Rodham Clinton (left) *being sworn in as secretary of state by Joe Biden* (right) *as Bill Clinton, Chelsea Clinton, and Dorothy Rodham look on, Feb. 2, 2009.* Michael Gross/U.S. Department of State

President George W. Bush's handling of the Iraq War. In 2003 Hillary's much-anticipated memoir of her White House years, *Living History*, was published and set sales records; she had received an advance of about $8 million for the book.

In 2006 she was easily reelected to the Senate. The following year Hillary announced that she would seek the Democratic Party's presidential nomination for 2008. She began the primary season as the front-runner for the nomination but placed a disappointing third in the first contest, the Iowa caucus, on Jan. 3, 2008. Her campaign quickly rebounded, and she won the New Hampshire primary five days later. On Super Tuesday, February 5, she won important states such as California, Massachusetts, and New York, but she failed to gain a significant lead over Barack Obama in the number of pledged convention delegates. Obama won 11 consecutive states following Super Tuesday to take over the delegate lead and become the new favourite for the nomination, but Hillary rebounded in early March with key victories in Ohio and Texas, and in April she added to her momentum by winning the Pennsylvania primary. However, her narrow victory in Indiana and substantial loss in North Carolina in early May severely limited the possibility of her garnering enough delegates to overtake Obama before the final primaries in June. On June 3, following the final primaries in Montana and South Dakota, Obama passed the delegate threshold and became the presumptive Democratic nominee. He officially secured the party's nomination on August 27 at the Democratic National Convention in Denver and went on to win the general election on November 4. In December 2008, Obama selected Hillary to serve as secretary of state, and she was easily confirmed by the Senate in January 2009.

OPRAH WINFREY

(b. Jan. 29, 1954, Kosciusko, Miss., U.S.)

One of the richest and most influential women in the United States is the American television personality, actress, and entrepreneur Oprah Winfrey. Her syndicated daily talk show was among the most popular of the genre.

Winfrey moved to Milwaukee, Wis., at age six to live with her mother. In her early teens she was sent to Nashville, Tenn., to live with her father, who proved to be a positive influence in her life.

At age 19, Winfrey became a news anchor for the local CBS television station. Following her graduation from Tennessee State University in 1976, she was made a reporter and coanchor for the ABC news affiliate in Baltimore, Maryland. She found herself constrained by the objectivity required of news reporting, and in 1977 she became cohost of the Baltimore morning show *People Are Talking*.

Winfrey excelled in the casual and personal talk-show format, and in 1984 she moved to host the faltering talk show *AM Chicago*. Winfrey's honest and engaging personality quickly turned the program into a success, and in 1985 it was renamed *The Oprah Winfrey Show*. Syndicated nationally in 1986, the program became the highest-rated television talk show in America and earned several Emmy Awards.

Winfrey broke new ground in 1996 by starting an on-air book club. She announced selections two to four weeks in advance and then discussed the book on her show with a select group of people. Each book chosen quickly rose to the top of the best-seller charts, and Winfrey's effect on the publishing industry was significant. Winfrey further expanded her presence in the publishing industry with the highly successful launch of *O, the Oprah* magazine in 2000 and with *O at Home*, launched in 2004.

Oprah Winfrey in The Color Purple *(1985)*. Gordon Parks/© 1985 Warner Bros., Inc.; photograph from a private collection

In 1985 Winfrey appeared in Steven Spielberg's adaptation of Alice Walker's 1982 novel *The Color Purple*. Her critically acclaimed performance led to other roles, including a performance in the television miniseries *The Women of Brewster Place* (1989). Winfrey formed her own television production company, Harpo Productions, Inc., in 1986, and a film production company, Harpo Films, in 1990. The companies began buying film rights to literary works, including Connie May Fowler's *Before Women Had Wings*, which appeared as a televised movie in 1997 with Winfrey as both star and producer, and Toni Morrison's *Beloved*, which appeared on the big screen in 1998, also with Winfrey in a starring role.

In 1998 Winfrey expanded her media entertainment empire when she cofounded Oxygen Media, which operates a cable television network for women. In 2006 the Oprah & Friends channel debuted on satellite radio. She brokered a partnership with Discovery Communications in 2008, through which the Oprah Winfrey Network (OWN) was scheduled to replace the Discovery Health Channel in 2009.

Winfrey has engaged in numerous philanthropic activities, including the creation of Oprah's Angel Network, which sponsors charitable initiatives worldwide. In 2007 she opened a $40-million school for disadvantaged girls in South Africa. She is an outspoken crusader against child abuse and has received many honours and awards from civic, philanthropic, and entertainment organizations.

RIGOBERTA MENCHÚ

(b. Jan. 9, 1959, Guatemala)

The Guatemalan Indian-rights activist Rigoberta Menchú was awarded the Nobel Prize for Peace in 1992. Menchú, of the Quiché Maya group, spent her childhood helping with her family's agricultural work; she also likely worked on coffee plantations. As a young woman, she became an activist in the local women's rights movement and joined with the Catholic church to advocate for social reform.

The activism of Menchú and her family led to persecution by Guatemala's military government. When a guerrilla organization became active in their region, her father, a leader of a peasant organization opposed to the government, was accused of guerrilla activities. During Guatemala's ensuing civil war, he died in a fire while protesting human rights abuses by the military. Menchú's younger brother was kidnapped, tortured, and killed by a military death squad in 1979, and her mother was kidnapped, raped, mutilated, and murdered by soldiers the following year.

Menchú fled to Mexico in 1981 and was cared for there by members of a liberal Roman Catholic group. She soon joined international efforts to make the Guatemalan government cease its brutal counterinsurgency campaigns against Indian peasants, becoming a skilled public speaker and organizer in the course of her efforts.

Menchú gained international prominence in 1983 with her widely translated book *I, Rigoberta Menchú*, in which she tells the story of her impoverished youth and recounts in horrifying detail the torture-murders of her brother and mother. She received the Nobel Peace Prize in 1992 for her continuing efforts to achieve social justice and mutual reconciliation in Guatemala; she used the prize money to found the Rigoberta Menchú Tum Foundation, an Indian advocacy organization. In the late 1990s her autobiography became the centre of controversy after its veracity was questioned, most notably by David Stoll in *Rigoberta Menchú and the Story of All Poor Guatemalans* (1999). Despite alleged inaccuracies in her story, Menchú continued to earn praise for bringing international attention to the situation in Guatemala. In 2004 she accepted President Óscar Berger's offer to help implement the country's peace accords.

Menchú created the Indian-led political movement Winaq (Mayan: "The Wholeness of the Human Being") in February 2007. That September, as the candidate of a coalition between Winaq and the left-wing Encounter for Guatemala party, she ran for president of Guatemala but earned less than 3 percent of the vote. The following year Menchú began the legal process of creating a formal Winaq political party. If formed, it would be the first Guatemalan political party to represent indigenous groups directly.

DIANA, PRINCESS OF WALES

(b. July 1, 1961, Sandringham, Norfolk, Eng. — d. Aug. 31, 1997, Paris, France)

One of the best-loved women of the 20th century was Diana, princess of Wales, the former consort (1981–96) of Charles, prince of Wales, and mother of the heir second in line to the British throne, Prince William of Wales.

Diana Frances Spencer was born at Park House, the home that her parents rented on Queen Elizabeth II's estate at Sandringham and where her childhood playmates were the queen's younger sons, Prince Andrew and Prince Edward. She was the third child and youngest daughter of Edward John Spencer, Viscount Althorp, heir to the 7th Earl Spencer, and his first wife, Frances Ruth Burke Roche (daughter of the 4th Baron Fermoy). She became Lady Diana Spencer when her father succeeded to the earldom in 1975. Riddlesworth Hall (near Thetford, Norfolk) and West Heath School (Sevenoaks, Kent) provided the young Diana's schooling. After attending the finishing school of Chateau d'Oex at Montreux, Switz., Diana returned to

England and became a kindergarten teacher at the fashionable Young England school in Pimlico.

She renewed her contacts with the royal family, and her friendship with Charles grew in 1980. On Feb. 24, 1981, their engagement was announced, and on July 29, 1981, they were married in St. Paul's Cathedral in a globally televised ceremony watched by an audience numbering in the hundreds of millions. Their first child, Prince William Arthur Philip Louis of Wales, was born on June 21, 1982, and their second, Prince Henry Charles Albert David, on Sept. 15, 1984. Marital difficulties led to a separation between Diana and Charles in 1992, though they continued to carry out their royal duties and jointly participate in raising their two children. They divorced on Aug. 28, 1996, with Diana receiving a substantial settlement.

After the divorce, Diana maintained her high public profile and continued many of the activities she had earlier undertaken on behalf of charities, supporting causes as diverse as the arts, children's issues, and AIDS patients. Her unprecedented popularity as a member of the royal family, both in Britain and throughout the world, attracted considerable attention from the press, and she became one of the most photographed women in the world. Although she used that celebrity to great effect in promoting her charitable work, the media (in particular the aggressive freelance photographers known as paparazzi) were often intrusive.

It was while attempting to evade journalists that Diana was killed, along with her companion, Dodi Fayed, and their driver, in an automobile accident in a tunnel under the streets of Paris.

Though the photographers were initially blamed for causing the accident, a French judge in 1999 cleared them of any wrongdoing, instead faulting the driver, who was found to have had a blood-alcohol level over the legal limit at the time of the crash and to have taken prescription

Diana, Princess of Wales. Jayne Fincher/Hulton Archive/Getty Images

drugs incompatible with alcohol. In 2006 a Scotland Yard inquiry into the incident also concluded that the driver was at fault. In April 2008, however, a British inquest jury ruled both the driver and the paparazzi guilty of unlawful killing through grossly negligent driving, though it found no evidence of a conspiracy to kill Diana or Fayed, an accusation long made by Fayed's father.

Diana's death and funeral produced unprecedented expressions of public mourning, testifying to her enormous hold on the British national psyche. Her life, and her death, polarized national feeling about the existing system of monarchy (and, in a sense, about the British identity), which appeared antiquated and unfeeling in a populist age of media celebrity, in which Diana herself was a central figure.

GLOSSARY

abjuration The act of renouncing or giving up, frequently under oath.

alcalde The administrative and judicial head of a town or village in Spain or in areas under Spanish control or influence.

apostolic age Early period in the Christian church dominated by the actions of those personally known to Jesus or his disciples.

ascetic Denying oneself pleasure, goods, and personal affectations as a sign of spiritual devoutness.

chattel Objects and people that are considered someone's personal property.

concubine A woman who lives with a man as his wife, without actually being married to him.

consort A companion or partner; the spouse of royalty.

courtesan A mistress or prostitute that has members of royalty or nobility as her clientele.

de facto A Latin phrase meaning "in reality"—e.g., one who has power although not officially being in power is a de facto ruler.

Enlightenment A 17th- and 18th-century philosophical movement that emphasized the use of reason over accepted doctrines and traditions.

equerry A worker in the British royal household who took care of horses and stables.

extant Still in existence.

feudalism A political and economic system in medieval Europe based on the power of landholders over their tenants, who worked the land on which they lived to benefit the landowner.

foolscap A standard sheet of writing or printing paper in England.

funerary Suitable for or associated with burial.

gibbet A cross-like device for displaying the bodies of people who had been executed.

governess A woman employed, usually in a private household, to teach someone's children and to act as their nanny.

gymnasium A European secondary school that prepares students for university.

hypostyle hall A building with a roof or ceiling supported by rows of columns.

legation A diplomatic mission/outpost, or a person on staff at a diplomatic mission.

lyceum A hall in which lectures and concerts are performed.

meretricious Superficially significant, showy but shallow.

neoclassicism Style reflecting the aesthetic sense of ancient Greece and Rome.

obelisk A tall, tapered, four-sided shaft of stone, usually with a pointed pyramidal top.

parody Imitating a style in such a way as to mock it.

pernicious Causing great harm or death.

pitchblende A mineral ore of uranium that fascinated Marie Curie and led to the discovery of polonium and radium.

regnal Calculated from the beginning of a monarch's reign.

Romanticism An artistic movement of the late 18th century characterized by an emphasis on the individual, the subjective, the irrational, the imaginative, the personal, the spontaneous, the emotional, the visionary, and the transcendental.

sarcophagus A highly decorated coffin that typically is not buried.

serf A commoner who is required to perform work for a landowner in exchange for certain rights and privileges.

stelae Stone slab used as a grave marker or a memorial device.

thiasos Greek term for a community of women.

titulary The royal protocol adopted by Egyptian sovereigns.

triumviral Having to do with one of three people sharing public administration in ancient Rome.

unguent A healing ointment.

utopian An ideal but impractical situation, thought, or location.

veneration To show profound respect.

vicissitude A sudden or unexpected change in one's life; the ability of life to change quickly and without warning.

vilify To make hateful or defamatory statements; to make someone or something a villain.

FOR FURTHER READING

Aschenbrenner, Joyce. *Katherine Dunham: Dancing a Life*. Champaign, IL: University of Illinois Press, 2002.

Bernhardt, Sarah. *My Double Life: The Memoirs*. Charleston, SC: BiblioBazaar, 2007.

Bostridge, Mark. *Florence Nightingale: The Making of an Icon*. New York, NY: Farrar, Strauss, and Giroux, 2008.

Brinkley, Douglas. *Rosa Parks: A Life*. New York, NY: Penguin Books, 2005.

Charles-Roux, Edmonde. *Chanel and Her World*. New York, NY: The Vendome Press, 2005.

Clinton, Catherine. *Harriet Tubman: The Road to Freedom*. New York, NY: Back Bay Books, 2005.

Dalby, Liza. *The Tale of Murasaki: A Novel*. New York, NY: Anchor Books (Random House), 2000.

Frieda, Leonie. *Catherine de Medicis: Renaissance Queen of France*. New York, NY: HarperCollins, 2006.

Goodman, Dena, ed. *Marie Antoinette: Writings on the Body of a Queen*. New York, NY: Routledge, 2003.

Gordon, Lyndall. *Vindication: A Life of Mary Wollstonecraft*. New York, NY: Harper Perennial, 2006.

Knight, Louise W. *Citizen: Jane Addams and the Struggle for Democracy*. Chicago, IL: University of Chicago Press, 2006.

Liss, Peggy K. *Isabelle the Queen: Life and Times*. Philadelphia, PA: University of Pennsylvania Press, 2004.

Maathai, Wangari. *Unbowed: My Autobiography*. New York, NY: Arrow Books Ltd., 2008.

Montessori, Maria. *The Absorbent Mind*. Radford, VA: Wilder Publications, LLC, 2009.

Pollock, Griselda. *Mary Cassatt*. Dulles, VA: Chaucer Press, 2005.

Purvis, June. *Emmeline Pankhurst: A Biography*. London, England: Routledge, 2004.

Roberts, Ronald Suresh. *No Cold Kitchen: A Biography of Nadine Gordimer*. Johannesburg, South Africa: STE Publishers, 2005.

Roosevelt, Eleanor. *You Learn By Living: Eleven Keys to a More Fulfilling Life*. Edinburgh, Scotland: Westminster John Knox Press, 2009.

Scaperlanda, Maria Ruiz. *The Seeker's Guide to Mary*. Chicago, IL: Loyola Press, 2002.

Tracy, Robert. *Goddess: Martha Graham's Dancers Remember*. New York, NY: Limelight Editions, 2004.

Truth, Sojourner. *The Narrative of Sojourner Truth*. New York, NY: Cosimo Classics, 2008.

Turner, Ralph V. *Eleanor of Aquitaine: Queen of France, Queen of England*. New Haven, CT: Yale University Press, 2009.

Tyldesley, Joyce. *Cleopatra: Last Queen of Egypt*. London, England: Profile Books, Ltd., 2008.

Ward, Geoffrey C., and Burns, Ken. *Not For Ourselves Alone: The Story of Elizabeth Cady Stanton and Susan B. Anthony*. New York, NY: Knopf, 2001.

Woo, X.L. *Empress Dowager Cixi: China's Last Dynasty and the Long Reign of a Formidable Concubine*. New York, NY: Algora Publishing, 2003.

INDEX

A

abolitionism, 147, 148, 171–173, 175, 176, 182–183, 184

Addams, Jane, 206–208

Advanced Montessori Method, The (Montessori), 216

Agnes Grey (Anne Brontë), 151, 158

Aida, 282

Akkumulation des Kapitals, Die/ The Accumulation of Capital (Luxemburg), 219

Allegory of Inclination (Gentileschi), 105

American Journal of Psychoanalysis, 262

Amurath to Amurath (Bell), 214

Anthony, Susan B., 12, 170–177, 224–225

Antony, Mark, 10, 25, 27–30

Antony and Cleopatra (Shakespeare), 31

Aphrodite, ode to (Sappho), 24, 25

Appalachian Spring, 265

Art du théâtre, L'/The Art of the Theatre (Bernhardt), 201

Art of Biography, The (Woolf), 251

Art of Fiction, The (Woolf), 247

Attente de Dieu/Waiting for God (Weil), 281

Aung San Suu Kyi, 329–330

Austen, Jane, 14, 136–144

Autobiography of Alice B. Toklas, The (Stein), 224

Autobiography of Billie Jean King, The (King), 327

Avision de Christine, L' (Christine de Pisan), 55

B

Ball, Lucille, 14, 288–291

Bandaranaike, Sirimavo R. D., 11, 296–298

Bath, The (Cassatt), 196

Becquerel, Henri, 210, 211

Bell, Gertrude, 213–214

Bernhardt, Sarah, 13–14, 197–201

Between the Acts (Woolf), 251, 252

Billie Jean (King), 327

birth control, 13, 229–230, 233–234

Birth Control Review, The, 230

Blackwell, Elizabeth, 13, 184–186

Blé en herbe, Le/The Ripening Seed (Colette), 222

Boleyn, Anne, 81, 91

Book of the Foundations (Teresa of
Ávila), 80
Brewsie and Willie (Stein), 225
Brontë, Anne, 151, 154, 155, 158
Brontë, Charlotte, 14, 151–159
Brontë, Emily, 14, 151–159
Brundtland, Gro Harlem,
318–319

C

Caesar, Julius, 10, 25, 26–27, 30
Cahiers/Notebooks (Weil), 281
Cannon, Annie Jump, 208–209
Cassatt, Mary, 195–197
Catherine de Médicis, 83–89
Catherine of Aragon, 10, 80,
81, 91
Catherine II, 115–125
Catt, Carrie Chapman, 174
Cave of the Heart, 265
Ces Plaisirs/Those Pleasures
(Colette), 222
Challenge for Africa, The
(Maathai), 320
Chamorro, Violeta Barrios de,
312–313
Chanel, Coco, 253–254
Chanel No. 5, 254
Charles, Prince, 11, 308, 309,
310, 342
Charles VII, 57–59, 60–62, 63,
64, 65, 66, 68, 70
Chatte, La/The Cat (Colette), 222
Chéri (Colette), 222
Chiang Kai-shek, 267–269
Christian Science, 186–192
Christian Science Monitor, The, 191
Christina, 107–110
Christine de Pisan, 54–55

Cixi, 192–195
Clark, William, 145, 146–147
*Claudine à l'école/Claudine at
School* (Colette), 221
*Claudine amoureuse/The Indulgent
Husband* (Colette), 221
Claudine à Paris/Claudine in Paris
(Colette), 221
*Claudine s'en va: Journal
d'Annie/The Innocent Wife*
(Colette), 221
Cleopatra, 9–10, 25–31
Clinton, Bill, 332, 333, 334, 335
Clinton, Hillary Rodham, 11–12,
332–337
Coiffure, The (Cassatt), 196
Colette, 220–223
Columbus, Christopher, 71, 74
Coming to Life (Nüsslein-
Volhard), 324
Common Reader, The (Woolf), 252
Common Reader, The: Second Series
(Woolf), 252
Composition and Explanation
(Stein), 224
Conceptions on the Love of God
(Teresa of Ávila), 80
Conservationist, The
(Gordimer), 306
*Considérations sur la Révolution
française/Considerations on the
Principal Events of the French
Revolution* (Staël), 135
*Contraception: Its Theory, History
and Practice* (Stopes), 234
Corinne (Staël), 134, 135
*Counsel to Parents on the Moral
Education of Their Children*
(Blackwell), 186

Curie, Marie, 209–213, 271
Curie, Pierre, 210, 211–212, 271

D

De la littérature considérée dans ses rapports avec les institutions sociales/A Treatise of Ancient and Modern Literature and The Influence of Literature upon Society (Staël), 134
De l'Allemagne/Germany (Staël), 135
De l'Angleterre (Staël), 135
De l'influence des passions sur le bonheur des individus et des nations/A Treatise on the Influence of the Passions upon the Happiness of Individuals and of Nations (Staël), 133
Delphine (Staël), 134
Democracy and Social Ethics (Addams), 208
Desert and the Sown, The (Bell), 214
Diana, Princess of Wales, 11, 310, 342–344
Diaries of Court Ladies of Old Japan, 45
Diary of a Young Girl, The (Frank), 14–15, 311–312
Dietrich, Marlene, 14, 276–279
Disraeli, Benjamin, 167, 168, 169
Ditié de Jehanne d'Arc, Le (Christine de Pisan), 55
Dix, Dorothea, 149–150
Dix Années d'exil/Ten Years' Exile (Staël), 134
Duncan, Isadora, 225–229
Dunham, Katherine, 281–282
Duo (Colette), 222

E

Earhart, Amelia, 270–271
Ebadi, Shirin, 330–331
Eddy, Mary Baker, 186–192
Education for a New World (Montessori), 216
Eighty Years and More (Stanton), 177
Eleanor of Aquitaine, 10, 47–50
Elizabeth I, 10–11, 89–103, 123
Elizabeth II, 11, 307–310
Emma (Austen), 137, 139, 140, 141, 143
Emma (Charlotte Brontë), 155
Enracinement, L'/The Need for Roots (Weil), 280–281
Entertaining (Stewart), 321
Envers du music-hall, L'/Music-Hall Sidelights (Colette), 221
Épistre au Dieu d'amours, L'/
"Letter to the God of Loves" (Christine de Pisan), 54
Errand into the Maze, 265
Essays in Medical Sociology (Blackwell), 186

F

Family Limitation (Sanger), 229
Feminine Psychology (Horney), 262
Ferdinand II, 71, 72, 73, 74, 75, 77
Fin de Chéri, La/The Last of Chéri (Colette), 222
Flush (Woolf), 249
Four Saints in Three Acts (Stein), 224
Frank, Anne, 14–15, 310–312
Frankenstein; or, The Modern Prometheus (Shelley), 130

Franklin, Rosalind, 13, 303–304
Freshwater (Woolf), 250
Freud, Sigmund, 260, 261
Frontier, 264
Fuller, Margaret, 131
Fun of It, The (Earhart), 270

G

Gage, Matilda, 174, 177
Gandhi, Indira, 11, 299–301
Genji monogatari/The Tale of Genji
    (Murasaki Shikibu), 14, 43–45
Gentileschi, Artemisia, 103–105
Get a Life (Gordimer), 307
Gigi (Colette), 222
Godwin, William, 130
Gordimer, Nadine, 306–307
Graham, Martha, 262–267
*Green Belt Movement, The: Sharing
    the Approach and the
    Experience* (Maathai), 320

H

Hatshepsut, 9, 17–19
Helen Keller's Journal (Keller), 232
Henry Draper Catalogue
    (Cannon), 209
Henry Draper Extension
    (Cannon), 209
Henry VIII, 10, 80, 81, 82–83,
    91–92, 96, 98
Hildegard, 45–47
*History and Documentation of
    Human Rights in Iran*
    (Ebadi), 331
History of Woman Suffrage
    (Anthony, Stanton, Gage),
    174, 177

Hodgkin, Dorothy Crowfoot,
    282–286
Horney, Karen, 260–262
Hull House, 206–208
Human Element in Sex, The
    (Blackwell), 186
Hypatia, 34–36

I

I Love Lucy, 14, 290
Interior Castle, The (Teresa of
    Ávila), 80
*Iran Awakening: From Prison to
    Peace Prize, One Woman's
    Struggle at the Crossroads*
    (Ebadi), 331
Irene, 41–43
I, Rigoberta Menchú (Menchú), 341
Isabella I, 71–78
Island Possessed (Dunham), 282
*It Takes a Village: And Other
    Lessons Children Teach Us*
    (Clinton), 335

J

Jacob's Room (Woolf), 245
Jane Eyre (Charlotte Brontë), 14,
    151, 154, 155, 156, 158
Jane Gray (Staël), 132
Jiang Qing, 292–295
Joan of Arc, 55–70
Johnson-Sirleaf, Ellen, 11, 316–318
Joliot-Curie, Irène, 211, 212, 213,
    271–273
Judith Beheading Holofernes
    (Gentileschi), 103
Justinian I, 36, 37, 38

K

Kabuki, 105, 106
Katherine Dunham's Journey to Accompong (Dunham), 282
Keller, Helen, 230–233
Kew Gardens (Woolf), 244
King, Billie Jean, 324–327
Krise der Sozialdemokratie, Die/ The Crisis in the German Social Democracy (Luxemburg), 219

L

Lady Susan (Austen), 137–138
Laws of Life, with Special Reference to the Physical Education of Girls, The (Blackwell), 185
Letter to the World, 265
Lettres sur les ouvrages et le caractère de J.-J. Rousseau/ Letters on the Works and the Character of J.-J. Rousseau (Staël), 132
Lewis and Clark Expedition, 144–146
Life Among the Piutes: Their Wrongs and Claims (Winnemucca), 202, 203
Life of the Mother Teresa of Jesus (Teresa of Ávila), 80
Living History (Clinton), 337
Living in Hope and History: Notes from Our Century (Gordimer), 307
Livre de la cité des dames, Le/The Book of the City of Ladies (Christine de Pisan), 55
Livre des fais et bonnes meurs du sage roy Charles V, Le/"Book of the Deeds and Good Morals of the Wise King Charles V" (Christine de Pisan), 55
Livre des trois vertus, Le/"Book of Three Virtues" (Christine de Pisan), 55
Louis XVI, 123, 126, 127, 128, 131, 133
Luxemburg, Rosa, 217–220
Lying Days, The (Gordimer), 306

M

Maathai, Wangari, 319–320
Ma Double Vie: mémoires de Sarah Bernhardt/My Double Life: Memoirs of Sarah Bernhardt (Bernhardt), 201
Maison de Claudine, La/My Mother's House (Colette), 222
Making of Americans, The (Stein), 224
Mansfield Park (Austen), 137, 139, 142, 143
Manual of The Mother Church (Eddy), 191
Mao Zedong, 292, 294, 295
Margaret Sanger: An Autobiography (Sanger), 230
Margaret I, 51–54
Maria Theresa, 110–115, 126
Marie-Antoinette, 114, 125, 126–128
Married Love (Stopes), 234
Martha Stewart's Hors d'Oeuvres (Stewart), 321
Mary (Virgin Mary), 31–34
Mary: A Fiction (Wollstonecraft), 129

Mary, Queen of Scots, 96, 99–100, 100–101

Mary I, 10, 11, 80–83, 91, 93, 94, 96

Massenstreik, Partei und Gewerkschaften/The Mass Strike, the Political Party, and the Trade Unions (Luxemburg), 218–219

Meir, Golda, 274–276

Melymbrosia (Woolf), 240–242

Menchú, Rigoberta, 340–342

mente assorbente, La/The Absorbent Mind (Montessori), 217

Mes Apprentissages/My Apprenticeships (Colette), 222

metodo della pedagogia scientifica, Il/The Montessori Method (Montessori), 216

Mira Bai, 70–71

Modern Novels (Woolf), 244

Monday or Tuesday (Woolf), 244

Montessori, Maria, 215–217

Montessori education system, 215–217

Mother and Child (Cassatt), 196

Mother of Us All, The (Stein), 224

Mott, Lucretia, 148, 175

Mr. Bennett and Mrs. Brown (Woolf), 245–246

Mrs. Dalloway (Woolf), 238, 245, 246

Murasaki Shikibu, 14, 43–45

My Fight for Birth Control (Sanger), 230

My Life (Duncan), 228

My Life (Meir), 276

My Own Story (Emmeline Pankhurst), 205

My Religion (Keller), 232

N

Napoleon, 126, 134, 135, 136

Narrative of Sojourner Truth, The (Truth), 148

Nefertiti, 19–22

Neurosis and Human Growth (Horney), 262

Neurotic Personality of Our Time, The (Horney), 261

New Biography, The (Woolf), 247, 249

Newer Ideals of Peace (Addams), 208

New Ways in Psychoanalysis (Horney), 261

Night and Day (Woolf), 243–244

Nightingale, Florence, 13, 166, 177–182, 185

Night Journey, 264–265

Northanger Abbey (Austen), 137, 138, 140, 141, 142, 143

Notebooks of Martha Graham, The (Graham), 267

Notes on Nursing: What It Is and What It Is Not (Nightingale), 181

Nüsslein-Volhard, Christiane, 323–324

O

O'Connor, Sandra Day, 313–315

Okuni, 105–107

On Re-Reading Novels (Woolf), 245

Open Door, The (Keller), 233

Oppression et Liberté/Oppression and Liberty (Weil), 281

Oprah Winfrey Show, The, 338

Optimism (Keller), 232

Orlando: A Biography (Woolf),
247–248
Our Inner Conflicts (Horney), 262

P

Pankhurst, Christabel, 12, 203–205
Pankhurst, Emmeline, 12, 203–205
Parallel Lives (Plutarch), 31
Pargiters, The: A Novel-Essay
(Woolf), 249, 250
Parks, Rosa, 291–292
Parr, Catherine, 92, 93
Pavlova, Anna, 235–237
Perón, Eva, 301–303
Perón, Juan, 301, 302
Persuasion (Austen), 137, 139–140,
141, 143
*Pesanteur et la grâce, La/Gravity
and Grace* (Weil), 280
Petite Idole (Bernhardt), 201
*Pioneer Work in Opening the
Medical Profession to Women*
(Blackwell), 186
*Plan of a Novel, According to Hints
from Various Quarters*
(Austen), 140
Plutarch, 26, 31
*Poems by Currer, Ellis and Acton
Bell* (Charlotte, Emily, and
Anne Brontë), 154, 158
Poems from the Divan of Hafiz
(Bell), 214
Potemkin, Grigory, 121–122, 124
*Pressure Is a Privilege: Lessons I've
Learned from Life and the
Battle of the Sexes* (King), 327
Pride and Prejudice (Austen), 137,
138, 139, 142, 143
Primitive Mysteries, 264

Professions for Women (Woolf),
248, 249
Professor, The: A Tale (Charlotte
Brontë), 154, 155–156

Q

"Q.E.D." (Stein), 225

R

Religion of Health, The
(Blackwell), 186
*Remarks on Prisons and Prison
Discipline in the United States*
(Dix), 150
Reminiscences (Woolf), 240
*Retraite sentimentale, La/Retreat
from Love* (Colette), 221
Revolt, 264
Revolution, The, 173, 176
*Rights of the Child, The: A Study of
Legal Aspects of Children's
Rights in Iran* (Ebadi), 331
Rights of Women, The (Ebadi), 331
Robinson, Mary, 11, 327–329
Room of One's Own, A (Woolf),
248, 249
Roosevelt, Eleanor, 12, 255–260
Roosevelt, Franklin, 255–257, 259
*Russische Revolution, Die/The
Russian Revolution*
(Luxemburg), 220

S

Sacagawea, 144–147
Safar Nameh (Bell), 214
Sanditon (Austen), 140
Sanger, Margaret, 13, 229–230
Sappho, 14, 23–25

Science and Health (Eddy), 188–189, 190, 191

Scivias (Hildegard), 46

Second Twenty Years at Hull-House, The (Addams), 208

Secret of Childhood, The (Montessori), 216

Sense and Sensibility (Austen), 137, 138, 139, 141, 143

Seymour, Thomas, 92–93

Shirley: A Tale (Charlotte Brontë), 155, 156–157

Sido (Colette), 222

Soft Voice of the Serpent, The (Gordimer), 306

Soong Mei-ling, 267–269

Sophie, ou les sentiments secrets (Staël), 132

Souvenirs de ma vie/Memoirs of Madame Vigée Lebrun (Vigée-Lebrun), 126

Sozialreform oder Revolution?/ Reform or Revolution? (Luxemburg), 218

Spiritual Relations, Exclamations of the Soul to God (Teresa of Ávila), 80

Staël, Germaine de, 126, 131–136

Stanton, Elizabeth Cady, 12, 131, 170–177

Starr, Ellen Gates, 206

Stein, Gertrude, 223–225

Stern, Elizabeth, 13, 295–296

Stewart, Martha, 320–322

Stopes, Marie, 233–234

Story of My Life, The (Keller), 232

Sullivan, Anne, 232

Sure Victory, The (Soong Mei-ling), 269

Susanna and the Elders (Gentileschi), 103

Symphonia armonie celestium revelationum (Hildegard), 46

T

Tenant of Wildfell Hall, The (Anne Brontë), 151

Tender Buttons (Stein), 224

Teresa, Mother, 286–288

Teresa of Ávila, 78–80

Theodora, 36–38

This Is Our China (Soong Mei-ling), 269

Thoughts on the Education of Daughters (Wollstonecraft), 129

Thousand and One Churches, The (Bell), 214

Three Guineas (Woolf), 250

Three Lives (Stein), 224

To Educate the Human Potential (Montessori), 217

To the Lighthouse (Woolf), 238, 246–247, 249

Touch of Innocence, A (Dunham), 282

Truth, Sojourner, 12, 147–149

Tubman, Harriet, 12, 182–183

20 Hrs., 40 Min. (Earhart), 270

Twenty Years at Hull-House (Addams), 208

U

Unbowed (Maathai), 320

Underground Railroad, 12, 182–183

V

Vagabonde, La/The Vagabond (Colette), 221

Victoria, 11, 123, 159–170, 180

Vigée-Lebrun, Elisabeth, 125–126

Villette (Charlotte Brontë), 155, 157

Vindication on the Rights of Woman, A (Wollstonecraft), 129, 130

Voyage Out, The (Woolf), 242, 244

W

Waves, The (Woolf), 248–249, 252

Way of Perfection, The (Teresa of Ávila), 80

Weddings (Stewart), 321

We Have Come a Long Way: The Story of Women's Tennis (King), 327

Weil, Simone, 279–281

What Every Mother Should Know (Sanger), 230

Winfrey, Oprah, 338–340

Winnemucca, Sarah, 201–203

Wise Parenthood (Stopes), 234

Wollstonecraft, Mary, 128–131

Woman Bathing (Cassatt), 196

Woman Rebel, The (Sanger), 229

Woman's Bible, The (Stanton), 177

women's rights/women's suffrage, 12, 37–38, 128, 129, 130–131, 147, 148, 169, 170–177, 192, 203–205, 207, 258, 302

Woolf, Virginia, 237–253

World I Live In, The (Keller), 232

Wuhou, 38–41

Wuthering Heights (Emily Brontë), 14, 151, 157, 158–159

Y

Yalow, Rosalyn S., 304–306

Years, The (Woolf), 250

Z

Zebrafish: A Practical Approach (Nüsslein-Volhard), 324

REF
YA
920.72   The 100 most
100   influential women of
ONE   all time.

$53.00   10/05/2010

DATE			